William Dearing Harden

An Inquiry Into the Truth of Dogmatic Christianity

Comprising a Discussion With a Bishop of the Roman Catholic Church

William Dearing Harden

An Inquiry Into the Truth of Dogmatic Christianity
Comprising a Discussion With a Bishop of the Roman Catholic Church

ISBN/EAN: 9783337008352

Printed in Europe, USA, Canada, Australia, Japan

Cover: Foto ©Lupo / pixelio.de

More available books at **www.hansebooks.com**

AN INQUIRY INTO

THE TRUTH OF DOGMATIC CHRISTIANITY

COMPRISING A DISCUSSION WITH A BISHOP OF
THE ROMAN CATHOLIC CHURCH

BY

WILLIAM DEARING HARDEN

"It is obvious that the most indispensable requisite in regard to Religion is that it should be true. No specious hopes or flattering promises can have the slightest value unless they be genuine and based upon substantial realities. Fear of the results of investigation, therefore, should deter no man, for the issue in any case is gain: emancipation from delusion, or increase of assurance. It is poor honor to sequester a creed from healthy handling, or to shrink from the serious examination of its doctrines. That which is true in Religion cannot be shaken; that which is false no one can desire to preserve."—*Supernatural Religion*, Preface to First Edition.

"It is absurd to assume what is beyond reason to account for what is opposed to reason."—*Ibid.* Part I., Chapter 3, Sec. 2.

G. P. PUTNAM'S SONS

NEW YORK
27 WEST TWENTY-THIRD ST.

LONDON
24 BEDFORD ST., STRAND

The Knickerbocker Press

1893

TO MY CHILDREN

for whose advantage even more than for my own this Search for Truth has been prosecuted, so much of this volume as I can fairly claim as my own, and therefore subject to such disposition, is most affectionately inscribed ; with the earnest, soul-full prayer that, if there be error in my views, the conviction of it may be brought to my mind before it can possibly affect theirs.

W. D. H.

PREFACE.

SOME time ago, for reasons of no interest to the public, I engaged in a friendly controversy on religious topics, running in a rather desultory way through several years, with a Bishop (since Archbishop) of the Roman Catholic Church. A mass of arguments on both sides of the question was thus accumulated, and friends, who think they have been benefited by reading the discussion, have urged its publication.

Thinking that it may reach and benefit some who would be deterred from undertaking an examination of the subject if the argument had assumed a more learned and profound shape; believing that the fact of its being an actual discussion, in which the side of orthodoxy is represented by a learned Bishop of her strongest Church, would lend an additional interest to the argument; knowing that it is a great advantage, in a search for truth, to have the argument on the one side directly contrasted with the argument on the other, the weakness of the one adding to the strength of the other; and, more than all, because the argument is in a form that can be understood without any previous theological education, and is therefore the better adapted to the ordinary lay reader, and every new argument, or new statement of an old argument, may convince some who had not been convinced before,—I have consented to give the discussion to the public.

In its original form the correspondence (which it is proper to state was probably written by both, certainly by me, without any idea of any future publication) contained much of a purely personal nature, and the argument was necessarily somewhat disjointed, each paper discussing a variety of subjects. I have therefore thought it best to re-arrange it so as to omit that which was purely personal and not pertinent to the argument, and to give it a more connected form, putting together all the correspondence on each subject and arranging the points in what seems a more natural sequence.

Further than this I have not interfered with the Bishop's presentation of his views. I have had no disposition to set up any specious or pretended arguments in order to refute them; I am too much in earnest for that. I did not even seek an inexperienced or unlearned layman with whom to discuss for the sake of confounding; but, on the contrary, I sought the most distinguished and learned Prelate within my reach, and if he has replied to, without answering, my arguments, it may be safely assumed that it is because they are unanswerable.

The correspondence was a real one,[1] and I have the right to use the Bishop's argument, which I think covers pretty much all that can be said for his Church, and I use it in his own words.

In my own argument I have dropped the epistolary form, and address myself directly to the reader.[2]

---

[1] The original is in the hands of the Publishers.

[2] The choice was before me to use the material for the purpose of writing a book, in which the entire argument on both sides would be in my own words—which might give the orthodox, if they felt themselves worsted, the

If there is any argument, other than those herein discussed, that can be urged against my views; any argument which does not depend upon the point at issue for one of its premises; any argument which is sustained by fact rather than by mere assertion, and which appeals to reason, and not alone to faith; any argument not entirely based on the authority of a doubtful scripture, or a still more doubtful tradition,—I will be more than pleased to hear it, come from what source it may, and will answer or yield.

But otherwise further discussion would, I fear, be but time wasted.

It is a fundamental principle of science that a theory is exploded whenever a single fact is produced, within the range of its application, which it does not explain or account for; the variance of fact and theory is always fatal to theory. I do not see why the same principle may not be applied to theology. So, if there be a single point in my argument which the Church cannot meet, the Church must go to the wall; not that I expect to be the means of accomplishing what so many abler and better men have failed to compass—the death of superstition. I know human nature too well for that; but I do hope to satisfy some of my readers that the dogmas of the Church are

chance to say that I had used only such arguments in behalf of the Church as I thought I could answer, leaving out the strongest, or emasculating them by my method of statement; or to give the correspondence substantially as it stood, with all its imperfections on both sides. I have chosen the latter course as being fairer to my opponent, and decidedly more interesting to the public, who might be attracted by the unusual fact of an actual controversy, and would not be repelled by finding itself entrapped into a dry and technical theological dissertation; and I might thus reach the people whom I sought above all others—those who, not realizing its importance, were not disposed to give much time or thought to the subject.

devised rather for its own perpetuation than their salvation; and if I shall succeed in bringing even one human soul from darkness into light—from superstition and death to freedom and life—I will not have thought and worked in vain.

CONTENTS.

	PAGE
INTRODUCTORY	1
THE POINTS TO BE DISCUSSED	7
PROPOSITION I. INFLUENCE OF THE CHURCH	11
PROPOSITION II. FREE-WILL	47
PROPOSITION III. ŒCUMENICAL COUNCILS	69
PROPOSITION IV. THE DIVINITY OF JESUS	114
PROPOSITION V. THE BETRAYAL	186
PROPOSITION VI. THE BIBLE	221
PROPOSITION VII. THE MASS. GOOD WORKS	237
CONCLUDING REMARKS	242

AN INQUIRY INTO THE TRUTH OF DOGMATIC CHRISTIANITY.

INTRODUCTORY.

IT is my belief that Dogmatic Christianity, Catholic and Protestant, contains, along with much that is pure, good, and elevating, much that is unreasonable, unauthorized, untrue, and pernicious.

That owing to this the good which it has undoubtedly accomplished, and may yet accomplish, has been, and is, fully, if not more than, counterbalanced by the harm it has done and is doing.

I believe, further, that the false may, to a great extent, be separated from the true, and that whatever can be clearly established as untrue should be discarded: and that once freed from its errors, retaining only its truths, Christianity will arise from the ashes of dogmatism purified, glorified; and men need no longer fear to examine their faith in the strong clear light of reason.

The object of my argument, therefore, is to point out in a simple, homely way, that all can understand, what I consider error in the Church's Creed, and why, and to show that with its errors expunged Christianity, so far from being injured or having its power for good impaired, will be in every way strengthened and improved.

I claim an earnest desire to benefit my fellow-man as far as I am able to do so without neglecting my personal duties, or injuring my private interests. I think that man will be benefited, here and hereafter, by having a true religion, pure and undefiled; and if I can help him to that, I will have helped him indeed.

Hence, writing with the wish to benefit those who differ with me in their theological ideas, and with the hope of bringing them to adopt my views, it has been my desire to say nothing which could in any way wound their susceptibilities: and if I should appear sometimes to be either caustic or flippant, it is because the argument of the Church, or the example of her defenders, seemed to call for it.

But I desire my orthodox readers and friends (and probably the larger portion of both readers and friends are, or think themselves, orthodox) to be assured that I speak with none but the kindliest feelings towards them personally; and I beg them to read me calmly and dispassionately, and to avoid coming to any conclusion until they have read it all. I beg them to read as I have studied and written, with the single object of ascertaining just how much of orthodoxy is true and beneficial, and how much false and hurtful; with the full assurance that, whether concurring with, or dissenting from, me, their honest conclusions will always be entitled to, and shall receive from me, that respect which is due to every conscientious conviction; and let us hope that some day, not this or that belief, but the actual, living truth will reach the minds of us all, and really deliver us from "envy, hatred, and malice, and all uncharitableness."

I know that I attack some beliefs which are cherished with the fondest reverence, the most affectionate devotion, and the deepest awe, and that such will be abandoned only with the greatest reluctance; but this should not be so: any belief that is shown to be unfounded in fact or reason should be discarded unhesitatingly, no matter how dear; for age cannot sanctify error, nor faith make truth.

But I am asked "cui bono?" Why should I seek to weaken any one's faith, unless I have something better with which to replace old beliefs?

I reply that I have something better with which to replace such beliefs as I attack: I propose to substitute truth for error. And I have no disposition to interfere with any faith the holding of which can be of any possible benefit here or hereafter. I would not leave humanity comfortless. But I would relieve it from the hideous incubus of superstition; from the fearful tyranny of an earth-devised Church; from the paralyzing clutches of a fear-inspiring clergy. I would elevate its conception of deity, and teach it that God is indeed love; that He hates nothing that He has made; that He has made us for other purposes than to administer to His vanity; that He is not subject to the worst of human frailties; that He has no favorites through whose importunities He can be induced to change His purposes; that He will not hurl the thunderbolts of His wrath at the poor mortal who may prefer to act in accordance with his own honest convictions, even though they may run counter to the dicta of the Church; that He is neither a supernatural Jew nor an incorporeal Christian.

God has given us reason: it is impossible for me to believe that He did not intend for us to use it: it can be fully used only when unrestrained, therefore I would set it free. Whatever is within its grasp, it should control; only that which is above, beyond it can be proper subject-matter for faith; and when faith and reason are antagonistic, faith must succumb; it should live only when in accord with, or, at least, unopposed by reason.

Then let us use our God-given reason cautiously, carefully, prayerfully, but honestly and fearlessly; and in the language of Paul "prove all things: hold fast that which is good." Surely no one can wish to worship a myth, or hang his hope of salvation on a shadow. So then, I say, let us reason together, not in the spirit of bitter sectarianism, but in the love of God, which is truth, and fear not the result. If our views remain unchanged, our convictions will have been strengthened, and our doubts dissipated: if we agree with the conclusions which I have reached, we will have indeed found that "peace of mind which passeth understanding." I speak from my personal experience, confirmatory of that of others; for, brought up with the usual views of a youth reared by Christian parents in a Christian country, I had become so harassed by doubts that would not down at the command of faith, that I was forced, in spite of myself, to investigate a subject which I considered too important to be left in uncertainty: and if ever a man sought earnestly for truth, if ever a man prayed fervently for light, I know I have; and if ever a man had his search rewarded and his prayer answered, I believe I have; and I feel as though I had come up out of the valley of the shadow of death into the pure bright light of God's truth shining, not for this or that creed, not for this or that nation, but for all humanity. Hence I know that when once we have freed ourselves from those terrible doctrines and dogmas which we have hitherto feared to even investigate; when we have cast aside the senseless errors and superstitions of the ignorant past as merely the outcome of the early gropings of primitive man; and study God as He has revealed Himself in nature, the truths of the present and the hopes of the future become actual living realities; and in the life-giving atmosphere of rationalism we fairly revel in moral health, and really love, instead of fearing, the great controlling Spirit of the universe.

How far I shall succeed in establishing that certain beliefs are not only not sustained, but are actually disproved, by reason, I cannot possibly foretell. I hope I may convince; but I will be satisfied if I induce the reader to think and investigate earnestly and conscientiously for himself; for earnest thought and conscientious investigation must certainly, as I think, lead to the absolute conviction of the truth of the propositions urged by me. And sure am I that if every doctrine I combat were destroyed, humanity would be the gainer.

The two commandments enunciated by Jesus, and which he said included all the law and the prophets, and which, being taught by all the old religions (except perhaps the Hebrew) may be considered as the ethical instinct of all humanity, contain all that is necessary as a rule of conduct; and the doctrine which I urge, that there is no escape from the consequences of wrong-doing, even by repentance, confession, or absolution—that no vicarious atonement can help us—that the penalties for transgressing the law are sure and proportionate, though not endless—would seem to furnish an all-sufficient motive to those who need the fear of punishment to induce them to observe the law.

I think, therefore, that I am justified in saying that I

seek to remove only such beliefs as are hurtful, because false, and try to hold fast to that which is good; and with the hope that I may bring truth to the minds of those who have it not, and strengthen it in the minds of those who already possess it, I proceed with the argument.

THE ARGUMENT.

THE POINTS TO BE DISCUSSED.

I HAVE found it convenient to divide the subject into distinct propositions, all tending, however, to the same end—the demonstration of the defects of Dogmatic Christianity—and will discuss them *seriatim*, giving, whenever I have it, the argument *contra* of my learned opponent.

While I thus subdivide the subject, it must be borne in mind that each proposition, while seemingly distinct in itself, is but a branch of the controversy, and is so interwoven with, and so overlaps, the others, that it is difficult to draw a very accurate dividing line between them, and much that is said under one head is equally appropriate to another; and there will necessarily be some repetition, the more especially as I have tried to make the argument on each point as complete in itself as the circumstances would permit.

I will endeavor to establish the following propositions, premising that by the term "Church" here, and in the argument, I mean Dogmatic Christianity in any of its phases, Catholic or Protestant.

I. The Church has exerted, and still exerts, a baleful influence upon mankind:

    a. by discouraging the study of nature and suppressing the use of reason, thereby checking progress and retarding civilization; and

    b. by insisting that belief is necessary to salvation, thereby driving many to despair and ruin;
and man's physical, mental, and spiritual advancement has been, and must be, through skepticism and free-thought, and in spite—and not because—of the Church.
II. The doctrine of free-will, as usually understood and as taught by the Church, is impossible if God be as He is represented. Attributing the origin of sin to man is absurd; and the idea of a continual strife between God and the Devil is blasphemous.
III. The councils of the Church by which her Creeds were formulated, were not inspired, but very fallible, assemblies of exceedingly natural men; and their decrees are conflicting, unreasonable, and utterly without authority.
IV. Jesus of Nazareth was not God, nor the son, in the sense of offspring, of God; he never claimed to be either, nor did others claim it for him until long after his death; and during his life he never sought or received divine honors.
He taught no new ethics; and the ethics of many of the "Pagans" were superior to those of the Jews, and equal to those of the Church.
V. If Jesus of Nazareth was God, he could not have been betrayed, and Judas Iscariot was but a helpless instrument in the hands of Omnipotence; if Judas was a traitor, Jesus was not God: and the doctrine of free-will does not relieve us from the dilemma, for the attempt to reconcile free-will with the attributes of God results only in attacking His absolute supremacy.

VI. The Bible is not a divinely inspired book; and being untrustworthy as to its facts cannot be relied on as infallible as to its theories.
VII. Arguments directed especially against the Roman Catholic form of orthodoxy:
Saying masses for the dead—for a pecuniary consideration—is either obtaining money under false pretences, or is selling the grace of God;
If repentance and confession are necessary to and will secure salvation, charity and other good works cannot affect our future condition—unless the forgiveness of God can be bought;
and the Church practising the one and teaching the other is in error and not infallible.

I realize the difficulties of the task, but I think it can be accomplished.

I shall endeavor, where I state arguments on the side of the Church otherwise than in the Bishop's own words, to state them fairly and candidly; and I will try to present those on my side clearly.

I may, doubtless will, have to say many things in the course of my remarks which will clash unpleasantly with the views of those who differ with me; but I shall say them with all respect for my opponents and their honest convictions; and I trust that even if my views be found objectionable, my language may never be offensive.

Some of my arguments will be recognized as old and familiar, for I have not hesitated to use any legitimate argument which I thought of without reference to, and frequently without knowing, where it came from. Some I have never heard from others; yet I cannot doubt but that even these have been used before. But age does not hurt an argument if it has not been refuted, and an argument, whether original or borrowed, is an argument still, and its value depends on its inherent strength, not on who may be its author.

THE ARGUMENT.

PROPOSITION I.

I. The Church has exerted, and still exerts, a baleful influence upon mankind :
    a. by discouraging the study of nature and suppressing the use of reason, thereby checking progress and retarding civilization ; and
    b. by insisting that belief is necessary to salvation, thereby driving many to despair and ruin ;
    and man's physical, mental, and spiritual advancement has been, and must be, through skepticism and free-thought, and in spite—and not because—of the Church.

The Church has so pertinaciously claimed that everything good comes from, through, or by it ; has so persistently appropriated to itself the credit of improving man's temporal condition as well as of providing for his future happiness, that it seldom occurs to any one to question its pretensions. But some have thought it worth while to look into the matter, and I purpose giving, very briefly, a summary of some of their researches into history, and also my own views on the subject, that we may form a more accurate opinion than some of us probably now have, as to the value of the Church's services to man in the past and now.

I think it necessary that I should state the actual truth,

because it is constantly urged on me, and many doubtless so think, that even if the Church be wrong in many of its dogmas and doctrines, it has done and is doing so much good that it should be helped, not hurt; that most certainly some religion is necessary to control, at least, the masses, and keep them in the paths of rectitude and virtue; and that Christianity, as taught by the Churches, Roman, Greek, and Protestant, is the best and highest form of religion known; and, even if not true, should not be interfered with; that a disbelief in the Church and the religion which it teaches would do much harm and no good.

I doubt the morality of the position, which is closely akin to the doctrine that evil may be done that good may follow. I think that what is false should perish because it is false, and that no other reason is necessary for combating it. And while I believe it to be a fact that it is a great advantage to any one to have a religion, I believe also that it is of grave importance that such religion should be true; and I do not, and cannot, believe that a false religion can do more good than a true one—that the spirit of falsehood is stronger for good than is the spirit of truth.

I make no war on religion. I attack only such phases of it as seem to me to be clearly wrong and hurtful; and I think that what is left, the true, is all that is worth preserving—is all that does any good. All the morality of Christianity, the outpouring of the ethical instincts of all humanity, should and must stand forever; the mere dogmatic teachings of ecclesiasticism with reference to beliefs, with no foundation in fact or reason, should be discarded. They may be useful to the Church in helping to sustain her power, wealth, and glory, but are exceedingly injurious in their effects on mankind. Christianity, as taught by the Church, may be the best form of organized religion known, but it is certainly not the best knowable, nor near so good as it will be with its errors expunged and only its truths left. And this I now attempt to show, beginning with the Church's past record.

(*a.*) I quote, and largely, from a little pamphlet called *The Influence of Christianity on Civilization*, by B. F. Underwood.

Having shown in detail the condition of Europe when it was under the absolute domination of the Church; when all learning, all science, all art, all history, all literature in Christendom were monopolized by the clergy, and no education worthy the name existed outside; when the light of the Church, in its full and unobstructed power, though shining so brilliantly for the clergy, shone so dimly for the rest of mankind that that period has ever since been known as the "Dark Ages,"—the mental and moral atmosphere sodden with ignorance and superstition until the mind of the laity began at last to hunger for wholesome air and nutritious food; he goes on to show how they were obtained.

He quotes Lecky (and I commence my selections on p. 63) thus:

"The influence of theology having for centuries benumbed and paralyzed the whole intellect of Christian Europe, the revival which forms the starting-point of our modern civilization, was mainly due to the fact that two spheres of intellect still remained uncontrolled by the sceptre of Catholicism. The Pagan literature of antiquity and the Mohammedan schools of science were the chief agencies in resuscitating the dormant energies of Christendom."[1]

[1] *Hist. of Morals*, p. 18. Appleton & Co., N. Y., 1869.

Mr. Underwood goes on to say:

"The Crusades, the main object of which was to get possession of an empty sepulchre, and which a writer justly says 'turned Syria into an Aceldama, and inundated with blood the fairest fields of Europe,' nevertheless, by bringing the Christians more generally and more directly in contrast with the Saracens, accomplished much good. 'They proved,' says Guizot, 'a great progress toward more extensive and liberal ideas. They, the Crusaders, also found themselves in juxtaposition with two civilizations, not only different from their own, but more advanced—the Greeks on the one hand, and the Mohammedans on the other. . . . It is curious to observe in the old Chronicles the impression which the Crusaders made upon the Mussulmans. These latter regarded them at first as barbarians; as the rudest, the most ferocious, and the most stupid class of men they had ever seen. The Crusaders, on their part, were struck with the riches and elegance of manners of the Mussulmans.'[1]

"Brought thus in contact with a people greatly their superiors in intelligence and culture, the Christians could not help receiving benefit from those whose country they invaded. That Christendom, in various ways, is vastly indebted to the Arabs, and especially to the Saracens, for the intellectual advancement that has been made within its limits, no person who has acquaintance with the history of the middle ages can deny. By them the learning and ethics of pagan antiquity were disinterred from the dust of centuries and transmitted and cultivated on the soil of modern Europe. And it was contact with the Saracens that quickened the energies and enlarged the minds of the European Christians, and prepared the way for advances in every direction. Knowledge and skepticism increased together. The rationalism of Abelard in the twelfth century, the heresies of the Waldenses, which gave the Church so much trouble and called forth her vengeance, the spirit of free-thought, of which general complaint was made in the thirteenth century, all furnish evidence of the existence of a strong and growing sentiment against the prevailing system. The poetry of Dante, in which he assigned several popes a place in hell for their vices, the sonnets of Petrarch, in some of which the Church of Rome is characterized as a harlot, and the tales of Boccaccio, wherein the vices of the monks and priests were freely exposed, among other works of less ability and note, tended to increase contempt for the Church and her unholy pretensions. The influence of Roger Bacon. . . . The invention of rag paper, and afterwards of printing.

[1] *Hist. Civilization*, vol. i., p. 154. See Hazlitt's translation, Appleton & Co., 1867, pp. 182.

... An acquaintance with the mariner's compass ... and a knowledge of gunpowder, proved of incalculable value to the cause of progress. ... Copernicus, and later Galileo, opened to the contemplation of man other worlds than our own; science and philosophy received more and more attention, and the heart of man seemed to beat with a more vigorous pulsation, and his mind, brought from heaven to earth, awakened to a life of activity and adventure. ... During all this struggle between intellectual life and intellectual death, which continued for ages, Christianity opposed most stubbornly every innovation and punished with imprisonment, torture, and death the votaries of science, philosophy, and reform. Roger Bacon was imprisoned ten years for his scientific investigations; the work of Copernicus was condemned as 'a false Pythagorean doctrine,' and the author, there is reason to believe, excommunicated; Bruno was burnt at the stake; Galileo was arrested and forced to renounce his scientific theories, and when released his steps were dogged until his death.

"If the Church became the friend of the serfs against the nobles of Europe, it was because a proud and powerful nobility, not always submissive to Ecclesiastical discipline, having almost unlimited control over the people, weakened the authority of the Church. The people once more under her power, she oppressed the nobles and the serfs alike.

"The Archbishop of Canterbury joined with the barons in extorting Magna Charta from King John. For this act he incurred the wrath of Pope Innocent III., who removed him from office, denounced the Charter, declared it null and void, and threatened the King with excommunication and the curses of the Church if he did not disregard it. . . .

"In Spain, the supremacy of Catholic Christianity was followed by the most disastrous results. Under the Saracens, as we have seen, that country was the most enlightened portion of Europe. Its decline commenced with the triumph of the Christian faith, when science decayed, manufactures gradually disappeared, industrial pursuits were abandoned, fields were uncultivated, and whole districts depopulated. The most valuable part of the Spanish population—the Moriscoes, a remnant of the people who had made Spain illustrious in preceding centuries—were expelled from Spanish soil. This monstrous wrong, the expulsion of 100,000 people from their native land, was urged on and compelled by the Spanish priests. 'When they were thrust out of Spain,' says Buckle, 'there was no one to fill their places; arts and manufactures either degenerated or were entirely lost, and immense regions of arable land were left deserted; . . . Whole districts were suddenly deserted, and down to the present day have never been repeopled. These solitudes gave refuge to smugglers and brigands, who succeeded the industrious inhabitants formerly occupying them; and it is said that from the expulsion of the Moriscoes is to be dated the existence of those organized bands of robbers, which after this period became the scourge of Spain, and which no subsequent government has been able entirely to extirpate.'[1]

"The expulsion of the Jews from Spain, who next to the Moriscoes were the best part of the population, still further contributed to the downfall of that priest-ridden country. The terrible effects of the Inquisition can never be computed. According to Llorente, 31,000 persons were burnt, and 290,000 condemned to other kinds of punishment by this institution in Spain alone. It destroyed all industry, stamped out all free-thought, and in spite of all the treasures which the new world poured into Spain, the people were reduced, largely through its influence, to a condition of poverty and degradation. In no way did the prevailing religion intentionally encourage the dissemination of learning or the improvement of man's unhappy condition in this world. On the contrary, the Church robbed and impoverished the people here, giving them in return promises of crowns of glory beyond the grave.

"Since man has to a considerable extent, in some portions of Christendom, emancipated himself from the thraldom of the Church he has made unprecedented progress. The advocates of Christianity now absurdly claim that the advancement thus made is justly attributable to their faith. As well might we ascribe the enlightenment of Spain from the ninth to the thirteenth century to the religion of the Koran. In those times the Mohammedan might have maintained the divine character and beneficent tendency of his religion by a comparison of Spain with the Christian countries of Europe with just as much reason and truth as the defenders of Christianity now argue in favor of the divinity and favorable tendency of their religion by comparing the Christian nations of to-day with pagan countries—with as much reason and truth as the Protestant endeavors to prove what the Protestant form of Christianity has accomplished by pointing to England and America, and contrasting them with Spain and Mexico as they are to-day.

"It is not uncommon for the defenders of Christianity to refer to the fact that nearly all the universities of learning in Christendom are sustained in the interests of the Christian religion, and that science, philosophy, and literature have been chiefly encouraged and cultivated by those who have been reared under the influence of this faith. The Saracens of Spain in the centuries named could have said the same in defence of Mohammedanism. The noblest universities in the world were Mohammedan institutions, and the cultivation of science and learning was brought up under and indoctri-

---

[1] *Hist. Civil.*, vol. ii., p. 53.

nated in the Mohammedan faith. But the universities and learning of Spain were surely not the result of the religion of the Saracens. Neither are the learning and the universities of England, Germany, and America the result of any form of Christianity. Mohammedanism was less unfavorable to intellectual progress in the middle ages than Mediæval Christianity. So Protestant Christianity as it exists in England or America is far less injurious in its tendency than Catholicism as it exists in Spain and Mexico ; but it is certainly absurd to maintain that the progress that has been made in the former countries should be put to the credit of Protestant Christianity. This form of Christianity, like Catholicism, has, in the past, opposed science, philosophy, and reform, and persecuted the pioneers of intellectual progress to the full extent of its power ; but happily, its power, never equal to that of the mother Church, has been growing less gradually until now it is so weak that, in this country especially, it can oppose but feebly the discoveries and innovations which contradict its assumptions and threaten to destroy it entirely. The policy that it now adopts to get a new lease of life is to conform, with the best possible grace, to the teachings of science and philosophy, and to acquiesce, as far as possible, in the reforms of the day.

" Hence it is now comparatively harmless in checking intellectual progress. Herein we see the liberalizing and elevating influence of those sciences and arts, and those pursuits of industrialism which have thus expanded the mind and enlightened the understanding, and, in consequence, shorn religion of its power, and forced it, in spite of its stubborn opposition at every step, to abandon many of its antiquated errors, and stop its cruel persecution of the benefactors of mankind. It is skepticism and freethought, not religion, that have contributed to the progress we have sketched.

" ' For more than three centuries,' says Lecky, ' decadence of theological influence has been one of the most invariable signs and means of our progress. In medicine, physical science, commercial interests, politics, and even ethics, the reformer has been confronted with theological affirmations which barred his way, which were all defended as of vital importance, and were all in turn compelled to yield before the secularizing influence of civilization.' [1]

" It is frequently asserted that in the most Christian countries the people are the most intellectual, moral, and happy. But the fact is, that in those countries in which skepticism and infidelity have acquired the greatest strength and influence, and in which Christianity has been modified to conform to the changed condition of affairs, the people are the most advanced."

[1] *Hist. Morals*, vol. ii., p. 18.

I hardly think it worth while to quote further. Any unsectarian history of the middle ages will afford cumulative and convincing proof of the prodigious harm worked by the Church.

I have not quoted Church writers; they are too apt to confound faith and fact, assertion and argument, and accept or reject without sufficient investigation. Nor do I think a rigid Churchman competent to investigate and judge in matters affecting his religion. It is only those who have emancipated themselves from " authority " and " faith "—who have. no theory to sustain, but who want truth and do not care what that truth may be—who can investigate impartially, and are apt to reach correct conclusions. All experience proves this, and until human nature becomes different from what it is it must continue to be so. But the facts which I have quoted cannot be successfully denied. They are undoubtedly true, and could not have been otherwise so long as the Church believed and taught the Bible literally, and held it to be the word of God; for under that state of facts any scientific demonstration which contradicted, or conflicted with, the statements of the Bible, must have been regarded as dangerous. The Church, for its own protection, was bound to see that no knowledge should find its way into any man's mind until it had been first inspected by its authority. I care not if a word of history had never been written; I care not if every word of history that ever has been written had been lost; it must follow, as a matter of necessity, that any religion which teaches that God Himself revealed to man what He had done and how He had done it, which goes into detail, and undertakes to explain nature; which represents that the natural facts contained in the Bible are the direct statements of the Creator Himself;

which, in short, includes a detailed cosmogony as well as a theology; must be a religion which discourages, if it does not forbid, investigation. Why question nature when God, its Creator, has explained? Why seek for further information, for more knowledge, when God has revealed all He thought necessary for man? And when some active, honest mind that would not be still, would observe, record, and report some fact in nature in seeming conflict with the sacred statement, it could not be otherwise than that he should be regarded as a heretic, an enemy of mankind; and when the religion taught that God Himself directed the slaughter of His and their enemies by His chosen people, it could hardly be that the people would restrain their brutish instincts in the face of what they would have been justified in considering a permission, if not an order, to turn them loose.

Hence, apart from the teachings of history, it could not have been otherwise than that the human mind was fettered, benumbed, paralyzed, and progress rendered wellnigh impossible either in science or religion, except where the Church could turn it to its own account.

Therefore the arts, and such sciences as did not conflict with—that is, did not touch—the statements of the Bible, would have flourished, but all others would have declined or died out,—notably the sciences of astronomy, geology, and medicine: the first two because it was supposed that the Bible told all that was necessary on the subjects; and the third because nearly all sickness, especially epidemics, was regarded as a direct visitation of Divine wrath, and therefore to be gotten rid of only by prayer or miracle. And this is just what history, as recorded by honest writers, tells us, and their accounts need no other confirmation. Just as a philologist will take a few words, and from them give a history of the people who used them; as a naturalist will from a single bone reconstruct in his mind and accurately describe the animal to which it had belonged, its appearance, habits, and disposition; so an historian might take the teachings of the Church and a knowledge of human nature, and tell just what effects such causes must have necessarily produced. And in looking over the conflicting statements of historians writing from different standpoints, for or against the Church, it is an easy matter for one at all versed in the business to tell the true from the false.

But we have further proofs of all this before us now. The world is still suffering from the influence of the Church, whether Catholic or Protestant. We still find the free discussion of science, ethics, and religion frowned down. The Church, thanks to the civilization brought about by the few brave men who were not afraid to think and speak their thoughts, has no longer the power to crush and punish, but she tries to frighten by her now powerless bulls, by excommunications and anathemas, by branding with such harmless epithets as "infidel," "deist," "atheist," "materialist," and still does all she can, in her small way, to check progress. Forced into the recognition of the demonstrated truths of astronomy, of geology, of geography, her own priests now study, and make discoveries, and hold opinions for which a few years ago they would have been burned at the stake. And we may thank infidelity for it. A very pious Protestant said to me, not long ago, that he hated infidelity, but believed God used it to advance the world in knowledge and freedom. And it is undoubtedly true. It is owing to the civilizing influences of infidelity that I can now thus publicly express my honest convictions, and that my views are patiently examined, and approved or disapproved, as the case may be, instead of my being denounced to the Grand Inquisitor. When the Church was in supreme power, I would not have dared to thus write, nor the public to read. Now the Church attempts to use no force, but leaves me unmolested. Surely it has changed for the better, through the civilizing effects of free-thought, or else civilization has pulled its teeth, cut its claws, and made it seem respectable.

And even yet we are not entirely free from the old superstition that plagues and epidemics are but the vengeance of God visited upon a sinful people; and we still hear of masses, processions, prayer-meetings, and various similar, but always unsuccessful, devices being used to prevent or get rid of them. But if the Church had never taught such an incorrect and blasphemous idea, but had taught that diseases are sent by God to punish man for his ignorance, or disregard of the laws of nature, and for no other sin, and only to teach him better, the time wasted in prayers, processions, fastings, and vigils, would have been applied to studying the laws of hygiene, and far more progress would have been made in stopping epidemics than has been. Nature warns but never forgives. Violate her laws, she warns by striking; continue to violate, and she strikes mortally. How much more important, then, to study nature as she is, than to spend time praying to God to change His laws to suit our views. Holy wafers, masses, relics, charms, and prayers will not do anything towards warding off sickness; but soap and water, ventilation, drainage, disinfection, and a proper diet will. The old superstitions are not all dead yet; but they are sickening, and some of them are gone; and by the grace of God, working through those who love Him and strive to do His commandments, not as taught by human churches and effete theology, but as gathered from His ever open and never-changing book of revelations, Nature, they will ultimately all be buried, and the world be freer, better, purer for it. And all of us, long since passed away, with our eyes opened to higher truths than we may know in this world now, forgetting all past differences of creed, will rejoice that the kingdom of God, not of the Church, has come at last to man.

But there were other influences than those just referred to at work to make it impossible that the Church should not have stayed progress and improvement of every sort.

These are indicated in the following passage from Darwin's *Descent of Man*[1]:

> "Who can positively say why the Spanish Nation, so dominant at one time, has been distanced in the race. The awakening of the Nations of Europe from the dark ages is a still more perplexing problem. At this early period, as Mr. Galton has remarked, almost all the men of gentle nature, those given to meditation or culture of the mind, had no refuge except in the bosom of the Church, which demanded celibacy : and this could hardly have failed to have a deteriorating influence on each successive generation. During the same period the Holy Inquisition selected with extreme care the freest and boldest men in order to burn or imprison them. In Spain alone some of the best men—those who doubted and questioned, and without doubting and questioning there can be no progress—were eliminated during three centuries at the rate of a thousand a year."

Talent, genius, bravery, nobility, gentleness, all of our good qualities and propensities, are as transmissible from father to son as are those that are bad ; and these two institutions of the Church, celibacy for the priests and the Inquisition for the laity, cut off the stream of good influences while the bad flowed steadily on.

And this does not reflect on the character of the men

[1] Vol. i., pp. 171, 172.

who worked this fearful harm on the world; it was the terrible nature of their creed. Believing, as they did, that celibacy was a virtue and that heresy was the worst of all crimes and forever damned those who were guilty of it, what wonder that they insisted on the one and tried to check the other, and used, to further their plans, the means with which Jehovah was wont to scourge His enemies. As Mr. Underwood remarks: "It is easy to believe Llorente when he says that the founders of the Spanish Inquisition were men whose characters were unstained by vice, and who acted from an earnest desire to save the souls of men."

It is claimed that the Church has been a boon to woman, and that it has immensely ameliorated her condition. This, too, is a mistake. Woman's condition, like man's, has been bettered by civilization and in spite of the Church. The fundamental fact in Scripture with reference to woman is that through her came sin into the world. "Adam was first formed, then Eve. And Adam was not deceived, but the woman being deceived was in the transgression."[1]

For this reason woman was to be in every way subject to man. She was not to speak in public, she was to yield implicit obedience to her husband, and man was made for the glory of God, while woman was made for the use of man. Her wishes were not to be consulted in the choice of a husband. She could be captured and put to the basest uses, and by the direct permission of God. She was an abject slave to man, submitting herself to him as to her God—and except as man has freed her, she so remains.

I am not an advocate of "woman's rights," so called; I believe in the division of labor, and think woman's sphere is different, in a great degree, from man's. But I think

[1] 1 Tim. ii., 13, 14.

she should be so educated as to bring out the full power and strength of her mind and body, and should be as free to discuss matters affecting her interest, and to express her views thereon, as man. And above all she should be relieved from the cowardly reproach of ages, " the woman tempted me, and I did eat." If we will believe the story, let us be men enough to bear the responsibilities of our own acts, and not try, like cringing school-boys, to shift the blame on helpless woman.

I have heard it frequently urged that we should not judge the Christian religion by the acts of its adherents in the early days of the Church ; that all men were then barbarous to some extent, and that it took time for Christianity to civilize them. A tree must be judged by its fruit. We can only judge the Church by its effect on mankind, and certainly it is fair to show its effect on its chief supporters and its own officers and priests.

We have seen the excesses which they committed when they held undisputed power, and we have seen that they became more moderate only in proportion as they lost their power ; and that there is abundant evidence that the Church is actuated yet by the same old intolerant spirit ; and I close this branch of my first proposition by a quotation in point from Huxley's *Lay Sermons*, p. 278.

" Who shall number the patient and earnest seekers after truth, from the days of Galilee until now, whose lives have been embittered and their good name blasted by the mistaken zeal of bibliolators ? Who shall count the host of weaker men whose sense of truth has been destroyed in the effort to harmonize impossibilities—whose life has been wasted in the attempt to force the generous new wine of science into the old bottles of Judaism, compelled by the outcry of the same strong party ?

" It is true that if philosophers have suffered, their cause has been amply avenged. Extinguished theologians lie about the cradle of every science as the strangled snakes beside that of Hercules; and history records that whenever science and orthodoxy have been fairly opposed, the latter has been forced to retire from the lists, bleeding and crushed, if not annihilated; scotched, if not slain. But orthodoxy is the Bourbon of the world of thought. It learns not, neither can it forget; and though at present bewildered and afraid to move, it is as willing as ever to insist that the first chapter of Genesis contains the beginning and the end of sound science, and to visit with such petty thunderbolts as its half-paralyzed hands can hurl, those who refuse to degrade nature to the level of primitive Judaism."

We have thus seen how, and why, the Church has discouraged the study of nature, and has sought to suppress the use of reason, thereby checking progress and retarding civilization; and that it still retains the same tendencies, though, on account of the gradual emancipation of man's mind, by skepticism and free-thought, from the slavery imposed by his superstitious fears, its power is materially lessened.

(*b.*) It now remains to go a little further, and to show that so long as the Church insists that belief in any creed or dogma is necessary to salvation, so long must it continue to exert, in the future, as in the past and present, a baleful influence on mankind, and to drive many to despair and ruin.

In order to be perfectly clear, it will be best, I think, to examine, somewhat in detail, but rapidly, how belief, of the kind being considered, originates, how it is maintained, and how the doctrine of its importance works harm; for knowing its origin we can the better judge of its correctness and consequent importance, and if it be found to be incorrect, and therefore the very reverse of important, we will the more fully appreciate the error of a system which makes belief a necessary preliminary to salvation.

Impressions made upon the infant mind, growing with our growth, increasing with our strength, are the most tenacious we have; and even when we think we have gotten rid of them, that they are finally effaced, we find that they have left a scar, like that of a badly healed wound, which sometimes breaks out afresh.

Among the strongest of our instincts (and surely the noblest) is love of, and respect for, our parents. The child looks up to father and mother, as father and mother look up to God. One or the other is appealed to for information, for sympathy, for help, for he has unlimited confidence in their knowledge, their affection, their power; and though experience comes later to show that knowledge and power were overestimated, their affection still remains undoubted and unchanged, and, as it should, casts a sacred, holy, charm over all they said and did.

Again, the child is like primitive man, certainly no further advanced in mental characteristics or powers. He sees, as saw primitive man, effects resulting from unknown causes, and, as with primitive man, his growing brain asks "why?" Why does the sun shine? Why does it rain? What is the awe-inspiring lightning, and the still more fearful thunder? What is the wind, and why does it blow? What holds up the stars? Why does it get dark? What, and why, are pain, and sickness, and death?

As primitive man, when questioned similarly by his thoughts, had gradually, if not solved these problems, at least quieted his mind, by at first personalizing the forces of nature, and later on, when they were recognized as powers, not persons, by putting them under the control of the personalities he had thus imagined; and guided by experience, having no other teacher, since he had come to recognize the necessity of a ruler among men, had assumed that there must be, and hence was, a superior and supreme personality in command of all the rest ; and so, by slow degrees, had built up a theological system, founded at first on his fancies alone, and subsequently merely modified as he learned to use his reason; and as this system, changing its dress as men changed their notions, the old gods and goddesses transformed into saints of either sex, shorn of much of their power, but still possessing some, or else, losing their personality, becoming attributes of the supreme God, has come down to our own times essentially the same old idea, modified in detail alone; so the father, under the domination of these inherited ideas, answers the queries of the child as primitive man answered his own aspirations for knowledge, his own yearning for the unknown—perhaps the unknowable—by referring all phenomena to a supernatural personal cause, individualized as God, telling him that all things may be explained as the acts of such God furthering His schemes of love and mercy, or of hatred and revenge ; for this God of his is very human in his nature, and is subject not only to the noblest, but also to the basest, passions of man ; and proceeds to teach him how to win God's love, how to avert God's anger; in other words, lays before him, by degrees, the Church's creed.

All men are superstitious, some to a greater some to a less degree. I do not think there exists one without superstition in some form—even if it be only a belief in "luck," and ways and means of changing it. The germ is there, though in many cases strength of will, or reason, or experience, or ridicule may have modified many of its expressions, and wellnigh, but not quite, destroyed itself. But in the child it is in its full force, and the theological system unfolded to him appeals directly to this strong instinct, and with it aiding the teachings of those in whom he has the most implicit confidence, how could it be otherwise than that he should receive as undoubted, undoubtable truth all that comes to him from such a source and under such circumstances?

And with most Christians, in fact with a majority so vast as to approach unanimity, this is the only foundation on which their faith is built,—the single source of their belief. Think of it. Our whole hope of the eternal future based on nothing more substantial than the teachings of those who knew no more than we, and who, like us, and like their teachers, believe only because taught to do so while children, or in the trusting mental condition of children, and, having never been taught differently, have never questioned what they thought unquestionable.

I do not mean to exaggerate. I do not think that I do. Let any one ask himself why he believes, and in nearly every case I am confident the answer, if intelligent and sincere, will prove that I am right. In nearly every instance he will find that the ultimate reason is that he has been taught to so believe by those in whom he had absolute confidence—his parents or his guardians in early life, his teachers and clergy later on. And the answer will be the same though in his turn he may now be parent, guardian, teacher, or priest. For even those who have investigated fully, as they think, the subject since they have become of maturer years, will find, by rigid self-examination, that their early beliefs and training have been all-important factors in their conclusions, that the *alpha* of their studies and the *omega* of their results, is FAITH, which I conceive to be a blind reliance on the views and assertions of others, and the utter suppression of reason.[1]

I do not wish to be misunderstood. I do not believe that all intelligence, wisdom, or knowledge is confined to those who doubt. I am perfectly well aware that some of the most brilliant intellects, the wisest minds, and the most learned men the world has ever known have been, and still are, conscientiously enlisted on the side of the

[1] This definition of faith seems to have aroused the indignation of the learned Bishop who did me the honor to discuss with me the points presented in this argument. I give his criticism :

"It is related of the famous Don Quixote that, lance in hand, he furiously attacked what he imagined to be a hostile giant. But alas! the foe of flesh and blood proved to be a windmill. This achievement of the knight of the rueful countenance is certainly ludicrous enough. But I don't think it is half so laughable as your gallant charges on 'faith.' You define faith to be a blind reliance on the views and assertions of others, and the utter suppression of the latter, *i. e.*, reason. And then you draw your gallant weapon against this ugly giant. But alas! Sir, it is only a windmill. For a windmill is about as much like an iron-clad knight as your definition is like to Catholic faith. You say I must use my own reason. Certainly ; we don't object to that. And don't you think it might have been using your reason to considerable advantage had you first learned what faith really was before penning such a caricature of it?

"Faith has been held to be the most sacred of things by such intellectual giants as a Copernicus, Michael-Angelo, Raphael, Dante, and hosts of others whose names are immortal in science and art. These mighty geniuses never for a moment dreamed that faith is a 'blind reliance on the views and assertions of others, and the utter suppression of reason'; for faith, instead of being the 'utter suppression of reason,' is reason's highest act."

To which I replied :

We now come to Don Quixote, and his windmill, to whom and which you are kind enough to liken me and my definition of faith.

At the time I had no intention of giving a regular definition of faith ; if I had, I would probably have given the famous one of Hood in his *Up the Rhine*. It is contained in a letter from Martha Penny to Rebecca Page, and is as follows :

"But as a party you don't know says, what's faith? As for beleavin what's

Church. But I do believe, and this is what I wish to convey, that such men either have never properly investigated in the pure spirit of truth, and nothing else, or, if with the proper spirit, have started at the wrong point; have taken for granted as an unquestioned fact something taught them in their early youth, but which is really the very point at issue, and, starting from false premises, have, by correct reasoning, been naturally brought to wrong conclusions.

That such men, not only wise but good, have believed, and still believe, the Church's creed, proves nothing, though it entitles their belief to a respectful considera-

only plain and probberble and nateral, says he, its no beleaf at all. But wen you beleav in things totally unpossible, and direct contrary to nater, that is real, true, downright faith, and to be sure, so it is."

And this reminds me of a sermon which a friend assures me he heard you preach, in which, while speaking of the sacrifices which the Church demanded of her children, you said (as he recollects it) that it even "demanded the sacrifice of our intellects," instancing the belief in the real presence.

But after carefully considering your objections, I am disposed to adopt, in cold blood, what I then said in my haste, and define faith as "a blind reliance on the views and assertions of others, and the utter suppression of reason." There, Sir, is the windmill, and you will excuse me if I turn your simile against you. Don Quixote did not make windmills; others made them, and he attacked them, as you do, and I really think you have been as successful as he, no more. If my definition is wrong, why have you not given me a better? You tell me that a number of "intellectual giants" have held faith "to be the most sacred of things," but that does not define it. You further say that they did not regard it as "a blind reliance on the views and assertions of others, and the utter suppression of reason," and you add "for faith, instead of being the utter suppression of reason, is reason's highest act." But why not define it? I do not know what the gentlemen whose names you give thought about faith, nor do I care. If their views were wrong, they ought to be suppressed; if they were right, they were right, not because *they* held them, but because of the reasons which induced them to hold them. Some eminently respectable gentlemen have believed that the earth was stationary, and that the sun revolved around it; indeed I am

tion and a careful examination. And that consideration and examination I have given it, and, so far as I have been able to ascertain, the basis of their belief, the foundation of their creed, is faith, as I have defined it, acquired as I have pointed out.

And yet the faith of such men, so acquired and maintained, is used as proof of the truth of their belief! Whereas, to restate with greater clearness what I have just said, the fact that any one believes or disbelieves a system is not, *per se*, any evidence that the system is either correct or incorrect. It may be evidence that it is not to be lightly rejected or accepted; but the reasons

not sure but that some of the popes, and other eminent luminaries of the Church, so held; but their belief did not make it so. Belief is now known not to influence facts; indeed it is doubted if the tractile or repellant power of faith can any longer remove a mountain, except figuratively, and it cannot be denied that mountains of fact, reason, or philosophy are to faith as if they were not.

But, seriously, I would like to know what is wrong about my definition. Let us examine it. It certainly is a belief in something of which we have no demonstration, or it would be knowledge—not faith. If we have no demonstration of it, it would seem to be a belief in the opinions or assertions of others, and any belief in the opinions or assertions of another, without other evidence, is blind reliance, even though we only give that sort of confidence to people whom we *think* we can trust; and the only possible use I can see of reason in the matter is in determining upon whom we shall rely; and in matters of religious faith (and that is the sort I am speaking of) that has generally been determined for us when we were children and could n't help ourselves.

So, really, I cannot see how faith can be reason's "highest act," except on the principle that the highest act of a king is abdication.

To this the Bishop has never replied; so I adhere to my definition until I can find a better one. Indeed the language ascribed to Jesus (Matt. xviii., 13), "except ye be converted, and become as little children, ye shall not enter into the kingdom of heaven," would seem to be an authoritative enunciation of the principle that inability to reason is essential to a perfect fulness of faith.

why such a one believes or rejects are of much more importance than the mere fact that he so believes or rejects. And upon the strength of the reasons for belief or disbelief, not on the belief or disbelief itself, should the case rest. And when we are told that we must believe or reject any doctrine because believed or rejected by another, or many others, whom we admire, love, and respect for both mental and moral qualities, if it be a matter of any importance, our self-respect and our duty to ourselves and others should require us to ascertain WHY such person, or persons, so held. Any other course would be to surrender our individuality, to dethrone our reason. And the WHY we have just examined, and have found it to be the faith of a little child.

But notwithstanding its origin and its want of real foundation, such faith is claimed to be proven true by the fact that so many live and die content, nay, happy, in its possession. Especially is this urged of the calm beatitude of so many dying Christians.

But if this proves anything, it proves too much, for exactly the same argument may legitimately be used, and with precisely the same effect, in support of any and every religion actually and earnestly believed.

And so, indeed, of all the arguments based on faith, or inner consciousness, or soul-intelligence, or gratified spiritual aspirations. They are all as applicable to one sincere religion as to another, and no more so. If the Christian religion can be so proved, so can any other, and perhaps more conclusively; for it is notorious that the adherents of many of the rival religions of the world are far more earnest, far more sincere in their absolute faith, far more conscientious in the observance of their rites and ceremonies, and far more self-sacrificing in life and property, than their more civilized Christian brethren. But the honesty and sincerity of its votaries cannot establish the truth of any religion. Faith may be very satisfactory and comforting to its possessor, but it is not proof—it is not even evidence.

Having thus rapidly traced what seems to be the origin of belief and, incidentally, its value as evidence, let us see what importance the Church attaches to it.

Under the teachings of the orthodox Christian Church belief in certain dogmas is essential to salvation. It is not necessary now to consider what are these particular dogmas; we will consider, at present, only one—the Divinity of Jesus. This, of course, includes the Incarnation, the Death of Atonement, and the Resurrection.

Belief of this is absolutely necessary.

"He that believeth and is baptized shall be saved; but he that believeth not shall be damned." Mark xvi., 16.

"And as Moses lifted up the serpent in the wilderness, even so must the Son of Man be lifted up; that whosoever believeth in him should not perish, but have eternal life. For God so loved the world that He gave His only begotten Son that whosoever believeth in him should not perish but have everlasting life. For God sent not His Son into the world to condemn the world: but that the world through him might be saved. He that believeth on him is not condemned, but he that believeth not is condemned already, because he hath not believed in the name of the only begotten Son of God." John iii., 14, 18. "He that believeth on the Son hath everlasting life; and he that believeth not the Son shall not see life: but the wrath of God abideth on him." John iii., 36.

Texts need not be multiplied, nor sermons quoted, to establish this point. So far as I am aware it is not denied by any of the orthodox. I believe that some of the more liberal say that such belief is not necessary for those who have never heard of Jesus, nor had the truth preached to them, and such may be saved without so believing. I do not know the scriptural authority for this idea; I suspect that civilization is reading a little more humanity into the creed. But it does not matter, for all are agreed, as I understand it, that so far as those who have heard the gospel are concerned, such belief is essential; or, in other words, that if one is told the fact and rejects it, he is lost. And I may here parenthetically remark, that if the more liberal idea be true—that is, that belief is essential only to those who have heard the truth, it is a conclusive argument against sending missionaries to the heathen: for since it must necessarily be that many who hear will not believe, sending them missionaries is to do good to none (since they could be saved without them), but to send damnation to many.

But apart from the scriptural texts pointing in that direction, it seems to me to be absolutely necessary that the Church, as an organization, should hold to the harsher doctrine of the importance and necessity of belief, without exception of any kind. If morality alone will save, if belief be unimportant, then the good man of any and every creed, or of no creed at all, will be as surely saved as the most orthodox and bigoted Christian, and the Church will have become confessedly a useless, even a hurtful institution: useless, because it needs no ordained or anointed priest to teach us that virtue, for itself alone, is better than vice; hurtful, because it drives thousands out of the paths of rectitude by insisting that they cannot be really good, really acceptable to God, cannot be saved, without possessing what it would then have admitted to be an unnecessary faith. Therefore, while the Church must teach with James that faith without works is dead, it would be suicidal for it to admit that works without faith may be life. As horrible as I purpose to show the doctrine to be, it must insist on the essentiality of belief, be the consequences what they may.

Now belief is not dependent on volition. We *accept*, without examination, many things as true, but this is not belief. Belief, or mental conviction, is the result of evidence and reason, and is involuntary. No one can believe or disbelieve by the mere exertion of his will. When one in whom we have confidence tells us something which is not contrary to our experience, not inconsistent with our reason, we may believe it because of those facts satisfying our minds, but not because we wish to. But if the statement is unusual, apparently unreasonable, new to our experience, and of sufficient importance to arouse our interest, we examine into the facts, and as the facts and reasons are, so will our belief be: all of us have, at times, been compelled by evidence to believe many unpleasant things which we would gladly not have believed, and no amount of mere volition could control our mental convictions, and we believed in spite of ourselves.

Having examined into how faith comes and is sustained, and having shown that, although belief is an involuntary condition of the mind, the Church insists on its importance, let us see how doubt may arise and destroy belief, and what the Church teaches may flow from such destruction.

Most people go through life quietly, satisfied with the creeds of their fathers, thinking very little about it, save in a very general way, and the less they think the better they are satisfied. But some, with a realizing sense of the importance of the matter, unwilling to rest their eternal future entirely on others' views, begin to examine for themselves their Church's somewhat voluminous creed, having determined that the most important of all their affairs shall no longer be the only one about which they do not think, and thought on this subject must bring doubt.

They have been taught, for instance, that there is one Supreme God; that He is omnipotent, omniscient, omnipresent, and eternal—without beginning as without end; that He is all-good, all-just, and all-love; that He is our loving Father, and we His wayward children; that He so loved us that He gave His only begotten and well beloved Son as a sacrifice for our good. They believe all this with an absolute faith, and have so believed for many years. But now, having begun to think, they see that if all this be true some of the rest of their creed must be false; that if God possessed all the attributes ascribed to Him He could not have been angry with man, and would not have resolved to exterminate the race He Himself had created as it was, for anger necessarily implies discontent, and discontent can only mean that matters have not turned out to suit Him—and it is absurd to think of a supreme, omnipotent, omnipresent, omniscient, but *disappointed*, God,—and yet if He was angry with man and "repented" (that is the word used in the sacred text) that He had made him, that is what He must have been.

They further reflect that if possessed of all these attributes He could have demonstrated His love for us, and could have changed the heart of man, and have made him all-good, by the mere exercise of His volition; and as there was so simple, sure, and obvious a method of accomplishing His supposed purpose, they begin to doubt whether He would have employed a plan so complex, so utterly at variance with and contrary to His usual methods as seen in nature, so cruel, so unnecessary, and, as they hear their clergy so constantly bewailing the world as growing worse, they must also conclude, so ineffectual as the Incarnation.

They are utterly unable to conceive that of the many plans which suggest themselves to their finite minds and limited wisdom, and which would surely have succeeded when backed by the unlimited power of the Almighty, none would have occurred to Infinite Wisdom itself, or, having so occurred to it, would have been rejected in favor of a plan that Omniscience must have known would never succeed,—at least until untold millions of His children's souls should have been forever lost.

Another thought is here suggested.[1]

There could have been no necessity for any scheme of SALVATION had there not been first a scheme of DAMNATION. This is inevitable. One must be in danger before there is any necessity to save him. Was God the author of both schemes? Or is there another Being more powerful for evil than God is for good? If, as they are told, the world is getting worse, notwithstanding the scheme of salvation; if, as they are further taught, more are damned than saved, the scheme of damnation is more successful than the counter scheme of salvation, and the author of the first more powerful than the author of the second. Or, if God be the author of both, when they are returning thanks for the ineffectual second scheme, what are they to say about the successful first?

These and other kindred thoughts cause them to doubt, and their doubts lead to investigation; so they look to the evidence adduced in support of the whole extraordinary system.

They admit, to the fullest extent, that anything which God does, or has done, must be right; could not be

[1] By my friend Dr. Richard J. Nunn.

otherwise. But before they admit as right that which is so utterly at variance with their reason, they must be fully satisfied that God really did it.

It is not necessary, now, to follow any of our doubters through his investigations. We will investigate for ourselves farther on. It is not even necessary to my present purpose to assume that the conclusions at which he arrives are correct; it will be sufficient to assume that they are honest; and that as the result of long, patient, faithful, and earnest investigations, our doubter, as so many others have done, finds his doubts resolved into the certainty, so far as his own mind is concerned, that there is absolutely no foundation in fact for the dogma of the Incarnation, the fundamental doctrine of the whole system; that Jesus of Nazareth was not God, nor the son, in the sense of offspring, of God; that he never claimed to be such, nor did others claim it for him until long after his death.

As I have said, it is entirely immaterial, so far as the point now being discussed is concerned, whether he is right or wrong, so long as he is sincere. He has tried to believe his Church's creed—would much prefer to—for the sake of peace and the good-will of his fellows, but he cannot, and he is too honest to pretend.

Now, under the teachings of orthodoxy what might result from this?

Let us suppose two persons: the one, A, upright, moral, honest, honorable, charitable, industrious, sober, and, in all respects, a useful, respected citizen, but who, after careful examination of the matter, has reached the conclusions just referred to as reached by our doubter. He observes all the ethics of the best and most rigid Churchman, and in his life is a model for all; but he cannot believe certain doctrines, belief in which is declared by the Church to be absolutely essential to salvation.

On the other hand, B is all that is vile, a thorough criminal in thought and deed, out of the pale of the Church and of decent society.

A prevents B from committing some crime, frustrates some scheme of unlawful money-getting, or of revenge, and so incurs B's enmity. B lies in wait for him, and on some dark night kills him.

If the Church has not deceived us, if this matter of belief is so important, so necessary, A, the just man, who never did a wrong act, goes at once to a cruel and endless doom, his only crime being that he did not believe what he could not: damned for a matter beyond his own control.

B is arrested, tried, convicted, and sentenced to death. In the seclusion of his cell, reflecting over his past life, as his end draws near his mind reverts to his innocent childhood when, kneeling at his mother's feet, his baby-tongue first learned to lisp " Our Father which art in heaven." He thinks of that dear, dear mother so cruelly neglected, dead, perhaps, from grief at his cause, and the man's heart is softened, and he bitterly regrets, nay, sincerely repents, his past misdeeds. Wretched, and without hope in this world, but with his mother's unheeded, though not forgotten, teachings pointing to hope and happiness in another life; with some good priest at his side earnestly urging the same cheerful view; without any knowledge or ideas of his own on the subject, and, in his helpless condition, clutching at anything that looks like hope; he cannot fail to accept and believe that which so coincides with his wishes, and of which he knows nothing to the contrary. He believes, believes sincerely, and, as I have said, sincerely repents, and so dies, and goes to endless bliss, while his recent victim is writhing in hell.

The man who never did a wrong forever punished—the man who never did a right forever rewarded; and purely because the one could not believe, since the evidence did not convince his mind, while the other did believe merely because he knew no better. Reason, God's chiefest gift to man, thus made out to be his worst enemy—for the use of it sends to hell, while its suppression leads to heaven.

Can we wonder that so many men refuse to accept a creed of such hideous possibilities; that they believe such teachings to be a slander against the Almighty, and prefer to worship God in their hearts alone rather than to listen to the vapid utterances of a theological automaton who either has not the brains to discover, or the manhood to avow, the errors of his system?

Nor is this all the harm contained in this doctrine that certain beliefs are absolutely essential to salvation. Not only may it, as we have just seen, damn the righteous dead, it may actually drive the living to their utter ruin.

When one first discovers that he does not really believe some cherished tenet of his Church, something which it is held sacrilegious to even doubt, he is usually shocked at himself, and carefully conceals what he considers his back-sliding; most probably prays that his faith be increased and strengthened—prays that he may become as a little child, that being, as we have seen, the most favorable condition for faith—until he unexpectedly finds that he is not alone in his skepticism, that many, if not most of his friends have very much the same doubts in their hearts, but to be expressed only under the seal of confidence, when, gaining courage from sympathy, he either investigates the whole subject fully and fearlessly, and so becomes a rationalist, and, ninety-nine times out of a hundred, an honest, useful member of society ; or, hiding his doubts, he becomes a hypocrite, an Amminadab Sleek, with God in his lips and Satan in his heart, his religion but a cloak, his piety but a sham ; or, as is very likely to be the case, by the force of reaction, from being a devout, earnest Christian, he becomes an open scorner, sneering at all virtue, because some are hypocrites, rejecting all because some are bad, throwing away the wheat as well as the chaff ; and so, if he had been dependent on his religion for his morality, goes to the bad : more especially if he, as he probably will, still has a lurking belief that for his heresy he is to be eternally damned as soon as he leaves this world ; for in that case he is apt to try to make the most of this life of which he is certain for fear of that of which he is ignorant, and, with the dreaded ban of the Church upon him, an outcast among his fellows, he lives with no object higher than the present gratification of his passions and dies without a hope for the future—wrecked, here and hereafter, by the false teachings of a priesthood who, while claiming to be but the followers of the meek and lowly Jesus—" poor miserable sinners "—and preaching humility for all, are in reality filled with an intolerant pride that brooks neither contradiction nor doubt. We must agree with them or take the consequences, the anathema of the Church. We must go to heaven by their road, in their conveyance ; we may prefer some other route, some other vehicle, and they may not be able to show why our way is not as good as theirs ; but it makes no difference, we must submit our reason to their dicta, or be damned, if they can bring it about.

And how could it be otherwise ? The system teaches that when God wished to communicate with man He did so through His priests; and that when man wished to learn anything of God he should use the same intermediaries as the only source of information. If the priests believe what they teach they must think that they are very near to God—His ministers-plenipotentiary and, like the ministers of earthly kings, entitled to supremacy over other men; and if they do not believe their own dogmas, if they teach as true what they think is false, they are the very men of all others to pretend that they are God's agents in order that they may take advantage of what their congregations are thus taught to consider their semi-divine position to exact all the obedience, consideration, honor, and profit that they can.

And they have neglected neither their interests nor their opportunities. It is not so very long since the Church assumed to govern in temporal as well as spiritual things, and the arrogant priest gave his orders to a king as that king would to his valet. And in any discussion, if such were allowed at all, the finality of all argument was the "dixi"—"I have said"—of the Church. And though modern thought has exploded many of the old ideas, and compelled the Church to greatly modify her claims, and has curtailed the privileges and prestige of the clergy, they are still regarded, perhaps regard themselves, as a class set apart and consecrated to purposes which lift them far above their fellows.

So their pride is natural, and their intolerance to be expected; for their past experience has taught them that, the more their people thought over and discussed their teachings, the less those teachings prevailed, and the more their power waned. Hence they must look with extreme aversion on any one who interferes by his doubts and questions, still more by his arguments, with them or their doctrines, and, so far as in them lies, fight against the advancing champions of religious freedom, by shaking the anathemas of the Church, their only remaining weapons, in the faces of their assailants, in the same manner, and with about the same effect, that the Chinese beat their tom-toms at the advancing hosts of civilization; for, so far from being frightened by the noisy anger of the Church, unbelievers are rather amused at the impotency of her wrath, the very epithets once used by her to bring her enemies into reproach and contempt are now looked upon as rather complimentary than otherwise, investigators and rationalists are getting to be in fashionable demand, and agnosticism stalks in high places.

Faith must give way to doubt, for faith accepts, doubt investigates; faith rests content, doubt advances; faith paralyzes, doubt invigorates; faith is death, doubt is life. All the progress man has ever made, will ever make, must be because he doubts if the goal is reached, and still struggles onward and upward. And so it will be, so it should be. The goal, the consummation of all hope, the end of all progress, must lie beyond infinity, cannot be reached this side of eternity; it is unattainable, in the nature of things, here or hereafter,—but we may continue to approach it nearer and nearer, forever moving forward and higher, the past then as now a teacher, the future still an enigma to be solved, the ever changing present made more and more a delight as we learn more and more what, and why, we are.

Nor is this a cheerless view of the future life. It seems to me happier, higher, nobler, to advance forever than to rest at any one point, whether physical or spiritual, even though that point be what is, at this time, considered perfection. The highest perfection which the mind of man can conceive must be infinitely lower than the absolute perfection of the Deity. We can never reach His level, for that would make us Gods; we must ever be at some point below; and, to my mind, there can be no higher destiny for the human soul than a continued progression towards the Godhead, forever getting nearer and nearer, even though never attaining, each step of progress bringing a happiness unconceived of before.

This faith in the power of doubt, if I may so express it, brings the conviction that investigation can injure only error; that the clergy do not possess all knowledge; that if God has ever really spoken to man He has not yet told him all he was to know; that the goal in the spiritual is no more reached than is the goal in the physical; and prompts man to ask for more light. And finding that to ask the Church is to ask in vain; that she has but one answer, drawn from the barbarous past, and which she admits is best suited for children,—an answer that cannot be understood by reason, but must be accepted by faith, and which includes as self-evident propositions the very doctrines which first aroused his doubts, he turns to nature and leaves the Church to women and children, who, trusting and confiding in their nature, and with strong superstitious instincts, used to subjection and dependent in disposition, may receive its teachings unquestioned.

But the Church could not and cannot satisfy the cravings of thoughtful, earnest men, for she discourages investigation; she cannot answer their cry for light, for she forbids the free use of their reason; she cannot advance, for she claims she has attained; and to those who, hungering for spiritual food, ask for the nutritious bread of life, she has always given a spiritually indigestible stone in the shape of the unchanged and unchanging myths of an ignorant past, unsupported by reason, unsustained by fact, and says "believe or be damned."

Am I not right when I say that the Church works great harm to man when she insists that belief is necessary to salvation?

If such doctrine be derived from the Almighty, if God really teaches that we must believe what our reason rejects, then no wonder that Paul has said (1 Cor. ii., 14): "But the natural man receiveth not the things of the Spirit of God, for they are foolishness to him; neither can he know them, because they are spiritually discerned."

But I think Paul said this because he recognized, with his astute intellect, the necessity of silencing the voice of reason, and therefore called to his aid the superstitious instincts of those whom he addressed, and used exactly the same class of assertions (for they are not arguments) that are used in support of all theological systems,—that the inner consciousness must be the supreme controller (if it agreed with the teacher), that instinct is superior to reason, that belief is proof.

But I do not and cannot believe that God has set a trap for His children, that they may be taken unawares and cruelly and endlessly tortured without even the hope of relief through final annihilation, by making it necessary for their escape from that fearful doom that they should believe and accept as His wisdom that which their God-given reason rejects as nonsense.

I cannot believe that He would condemn me to punishment for a matter beyond my own control—belief.

I cannot believe that He would endow me with reason, and damn me, unwarned, for consciously using it.

And thousands think the same, and no longer bow to the behests of orthodoxy.

The glamour which her priests have thrown around her rites and doctrines is fast fading away, and the inconsistencies and incongruities of the Church are becoming more and more visible. Men are, by degrees, getting bold enough to deny that God is but an exaggerated man, and to assert that what is foolishness to the natural man cannot be of the Spirit of God. We may believe what is above and beyond our reason, for it is only where the realm of reason ends that the domain of faith properly begins; and in the legitimate domain of faith reason is silent, for she knows nothing which contradicts. But when *our* reason can clearly see why anything cannot be—when anything is palpably folly to us—how infinitely below the wisdom of God must it be. And before we admit that the highest type of Divine wisdom just reaches the level of our conception of nonsense; before we slander the Almighty by believing him absurd; before we stultify ourselves and insult Him by believing that what would be imbecility in us would be intelligence in Him; let us require absolute demonstration that He really is what His self-appointed priests have painted Him, and until such demonstration is made, let us continue to believe Him what nature tells us He is, an all-pervading, living, loving, unchanging God, ruling, not by caprice, but by fixed and immutable, because perfect, law.

THE ARGUMENT.

PROPOSITION II.

II. The Doctrine of Free-will, as usually understood, and as taught by the Church, is impossible if God be as He is represented: attributing the origin of sin to man is absurd; and the idea of a continual strife between God and the Devil is blasphemous.

In the course of my correspondence with the Bishop I had occasion to express my doubts as to the doctrine of free-will as taught by the Church. Whereupon he very kindly gave me his views (which I take to be also those of his Church) on this interesting and puzzling question, as follows.

I quote from his second letter:

"I must confess that I had not expected that you would deny to us free-will. In treating of the morality of human actions, philosophers and theologians regard liberty as a 'conditio sine qua non.' Where there is no liberty there can be no moral act. A twofold liberty is spoken of, viz: 'Libertas a coactione; libertas a necessitate.'

"'Libertas a coactione' is the freedom from exterior violence offered to me. For instance, if a man stronger than I would overpower me and force my hand, unable to resist, to stab another, no court would call my action a murder, since my will did not possess the 'libertas a coactione.'

"The 'libertas a necessitate' is defined ordinarily:

'Libertas qua voluntas non solum sponte ac liberter agit, sed cum tali suorum actuum dominio ut possit æque non eligere vel eligere, agere vel non agere.' It is also defined to be 'vis electiva, seu facultas eligendi vel non eligendi pro libitu.' This is in reality the true liberty which has its seat essentially in the intellectual soul, and no power of man or devils can rob us of it. No man or devil can force my will to consent to, or take pleasure in, an improper action. The very pagan Seneca says 'corpora obnoxia sunt dominis, mens sui juris est.' But if a man has lost, or never did possess, this 'libertas a necessitate,' he will not be punished for an act which *in se* would be a crime. Thus an idiot, who has killed a man, could not be punished for the act. But it is just this freedom of the will which you deny. To prove that man has no free-will, you bring the example of the drunkard. He falls into drunkenness and you very illogically conclude that therefore he has no free-will. You can logically conclude that the individual in question has preferred drunkenness to temperance—and nothing else. Hence we note thousands of instances of men who have preferred temperance to the allurements of drunkenness. I have seen in New York and other cities, what almost every Catholic priest can tell you of, how poor women have emerged from the lowest sinks of the great city, and, by a life of piety, redeemed the past. I have seen many and many a man who has been a drunkard, arise, and by a life of temperance bring back comfort and happiness to his family. From your example of the drunkard you can logically conclude that the poor fellow prefers the momentary gratification of his palate to the pleasures purchased only by checking the unlawful desires of the senses—and not a jot more can be logically concluded.

"Because some men always yield to their cravings for liquor and other improper gratifications of the flesh, to conclude that therefore 'an irresistible force' controls them, and thence to deny free-will—is certainly most illogical. Deny free-will to man, and you destroy all distinction between virtue and vice. If, as you say, 'the poor man is helpless'—if an 'irresistible force' controls him, the drunkard, the adulterer, the murderer, is to be pitied when he gets drunk, commits adultery, murder, and other crimes. But surely a man ought not to be punished for what he cannot help. In therefore denying free-will to man, you open the famous and terrible question: 'Whence the origin of evil?' That grave question puzzled the wisest heads of antiquity. Whence came all the evil—the countless woes, physical and moral, which we see in this world? How does it happen that the poor little babe must die in such agony as to melt the hardest bosom? How come those cruel diseases, fearful epidemics, and the countless woes that flesh is heir to from the cradle to the grave? To say that God purposely created man, who, without any fault of his own, is to endure the agonies, the pains, the death, which are so fearful in the history of man—is to make of God a tyrant, in comparison with whom Nero and Robespierre were gentle doves. Hence the ancients were all puzzled over this question. Hence their theories about a blind and eternal fate, about the dual principles, etc., etc. The only logical answer to this fearful question is what the Christian dogma gives. For the Christian dogma places the origin of all evil in the revolt of the free-will of the creature against the most lawful and mild command of Him who was more than friend, benefactor, father to man—for He was God. God created man with a nature perfect and free from disease and death. God placed man in a world free from all that is noxious, and replete with the good and beautiful. But man had a free-will—and he consequently could make a bad use of that beautiful freedom; and he did. He dared to insult the infinite majesty of God by revolting against His commands. Our sense of justice tells us that sin must be punished. Now the punishment must be in proportion to the enormity of the crime. Hence the man who may have stolen a few pennies is not to receive the same punishment as he who has committed murder. The enormity of the crime is also measured by the dignity of the person insulted. Hence the boy who slaps the face of one of his little playmates has not committed as grievous a fault as he who has slapped the face of his own mother. The dignity of the mother insulted being so much greater than the dignity of the little playmate, causes the difference. But He who is insulted by man's sin is a God of infinite dignity. Hence when death and his train of temporal punishments came into this world, the philosophic mind can justly regard all this as a punishment due to sin. 'Per peccatum mors intravit in hunc mundum'—by sin has death entered into this world. Moreover, God sent a Redeemer to fallen man,—and if man will but have a good will, God's wisdom will convert man's very fall into such wonderful dignities flowing from the redemption that for all eternity he will sing: 'O felix culpa quæ talem et tantum meruiti Redemptorem.' The bodily ills and miseries of life, if patiently endured by the Christian, cease to be ills. For they will merit such a glorious reward after this brief life that with Christ we say: 'Blessed are the poor; blessed are ye that mourn and weep; blessed are they that suffer persecutions.' As to moral evils, (and take them away, would you not be taking away the vast, I had almost said all, the evils which afflict mankind,) our dogma is here most reasonable. Catholic dogma tells us that our will is free—and consequently there is no 'irresistible force' to compel me, or any other human being, to get drunk, murder, or commit any other moral evil. If moral evil exists man's abuse of that wonderful gift—our free-will—is to blame for it and its consequences.

" But you deny that man has a free-will—you assert that an '*irresistible* force controls him.' Then we have the right to say that a just judge cannot punish man for doing what he is constrained to by 'an irresistible force.'

" I have a right then to ask you, whence then all these evils in this world? I can ask, why then does God make man suffer such cruel ills and horrid death? Can a God who is infinitely good create poor beings who without any fault of their own are so miserable as we—who having done no sin (as they have no free-will) enter this vale of tears, ' primam vocem lachrymans,' and leave this world amid groans and agonies which make the bystanders shudder with horror? Not having a free-will, man did nothing to merit all these punishments—and how could a God be just and punish man for sins which he could not avoid? Consequently there is no escape; deny a man free-will, and you must believe in the existence of an unjust and cruel God, which is an absurdity. Admit that man has a free will, and philosophy can tell you that sin deserves punishment; that death and the other evils of this life are not too severe punishments for sins committed against a person of infinite dignity.

" 'Tis true, I do not deny that there are difficulties. But these difficulties arise from the fact that we do not know in life the Infinite Being—God. The dignity of a father and mother we know. And hence when that dignity is insulted our sense of justice appreciates the justice of the punishment. The Infinite, however, we have never seen. Hence what is due to infinite dignity insulted will always appear more or less obscure, more or less attended with difficulty to the poor weak mind of the finite being.

"The Eternal Infinite, Omniscient, we have never seen, consequently we will always find difficulties in the action of the Eternal, Omniscient, Infinite God, with and upon the finite free-will of man. It is the very nature of things to expect difficulties here. For to comprehend clearly and without difficulties with our limited intellects, we must first know the Eternal Infinite. Hence it is impossible, in this life, fully to realize the enormity of sin—for we do not know in this life the infinite dignity of the God insulted by sin. The Infinite, the Eternal, have never yet fallen under the apprehension of our senses. We have really no true and adequate conception of the Infinite. But this should not surprise us. In our very body there are many things whose existence we must admit, but which give rise to difficulties which will never be explained. But to endeavor to remove difficulties by altogether denying well-established facts, is only to fall into inextricable absurdities. So in things divine. There are, no doubt, difficulties arising from acknowledging the free-will in man and the ever Omniscient, Infinite, Eternal God. But these difficulties must be in all reason expected to arise in our minds. For we are so limited. In this world our knowledge of the Omniscient, Infinite God is extremely little. We see God here only 'in œnigmate et quasi in speculo'—consequently the relations between an Infinite, Omniscient, Eternal Being, and beings like us, finite and subject to many weaknesses, must necessarily present difficulties to our mind, which has never seen the Infinite, the Eternal, the Omniscient.

"But because of difficulties to deny point-blank the existence of free-will in man, is to deny the belief of all mankind. Mankind has always been conscious that there is no 'irresistible force' which compels a man to get drunk, commit adultery, murder, and other sins. If a man does these acts, the voice of the entire human family says he himself is to blame,—and so conscious is the human family of this that they have always punished most terribly the men who dared commit those crimes. But deny free-will and you encounter a greater evil. You open the then countless and wholly unanswerable questions: how came evil into this world? Why does God, infinitely good, send sickness, miseries, and death upon his own, in that case, helpless, as well as hapless, creatures? What have they done to deserve all these miseries? They have not committed sin—for sin is impossible where there is no free-will. These actions are not sins; for an 'irresistible force,' which God Himself created, compelled them to get drunk and do other things—where then the justice in punishing them?

"Whereas by admitting that man has a free will we are in accord with the universal belief of mankind. If all mankind has been so wofully deceived that after all we have no free-will, the human intellect could no longer be trusted. We also find here the rational answer to the grave question: how came evil into this world? Moreover, I have said before that the omniscience of God is perfectly reconcilable with man's free-will."

It will be observed, I think, that this very interesting statement of the Church's side of the question is fairly reducible to this: The doctrine of free-will is a theory devised by the Church to explain certain mysterious facts and to answer certain very inconvenient questions. It does not seem to be claimed as a fact revealed by the Almighty, but is an assumption of the Church. It is frankly admitted that the subject is naturally full of difficulties, and it is practically confessed that the Church's dogma is only a partial solution; and the main arguments in favor of its correctness, when reduced to their last analysis, seem to be:

1st. That though not explaining satisfactorily, it explains better than any other theory; and

2d. All mankind believe it.

To these two arguments I reply:

1st. A theory that does not explain all the facts it attempts to account for is unfit for the purposes for which it was intended; and

2d. Even if all mankind believed it, (which I think is rather too broad an assertion), it would not be any evidence of its truth. It would be a very dangerous precedent to establish that a theory was true or false according to the number of those who accept or reject it, for, in that case, having in view "all mankind," the Christian religion would be in a hopeless minority, and consequently could not be held to be true.

And this ought to dispose of this class of arguments so common with the Church.

The Bishop's method of reconciling the omniscience of God with man's free-will, will be given and commented on under Proposition V, when we come to speak of the deductions to be drawn from the history of the betrayal by Judas.

I agree with the Bishop that the question of free-will is one of difficulty, very grave difficulty. I will even admit that the difficulty is, in our present state of knowledge, insolvable. So with the questions of the origin of the evil, and reconciling the existence of evil with the goodness of God. I have thought much, and read much on these subjects, and candidly admit that I have only partially satisfied my own mind. We are all equally in the dark, churchmen and laymen; but some little light is beginning to shine upon the question of why evil exists, or, more properly, of the uses and advantages of what we call evil, and I need hardly say the light does not come from the direction of the Church; it comes from a better acquaintance with nature.

Although whether I am right or wrong in my views upon these intricate and interesting questions cannot really affect the main points under discussion, except that if I am right the Church must be wrong, and therefore by no means infallible; and although the known facts are too few and too little understood to permit either side to do more than argue the probability of its views; I will, very briefly, considering the magnitude of the subject, give such conclusions as I have reached, with my reasons.

I understand there are those who believe in what is called "predestination," and that such urge that we are, with reference to God, as clay in the potter's hands, that our every act is foreseen, that our eternal fate is foreordained, but yet insist (by a contradiction which is absurd to all except theologians, to whom it is incomprehensible) that we are free agents. I do not address my argument to such, for they would seem to be on both sides of the question at once, and ready to agree with any one in any conclusion. I wish to reach a definite conclusion, not repugnant to reason, and which will at least have the merit of letting us know just what we do believe; and I will reason from analogy, and not from authority.

I believe, because I can see no reason to the contrary, but much in its favor, that there is a God, and that He is necessarily, or He would not be God, omnipotent, omniscient, and prescient, as well as all good. I also believe that He pervades all nature, and that everything exists by and through Him, and that without Him nothing could exist. I think this much can be logically deduced from nature, and as the Church and I agree on this point it is hardly necessary to argue it. I also believe, as a necessary corollary from these facts, that this universe is governed by His will; and as it has been demonstrated that the universe is governed by law, it must be, if my belief is right, that God's will is that law. This means, taken in connection with the attributes above specified, that everything, all nature, animate and inanimate, originated, exists, changes, grows, decays, dies, under fixed and inalterable law, not caprice; for caprice is not law, in the sense in which I am using the term, even if it be the caprice of a God.

All we *know*, in contra-distinction to *believe*, of God, we have learned from nature. *How* He works we may observe and learn; *why* He does it, we may never *know*, we can only *guess*. Or as I expressed the same idea in a public address more than twenty years ago: "We are not permitted to scrutinize the reasons of the Almighty, but we are permitted to observe phenomena and from them to learn His laws."

From the observation of these phenomena it is demonstrated with absolute certainty that under certain circumstances the desire to do certain acts amounts to mania, is a disease, and is irresistible. Hence dipsomania, nymphomania or gynæcomania, kleptomania, and other diseases which, though theology may teach the contrary, irresistibly impel men and women to do acts which, were their wills free, they would not do. These are scientific facts which the Church has not yet learned. Further investigation may, and probably will, establish the fact that even when one is apparently acting the most deliberately, he is acting under irresistible impulses, induced by causes beyond his control; and, of course, the same applies with more force to actions not deliberate. For example, suppose a man of violent temper marries a woman equally excitable; their offspring will almost certainly possess an ungovernable temper, and will do many things under its influence which he would not do if his parents had not forced, under the inexorable law of heredity, such disposition on him. His reason and judgment, his will, may be to be mild and gentle; he strives hard to control his inherited ferocity, but causes which on one more favorably born would have no effect, will goad him into a frenzy that makes him blind, and in his rage he knows not what he does. So, too, with the man who inherits the desire for drink. In his sober moments he resolves earnestly and honestly never to touch alcohol in any shape; he avoids temptation; but his desire is stronger than his will, and he falls again and again. Where is his free-will? Who is responsible for the irresistible force which controls his will? He is not to blame for it, his father, or his grandfather, or some other ancestor bequeathed it to him, and he cannot get rid of it. God made the law of heredity, and under its operation the poor man is helpless. Though we are not controlled by visible powers, we are none the less controlled. Disposition, the peculiar structure of our brains, surrounding circumstances, all or any, may control our wills, and they are all beyond our control; and I cannot doubt that in the final settlement of our accounts, whenever and wherever that may take place, our inherited disposition and character will enter very largely into it, and immensely modify the psychological consequences of our acts.

And yet, in the absence of visible physical force, in our inordinate human vanity, we, men, the creatures of circumstances beyond our control, arrogate to ourselves free-will, and think we are but a little lower than the angels.

A man cannot be truly said to possess a free will unless he can control *all* that goes to make up that will. One man is, as we have seen, by a nature for which he is not responsible, made cold and phlegmatic, while another, equally without his fault, is hot and impetuous. Each one's will is controlled by his natural disposition, and his natural disposition is forced upon him not by his own act. He may, by proper training and favorable circumstances, modify his nature, or, rather, to some extent restrain it; but never to that degree that he can be truly said to have entire free-will. One will find temptation irresistible, the other is not moved by it; it may be that neither is influenced by principle, but only by his natural disposition; or it may be that natural disposition in one is so much stronger than in the other that it controls and subordinates principle; yet in either case the will, and the choice made by it, is the result of that disposition which, come from what source it may, is not his fault; and therefore while his will may seem to choose, the choice is by no means free.

But the Bishop says that drunken men and fallen women may, and do, reform. This is true, though rare ; but it shows nothing to the contrary of, nor does it conflict with, what I have just said. Many, perhaps most, who fall are sorely tempted by present circumstances, frequently deceived and entrapped, in the case of women, or led astray by evil associations, or the desire to forget trouble, in the case of men, and are not impelled by pre-natal causes, though the facility of the yielding or the vigor of the resistance may be affected by them. And the reform may be because the experiment has satisfied the person that there was more happiness in a more moral life, his mind having, by satiety or other natural cause, been brought to that condition where it in its turn subordinated his wasted passions. Each case of reform, like each case of sin, must be examined in all its details before we can give any satisfatory explanation of how it has been brought about. But in each case the reform must depend, like the yielding, more on the effect of circumstances on the natural disposition, than on the mere volition, or free-will. There may be a line within which man is free to act as he wishes, and can control his will, or act contrary to his desires. But where that line is I do not know, and it must vary in each individual; but the probability is that every act, no matter how trivial, is done in strict accordance with some law, though we may not know or understand it; and that there are other laws which, by counteracting the first, may permit us a certain freedom within certain undefined and restricted bounds; and it is therefore probable that a better acquaintance with the laws of nature may teach us a better way of controlling unlawful desires than by praying for the grace of God, which experience shows us is, to put it with extreme mildness, a very uncertain method.

The study of the operations of the mind seems to point in the same direction. What I have already said in discussing the involuntary character of belief appears to me to illustrate this. If I had a free will in the sense in which the Church uses the term, and if to believe as I do be a sin, as the Church must certainly hold, then, on the Church's theory, I hold my views by virtue of my own free-will, and have the power (else I have not free-will), to change them and believe as the Church teaches. But I know that I am as powerless to believe the dogmas of the Church as I am to believe that my existence is a myth; so whatever the Church's theory may say, I *know* that I am not free to change my views. Were argument to be adduced sufficient to convince my mind, my views would change themselves, but my will would have nothing to do with it. And if my belief be a sin, it is a sin I cannot help committing. The Church might say that my free-will led me into a course of study which has produced the present result. But I say no; the study succeeded the doubt, and was the result of an earnest desire to get truth, a desire so strong that it absorbed even the wish to resist; and he is unfortunate indeed who wishes to resist the desire for truth; I am thankful that I do not.

It has been urged that on the theory which I advocate it is wrong to impose punishment upon criminals, certainly upon those who commit crimes under the impulsion of pre-natal causes. There is absolutely nothing in this beyond its seeming plausibility. In the first place, juries must convict and judges sentence without reference to their personal ideas of propriety, because it is their duty to execute all the laws which actually exist, not merely those which they approve. And in the next place the criminal laws, as they now exist, as a rule, are right. We have seen that these pre-natal causes impel with varying force, sometimes irresistibly, sometimes with less power. One force in nature frequently overcomes another. The cohesion of a string may counteract the attraction of gravity and hold a weight suspended in the air. Gravitation exists and is acting; cohesion exists and is acting. If gravitation is the stronger, the string breaks and the weight falls; otherwise the weight remains acted on but unmoved by gravity. So one emotion or passion may counterbalance or restrain another; and the dread of the publicity of a trial and the probability of a conviction, and, in that case, the certainty of punishment, may, and does frequently, overcome the desire to commit a wrong act, where the desire is merely strong but not irresistible; and in that way the law prevents or lessens crime. If the desire be stronger than the fear, then the crime is committed, and the law imposes its penalty not so much as an avenger as for the purpose of deterring others, through that same law of counteracting forces, by showing that the result of the crime is actual, practical pain and suffering; and for the purpose of separating from his fellows, for his own and their good, one who has shown that he cannot with safety be left at large. No one attaches the idea of crime to a mad dog, but nevertheless he must be put out of the way. So with certain classes of criminals. They may not be morally responsible for their acts, but if their acts are dangerous to the persons or property of the community they should be put where they can do no more harm even if they can do no good.

From his argument the Bishop seems to think that free-will is the only theory that can reconcile the existence of evil with the goodness of God, and that that theory does it, because by that theory evil comes from the free-will of man and not from God. This does not solve the difficulty, it only temporizes with it; for if sin and its attendant and consequent evils arose from free-will, then they arose because God chose to give men free-will, and the proposition is presented in this light: God is omnipotent and prescient; He made man, including his character and disposition; He knew that if He gave him free-will he would sin, and that, as a consequence, evil would come into the world; He need not have given him free-will, but could have controlled his will so that all his desires should have been pure; but He deliberately acted otherwise, and so made man that He knew sin and evil would result from it.

It seems to me that this is very far from solving the difficulty and carries us just where we did not want to go. The object of the theory is to remove the responsibility of sin from God; but clearly it does not do it.

Another effort in the same direction was inventing the devil; for it seems to have been thought that if putting the origin of sin on man did not relieve God from responsibility for it, putting it on the devil would. But that helps the matter no more than does the other theory, unless it be held that God did not make the devil, that the devil is the more powerful of the two, and that God cannot control him; otherwise he must be acting by the permission of God, doing just what God permits and wishes, for if He can without trouble or danger stop him, and does not, He must wish him to continue as he is doing; and the responsibility for all his acts would be with God.

None of the Church theories helps us, for in order to make any of them available God must be shorn of His chiefest attributes, or be dethroned.

But nature helps us a little—not very much. As I have indicated before, the *How* is within our reach. The *Why* must necessarily remain beyond.

God has made a set of laws which we may divide into physical and moral, the two covering all the phenomena of nature—physical, mental, and psychological.

The violation of any physical law carries punishment with it without reference to intention. Poison will produce sickness or death, whether taken ignorantly, intentionally, or accidentally. A law of nature has been violated, and all the consequences of violation follow. As I have said elsewhere in this discussion, nature warns with a blow, but the blow is usually given after, not before, the violation of her laws. This punishment, if we may so call it, is nature's protest against ignorance, and is her command to study her phenomena and learn her laws. Try to change, disguise, or explain it as we may, this is God's law in physical nature. No revelation is claimed to have ever been attempted in this direction: experience is the only teacher, reason the only guide; and they have been found to be sufficient when left free to assert themselves.

Now what warrant have we for assuming that God's moral law is so totally different from His physical law that it must be studied and learned in a totally different way; that in the place of experience and reason we must rely upon revelation and faith?

So far as I have been able to ascertain, only a supposed revelation to the Jews, a revelation which, like an ancient deed, is assumed to prove itself, and manifestly for the same reason—there is no other way to prove it. Proof being out of the question, it is taken for granted rather than raise perplexing and annoying questions and controversies. A revelation which was seemingly so unimportant that they were permitted to lose it, and be without it, until it was found by Hilkiah; a revelation of which the rest (and by far the largest part) of the world were permitted to be in entire ignorance until the translation at Alexandria against the will of the Chosen People.

And what did the rest of the world do during all this time? Why, nearly every nation had a "revelation" of its own, and so similar, in many instances, to that of the Jews as to suggest the idea of a common origin, the Jewish being about the youngest, and to a great extent the most repulsive. That common origin seems to have been the mind of man endeavoring to explain phenomena which he could not comprehend, by referring them to a Deity who was always only an exaggerated copy of the ideal man of the people over whom He was supposed to preside.

I think we are therefore authorized to assume that what has been called "revelation" is nothing more, nothing less, than an expression of the theories of the past based on imperfectly, or not at all, understood natural, mental, and psychological phenomena, and crude ideas of ethics and sociology, derived from limited experience and worked up by uncultivated minds. Hence, if this view be correct, as I think it is, the value of revelation as a guide is not particularly great, and it would be safer to look for the moral law as we do for the physical, by accurate observation and careful deduction. We may go astray, and most assuredly often do, but not so far as the Church would lead us, for that would carry us back to the dawn of civilization and keep us there. But the errors of the past lead to the truths of the future; past failures make future successes, when investigation and study are not annulled by dogmatism.

I see no reason, then, for supposing that the moral law, in its action, differs in any respect from the physical, and I deduce that an infraction of it is assuredly punished, in this world or the next, or both, whether the violation be voluntary, forced, or through ignorance. Every violation of the physical law, as we have seen, is followed by what we *may* call punishment, as the natural result of the act, without reference to how or why the violation was caused; and it seems exceedingly probable that in the same way, and for the same reasons, any violation of the moral law, equally without reference to why or how the violation was caused, will be followed by what we *do* call punishment, though equally only the natural result of the act. So, even without free-will, infractions of the law would result in evil (or punishment) enough to at least teach us better, and the consequences would be repeated and increased, with each infraction, until we did better, here or hereafter. In other words, my idea is that God is never vindictive, and never inflicts punishment, as the word is usually understood, but that He has so arranged His plan of human progress that man can work his way upward only through much tribulation and sorrow, the pains and penalties visited on him being only apparent evils, but really necessary educators to enable him to work out his own salvation, and teach him not to rely on others to do it for him; that it is only in Jewish and Christian (or other) fiction that there can be a scape-goat, and that man must bear the consequences of his ignorance and work out his own redemption, advancing step by step in knowledge, and growing better as he grows wiser, the same law of growth applying to his moral, that applies to his physical and mental nature.

This seems to be HOW God works. WHY He should have adopted such a plan ; why growth and decay should have been made a law of nature in every department— physical, mental, psychic ; why we should be left to our own efforts to learn the lessons necessary for our being and progress, I cannot even guess. It is sufficient for me to know that He has adopted it, and that in this view there is no conflict between His goodness and our temporary sufferings.

For I gather from these theories (though they are but imperfect at best) that evil is the result, in physical, mental, and psychological nature, of ignorance, and is the means of instruction and progress. Sin is ignorance, evil is instruction, study the remedy, and knowledge the reward : and all are but the means of carrying out God's great laws—Evolution and Compensation.

Physical pain and disease are the results of the violation of physical laws, and are warnings against further infractions ; and the unpleasant results of the violation of the moral law, whether the suffering be here or hereafter, serve to recall us to our duty : and all are educators, as I have just said. Grief, and pains of that character, are the price we pay for purification, progress, and the capacity to rejoice. They are the minor chords that give a tender melancholy to, and soften the asperities of, the music of our lives; the sharp dissonances which, harsh and unpleasant by themselves, yet lead to higher harmonies than we have known before. Without contrasts pleasure would only pall ; happiness itself would cloy.

Death is considered a fearful evil. So it is to the living, but I doubt if it be so to the dead. Could the worm formulate its thoughts, it would probably think death an unmixed evil, but the butterfly would probably regard it as a wondrous blessing. And I think it is so with man. It is but a " going before "; the birth of the spirit. And the grief and desolation of those who stay behind are the result in a great measure of the fearful teachings of the Church. Could we but believe that the parting was merely temporary, and that while punishment was inevitable, it was not endless, that it was proportionate and just (and nature points in that direction) rather than vindictive, and that it would certainly finally result in the eternal benefit and happiness of the dead, many of the pangs of grief would be assuaged.

I believe, therefore, that much of what we call sin and evil are so but seemingly, and are the means, in God's providence, of working out the progress of man here and hereafter; and in this view of the case the existence of evil and the goodness of God, though mysterious, and in a great degree incomprehensible, are not necessarily inharmonious.

Another very serious objection to the doctrine of freewill, in connection with the theory of the Devil, is that it forces the Church to represent God on the one hand and the Devil on the other, each engaged in endeavoring to lead mankind to himself: the one urging upon him the advantage of a life of temporary self-denial here, to be followed by an eternity of bliss hereafter; the other suggesting the wisdom of making the most of the present rather than trusting to an unknown future; and as in the only other instance in which the Devil is represented as contradicting God it turned out that the Devil was right

(Gen. ii., 16, 17; iii., 4), men are disposed to listen to the blandishments of the Enemy, and accept present pleasure rather than postpone their enjoyment to an uncertain hereafter. All of which—this idea of strife between the supreme God and the supreme Devil—this struggle for supremacy, this electioneering, so to speak, on the part of the almighty Ruler of heaven and earth, with the advantage rather on the side of the Devil—is to my mind sheer blasphemy, pure and unadulterated, unworthy of the age in which we live, degrading to those who believe it.

THE ARGUMENT.

PROPOSITION III.

III. The councils of the Church, by which her creeds were formulated, were not inspired, but very fallible, assemblies of exceedingly natural men; and their decrees are conflicting, unreasonable, and utterly without authority.

I give the remarks contained in my first communication to the Bishop which, with his reply, brought on the discussion of this point:

Nearly every dogma of any of the Churches has been established through debate, by argument and discussion, and determined by vote. Reasoning is permitted, nay, encouraged, so long as it is on the side of the majority. The subject only becomes too sacred for discussion after it has been voted a dogma. Reason may be used to determine what is true, but having once been decided to be true, by a majority vote, Reason must be ever after silent, unless a majority "go back" on the old truth, and so declare by another vote, when the old truth becomes error, and the old error, by the magic of numerical strength, becomes truth, and, in its turn, sacred and unassailable.

To which the Bishop said:

"Your remarks about dogmas are to me extremely novel. You assert that what at one time have been held to be dogmas 'too sacred for discussion,' have in the lapse of time been 'by the magic of numerical strength' declared errors. I reply to this assertion by simply challenging you to show one solitary dogma which the Roman Catholic Church taught in one age as a dogma of revealed religion, and which she afterwards repudiated as an error; or that what she repudiated in one age as an error, she in a succeeding age propounded as a dogma."

This drew from me the following reply which I give, changing the pronouns so as to relieve it from its epistolary character, and making some merely verbal alterations:

I am challenged to adduce one solitary dogma which the Roman Catholic Church taught as true and afterwards repudiated; or to show that she repudiated as error in one age what she afterwards propounded as a dogma.

I think that examples may be found in the facts which I give below, but I give them with a full knowledge that they may be explained away in a manner highly satisfactory to the faithful by either denying the authority of the council, or claiming that the view was always held, though not made a dogma. I will endeavor to anticipate such explanations as I go along, to save time.

My authority for the facts which follow is Voltaire's *Dictionnaire Philosophique*, Edition-Touquet, Paris, 1822, titles "Conciles," "Christianisme," from which I translate freely. I know that Voltaire is in very bad odor with orthodox Christians, but these facts are, I believe, undisputed, and can be found stated by other authors. I have used Voltaire because his book is the most convenient to my hand.

The first œcumenical council was convoked by Constantine (not a very exemplary Christian) at Nice in the year 325. The occasion of this council seems to have been certain disputes among the clergy of Alexandria touching the divinity of Jesus. Constantine sent a letter to them by Hosius, Bishop of Cordova, remonstrating with them for quarrelling over so small a matter; but his letter not having the effect he expected, he convoked the council to set the matter at rest. At that council some held the opinions of Origen, as set forth in his 6th chapter against Celsus:[1] "We present our prayers to God by Jesus, who holds the middle between natures created and natures uncreated, who brings us the grace of his father, and presents our prayers to the great God in the quality of our Pontiff." They based their position on Jesus' saying "My father is greater than I"; and they regarded Jesus as the first-born of the creation, and the purest emanation of the Supreme Being, but not precisely as God. Their opponents, on the strength of the text "My father and I are one," took the position that Jesus was God, in spite of the explanation that, in view of the other saying, this last meant: "My father and I have the same design, the same will; I have no other desires than those of my father." But Eusebius of Nicomedia, with seventeen other bishops, and a number of priests, including Arius, were voted down by a vote of 299 to 18, and the council decided that "Jesus is the only son of God, begotten of the Father, God of God, light of light, very God of very God, consubstantial with the Father. We believe also in the Holy Ghost," etc.

Up to this time the priests of the Church certainly taught different views upon the subject (or it were unnecessary to call the council), and it is to be hoped that some of both sides were saved. But this council, not

[1] *Cf.* Bk. v., ch. iv. ; Bk. vi., ch. xlvii.–xlviii. ; Bk. viii., ch. xiii.–xxvi.

convoked by the Church, but by an Emperor who was at that time not even baptized (that ceremony having been performed on his death-bed), decided that *henceforth* the belief thus formulated must be held under pain of damnation.

In 359 the Emperor Constantius assembled the two councils of Rimini and Seleucis, corresponding with each other, and composed of 600 bishops and a large number of priests, and these councils undid the work of the council of Nice, and rejected the word "consubstantial"; but these two councils are not recognized as valid by the Church; why, I know not, except that their action was afterwards found to be distasteful to a majority. Be that as it may, a grand council met, by order of the Emperor Theodosius, at Constantinople in 381, with 150 bishops, and this council anathematized that of Rimini. That is to say, these 150 bishops undid what the 600 bishops had done. St. Gregory Nazienzen presided,—the same who wrote to Procopius: "I fear these councils; I have never known one which did not do more harm than good, or which had a good end; the spirit of disputation, vanity, ambition, rule in them; he who wishes to reform the wicked exposes himself to be denounced without succeeding in his corrections."

This council added to the Nicene creed: "Jesus Christ is incarnate by the Holy Ghost, and of the Virgin Mary. He was crucified for us under Pontius Pilate. He was buried, and rose again the third day, according to the Scriptures. He is seated on the right of the Father: We believe in the Holy Ghost, vivifying Lord, who proceeds from the Father, and is glorified with the Father and the Son."

Here again we have more things made necessary to be

believed, which, while perhaps taught by many before, were not declared essential until then. And remark that this council did not find out that the Holy Ghost proceeded from both the Father and the Son, but announces it as proceeding only from the Father; so that we might then have been saved without believing that it proceeded from both. It was toward the ninth century that the Latin Church discovered, by degrees, that the Holy Ghost proceeded from both the Father and the Son, when it so announced, though Pope John VIII. had declared "Judas" those who so believed.

In 431 Theodosius II. convoked the grand council of Ephesus. Nestorius, Bishop of Constantinople, who had persecuted many for not agreeing with him in theology, was, in his turn, persecuted for holding that the Holy Virgin, mother of Jesus Christ, was not the mother of God, because, as he said, Jesus being the Word, Son of God, consubstantial with the Father, Mary could not be at the same time, mother of God the Father and God the Son. St. Cyril bitterly opposed him. Nestorius demanded and obtained an œcumenical council. Nestorius was condemned; but Cyril was deposed by a committee of the council.

The Emperor undid what the council did, but permitted it to reassemble. Rome sent deputies, but they arrived very late. Trouble increasing, the Emperor arrested both Nestorius and Cyril, and ordered all the bishops to their respective churches, and no conclusion was reached. Such was the famous council of Ephesus.

Another grand council at Ephesus in 449. The bishops said that those who would divide Jesus in two should themselves be torn in two. Dioscorus, Bishop of Alexandria, presided. The two natures of Jesus were anathematized. The disputants fought in full council; neither the first nor the last attempt to determine questions of faith by physical force.

In 451 the grand council of Chalcedon established that Jesus had two natures and one person.

Having established one person and two natures, it became necessary to determine how many wills Jesus had. So, in 680, more than two hundred years later, a general council at Constantinople decided that Jesus had two wills, and condemned Pope Honorius I., who held that Jesus had but one. This was before the Pope had been ascertained to be infallible.

In 787 was convoked the second council of Nice, by Irene, mother of Constantine, but in the name of her son. Her husband had abolished the adoration of images as contrary to the simplicity of the first centuries, and favoring idolatry; Irene re-established it; she spoke in the council. Two legates of Pope Adrian IV. were present, but did not speak, as they did not understand Greek.

In 794 Charlemagne called a numerous council at Frankfort. It characterized the second council of Nice as an impertinent and arrogant synod held in Greece for the adoration of pictures.

In 842 another grand council at Constantinople, convoked by the Empress Theodora, where the adoration of images was solemnly established.

Omitting the numerous intervening councils as not being necessary to the present discussion, we find that the dogmas of transubstantiation and confession were first announced at the council of Lateran, in 1215, under Pope Innocent III.

However much the doctrine of penance, as it is now called, may have been taught or practised by the Christian Church (as it was, and is, by many others) before that time, it was then that confession was made obligatory. Before that time God would forgive sins without confession to a man, be he priest or otherwise, or an infallible Church would surely not have waited twelve hundred years to inform the faithful to the contrary; but from and after that time confession, at least once a year, became necessary to attain that forgiveness.

And so, to be brief, with the very modern dogmas of the immaculate conception of the Virgin Mary, 1854, and papal infallibility, 1870.

I here stated that I knew that the Bishop would say that some of these councils were good and some bad, and that the good councils have always agreed, and were called to crush out heresies which had taken possession of some priests, and only announced what had always been believed. But in that case how are we to tell the true from the false? Called by the same power, consisting of the same class of men, some recognized by Rome and condemned by Constantinople, others recognized by Constantinople and condemned by Rome, who is to decide? The Roman Catholic Church accepts what pleases it; the Greek Catholic Church adopts what it likes. According to Hefele, Bishop of Rottenberg, the Roman Church recognizes twenty councils, while, according to the *Encyclopædia Britannica*, the Greek Church recognizes but seven, and the English Church practically only the first five. Of course the Bishop would claim that the Roman Catholic Church must be right, as it is infallible. But as that infallibility is one of the points at issue, that would hardly be an answer.

Let us try to look at the question by the aid of a little unfettered reason, outside of these councils and the

Church where it has been hampered and tied down by edicts, dogmas, and creeds, made by other mortals like ourselves, and forced down our throats under the most fearful penalties.

A council is, necessarily, either to establish or condemn—that is, its object and result must be either to establish as a dogma, or belief, of the Church something which had not before been a dogma, or belief; or to stamp with the seal of its disapprobation some idea or belief which was becoming sufficiently prevalent to be dangerous. In the first case, that is if the object be to establish, it follows, necessarily, as I think, that it is convoked because in the course of time theologians have diverged in their views, some one or more entertaining a doctrine that the others did not. His or their views were adopted at first by a few, then by more and more, until in the course, perhaps, of centuries they were entertained by a majority of the bishops, the views of the lesser priests counting for little or nothing. New ideas being always aggressive, those who held such, as soon as they felt sure that they were a majority and could therefore control it, called a council, and the new idea then became a dogma, and belief in it an essential of salvation.

Or, in the second case, that is, where the council is convened to condemn, it means nothing more or less than that those with the old idea, finding the new idea gaining ground so rapidly as to threaten to become dangerous to the old, were shrewd enough to call a council while they, the old-idea men, were yet in the majority, and therefore had a certainty of success on their side.

In either case the will of the majority is declared to be the will of God. An idea prevails, and is true, not from its inherent qualities, but from the number of adherents it can muster, no matter what the motive may be that prompts men to its support. Many men lack the moral and physical courage to boldly express their views when they have the full assurance that, because they differ from the majority, or controlling power, they will be certainly anathematized, and probably banished or condemned to death; and in the "ages of faith" such a fate was by no means unusual to a man who followed his own conscience instead of the wishes of his superiors. Therefore, if God would not allow His councils to err, it would seem that He has permitted the successors of His apostles to use some exceedingly human, but not very creditable, methods of convincing; and has not hesitated to allow His cause to be supported and advanced by the crimes of His most prominent and honored adherents, rewarding them with riches and power in this life, and glory and saintship in the next. Or, if this be not true, if God did not sanction such methods of argument, then it would perhaps be difficult to accurately determine which of the councils He was with and which were controlled by another power.

But leaving out of view the means used to influence votes, which, as we have seen, history would seem to indicate were not always entirely reputable, there is another view to be taken of these councils.

Belief is, as I have already argued (Prop. I., b.), an involuntary condition of the mind, influenced and controlled, it may be, by argument and facts, but entirely free from the control of the mere will. All that the will has to do with it is that it may cause one to seek for or avoid facts or reasons to influence it. Those facts or reasons may be mere confidence in another, which is the case generally. But having once formed a belief (and I do not mean a mere acceptance of a fact or idea), that belief cannot be gotten rid of by a mere desire, no matter how strong that desire may be. We are forced to believe much that is disagreeable, much that we would give worlds to disbelieve ; but nothing short of proof, or what is considered proof, to the mind, will change belief to doubt, or doubt to belief. And this is particularly the case with educated thoughtful persons, not because they are under a different rule, but because they require stronger reasons and better attested facts. Therefore those who in the discussions in the general councils remain unconvinced and vote according to their consciences, if they are the minority, must not only outwardly conform to the new order of things, and teach as truth what in their souls they condemn as error, but they must actually forcibly change their belief, not from reasons or facts, but by the command of the majority, or be forever damned.

And is this the law of God? Justice, mercy, truth, all of His attributes forbid. That which for centuries was not a dogma, and not a necessity of salvation, has by the force of numbers, and nothing else, become essential to save us in the future ; for if not necessary, why should the Church insist upon it? The task of salvation, taught by the Church to be only possible through the mercy of God and the atoning blood of Jesus, has still more difficulties thrown around it by a Church, which claims that it bears God's own and only commission to lead the world to Him. Millions have been saved without believing in it in the past, but in the future there is to be one more requirement, one more difficulty to conquer, one more strain on an already severely taxed faith, one more thing (and that frequently an impossibility) to be believed, before it will extend its all powerful and only aid to poor, weak, erring humanity. If the Church's ways are God's ways, truly the peace of God passeth understanding.

Such are my reasons for saying, in my first paper:

> "Nearly every dogma of any of the Churches has been established through debate, by argument and discussion, and determined by vote. Reasoning is permitted, nay, encouraged, so long as it is on the side of the majority. The subject only becomes too sacred for discussion after it has been voted a dogma. Reason may be used to determine what is true, but having once been decided to be true, by a majority vote, reason must be ever after silent, unless a majority 'go back' on the old truth, and so declare by another vote, when the old truth becomes error, and the old error, by the magic of numerical strength, becomes truth, and, in its turn, sacred and unassailable."

Councils of the bishops of the Church have decided points, and other councils of the same sort have reversed their decisions. Popes have held views which other popes have condemned. The Church requires, as essential, that its children now believe what in former years they were not required to believe; for when a dogma is established by a council, belief in it is essential, though until so established disbelief is countenanced. Notably is this the case with the doctrine of the Immaculate Conception. Pope Sixtus IV. directed that those who held different views on the subject should be tolerant towards each other under pain of excommunication. I hardly think Leo XIII. would issue such a bull.

It does not seem to me to be a sufficient answer to say that this or that council should not be recognized; or that this or that pope was not authority as he spoke only as a man, and not as the head of the Church—not *ex cathedra*. I should suppose 600 bishops at Rimini and Seleucis as apt to have God with them, and be right, as 150 bishops at Constantinople twenty-two years later. I should think that St. Gregory's opinion of such councils is entitled to some respect inasmuch as he had presided over one of them. I should consider Honorius I. as infallible as Pius IX., and would not expect either to have announced, as the head of the Church, that to be true which as a man he did not believe.

In fact I would be afraid to blindly believe in any pope or council for fear that some other pope or council might hereafter condemn the one I followed—for if I had gone to heaven for agreeing with Honorius I., I might have been translated to hell for differing from Pius IX.

So, as this whole question of religion is, in my opinion, by far the most important a man can consider, I have preferred to do my own thinking.

This is called an "infidel age." If that means that it is disposed to be unfaithful to creeds that have no other claim to respectability than age, and the names of those who have held them, I think the age correctly named. Modern cultivated thought tends to reject anything and everything which depends alone upon "authority"—that is, on any man's or men's dictum. And this I think is because, as the mind of man is developed by contact with others, and enlarged by experience and more extended observation and study; as it finds that the ideas so reverently held by one are utterly disbelieved by others who are as well informed, as intelligent, as learned, as good; as it realizes the fact of the utter inability of a man to control his belief, it begins to doubt the correctness of a theology which teaches that salvation is dependent upon that which is beyond the man's control; it refuses to believe that a pure, just, all-powerful God will condemn the man who hears, who thinks, who prays, who reasons, who seeks for truth with all the means at his command, and finds that which he in his soul holds true, because forsooth the truth thus found is not accepted by a self-complacent fraction of His people; and doubt thus entering into the mind, freeing it from the thraldom of the past, the whole subject has been taken up by classes of people who had hitherto been blind followers of precedent, and more true thought is now given to theology, in its largest sense, than ever before.

And this, I think, accounts for the increased and increasing opposition, in quantity and quality, to modern dogmatic Christianity.

I have thought it best to give the whole of this part of the correspondence, including my numerous very freely translated excerpts from Voltaire, though I might have cited the same facts from more generally approved writers: because it permits me to show by the Bishop's next letter, and my reply, the sort of personal arguments used by the Church when she is hard pressed, and because I wish to vindicate by the simple truth one whom I regard as an able, earnest, and conscientious friend of humanity, who battled gloriously in behalf of truth and free-thought; and whom, because he was such, and therefore her enemy, the Church, taking advantage of and magnifying defects and weaknesses without which he would hardly have been human, has pursued with relentless vindictiveness and unscrupulous malignity into his grave, and whose memory she has striven to blacken by scandalous falsehoods fabricated and uttered in the name of God.

To which the Bishop replied:

"You have treated me, in your second paper, to a long history of Church councils. You triumphantly exclaim, here are councils in which one contradicts what another has asserted; and you add: 'I know that you will say that some of these councils were good and some were bad, and that the good councils have always agreed. But how are we to tell the true from the false?' I am astonished that you should take as your guide in matters of Christian Church history such a writer as Voltaire. You seem to have the luck of falling in with very unreliable authors. Viscount Amberly is bad enough for theology—but he is a cherub when compared with Voltaire on Christian history. Were a man to quote the descriptions of Thaddeus Stevens and Ben Butler as a reliable history of the councils of the leaders of the late Confederacy, every sensible man would smile at his simplicity. But the well-known prejudice and blind passion of T. Stevens and B. F. Butler against the leaders of the Confederacy are as nothing when compared to the demoniacal hatred towards Christianity borne by that Voltaire whose constant expression was '*écrasez l'infame.*' I don't wish, however, to complain of the unfairness of asking me to take as unbiased honest history the garbled accounts of this sworn enemy of Jesus Christ, and whose private life was, if possible, more shameful than his public career in the courts of Prussia and France; but what does surprise me is that you should thus place on the witness-stand a liar and modestly ask me to admit, as unqualified truth, his testimony. That Voltaire is a liar, it suffices for me to refer to the *American Encylopedia* — which in its very moderate and impartial article on Voltaire is compelled to declare him utterly untrustworthy as an historian. But you would have been saved all reference to Voltaire had you been acquainted with the organization of the Catholic Church. The Catholic Church is the kingdom of Christ in this world. Christ chose as the visible head of that Church St. Peter. For Christ said: 'I will give to thee the keys of the kingdom of heaven, and whatsoever thou shalt bind upon earth shall be bound in heaven—and whatsoever thou wilt loosen on earth shall be loosened in heaven.' Hence St. Peter and his lawful successors have always been held to be the visible head in that great kingdom—the Catholic Church. No parliamentary assembly, however numerous, would be considered a legal body unless legitimately convoked by the sovereign's approbation;—and even 600 members assembling without the royal writ would not be regarded as a legal body, and their enactments would be worthless in point of law. Had you remembered this you would not have said: 'I suppose the 600 bishops at Rimini as apt . . . to be right as 150 bishops at Constantinople'; Rimini was wanting in its most essential characteristic. For the enactments of the bishops at Rimini were all rejected by the head of Christ's kingdom on earth,—the successor of St. Peter,—the Bishop of Rome. But the comparison between earthly kingdoms and Christ's immortal kingdom on earth '*claudicat*,' like all comparisons. For Christ not only placed Peter at the head in giving him the keys of his kingdom, but he gave Peter the command to strengthen in their faith all, even the apostles,—'*confirma fratres tuos*.' That Peter might be able to do that, Christ assured them that he had prayed himself for Peter's faith, which consequently would never fail. For that reason the successors of Peter have often, in assembling bishops, written to them directing and ordering them the manner in which they should treat subjects which were to be broached in the councils. Hence when you ask, 'How shall we tell the true from the false councils?' you need not have added the nonsense: 'I know that you will say some of these councils were good and some were bad, and the good have always agreed'—I will say no such foolishness. It was perfectly gratuitous in you to place such assertions in my mouth. For like every true Catholic I will say that only those councils are good whose decrees have met the sanction of the Vicar of Christ, the visible head of the Church. Hence Rimini, and many others which you cite from Voltaire, have always been rejected by Catholics because they have been rejected by the head of the Church.

"When again, copying from the worthless statements of Voltaire, you say: 'Dogmas of transubstantiation and confession were first announced at the council of Lateran, in 1215,' you must thank such a guide for leading you into a most palpable untruth. Into a falsehood equally absurd has Voltaire led you, when you assert in '842 another grand council at Constantinople . . . the adoration of images was solemnly established.' But I have not the time to follow all the crude ideas and infinitely false assertions contained in Voltaire's account, and quoted by you. Nor, in logic is it at all necessary. For a lying witness is no witness. We believe that there is a God. Consequently the question comes, What must I do to please and serve God? Man of himself can have but a faint knowledge of God. None of us have seen the things of the next world. Consequently what can we, when left to ourselves, know of the mysterious things of that dark eternity which none of us have ever seen—and from whose bourne no traveller has returned to tell the tale. If man cannot of himself know the things of the next life; if he cannot know what he must do to please God—then God must Himself impart such knowledge of Himself and the next world as may be necessary for man. And this God has done; first of all to Adam and Eve in Paradise; after, by the ministry of Moses; and finally, God has sent his only begotten son, Jesus Christ. He, taking on human nature, walked on earth and taught with unerring certainty what man should do to please God; and revealed not all things of eternity, but as much concerning them as it was pleasing to God that we should know in this brief transit through time to eternity. We believe, therefore, all the doctrines of Christ. But the question arises, How are we to know the genuine doctrines of Christ? What means did Christ adopt, by which all of his doctrines might be conveyed to future ages, pure and unadulterated? Christ formed a corporate body. He chose the first twelve of that body himself. He organized that body by selecting and placing at their head one called Peter. These he carefully instructed himself for several years; and even stayed forty days on earth after his resurrection instructing them. Now, having fully imparted to them his doctrines before leaving the earth, he gave them the broad commission: 'Go ye therefore and teach all nations.' 'I am with you all days, even until the end of the world.' These individual twelve men could not teach all nations, could not live 'till the end of the world.' It was therefore a corporate body formed by Christ, the individuals of which might die, but their successors in the corporate body were to teach all nations 'until the end of the world.' This body corporate was made by God, not by man. God can impart perpetuity to His works—man cannot. This corporate body is not an institution gotten up by man. For the one who established it, being God, could say: 'I am with you all days, even to the consummation of the world.' The constant, perpetual, in-dwelling and abiding of Christ, in and with that corporate teaching body, was promised by Christ repeatedly, and under a variety of expressions. We believe, therefore, that Christ is with this corporate teaching body, constantly upholding, preserving, and keeping it from error—even as the soul dwells in the body and gives it life. Consequently, we have only to look around and see where have been the legitimate successors in that corporate body, established by Christ, and to which Christ gave the commission to teach all nations, even until the end of the world. In all days, from the time when Christ instituted that corporate body, have there been the bishops who can trace their line of succession from the present time back to the apostolic age. This corporate body, always existing under the guidance and leadership of one visible head as Christ had in the beginning established it, has the commission from Christ to teach, and has taught the world. This corporate body is not an institution of man—else it would have shared the fate of the rest of human institutions, and would have gone to pieces long ago. But it is a divine institution, and hence has resisted the shock of ages. Hence, Christ said: 'I am with *you* all days.' Now this corporate body is the means established by Christ to teach all nations his doctrines. It is, therefore, to teach his doctrines—nothing more—nothing less. Hence, you will understand my expression, which is of such frequent occurrence with Catholic writers from the beginning—*i.e.* 'the sacred deposit of doctrines.' By this sacred deposit of doctrines, we mean the doctrines deposited with the apostles — this corporate teaching body. Hence the Catholic tradition—which is the doctrine handed down from age to age by the ministry of the corporate body of teachers established by Christ. Hence the Catholic Church makes no new revelation of doctrines—she adds nothing and takes away nothing from those original doctrines. She teaches those doctrines—but makes no new doctrines. But when, in the long course of ages, men ask for fuller explanations of these same doctrines; or when assertions are made in enmity to these doctrines, she must, in her capacity and divine commission be also able to speak with infallible authority. Just as a judge makes no new law, but simply expounds what is law—and has been law. For a decision we must take, not the popular reports or accounts concerning judicial decisions, but the very matter of fact of the law decided. To exemplify what I say, take the famous Arian heresy. What was really decided by the council of Nice? Why, that the Son was 'consubstantialis'—$\delta\mu oo\dot{\nu}\sigma\iota o\varsigma$—'consubstantial' with the Father. Arius was willing to call Christ the Son of God, the only-begotten—and, indeed, read the creeds drawn up from time to time by the Arians, and almost any person would say that they were identical in meaning with the famous Nicene creed. In fact, the learned do not yet agree as to what Arius really believed about Christ. One thing is certain—Arius denied that the Son was consubstantial with the Father, and it was just this which the Nicene council insisted upon. For read the speeches and works of an Athanasius, and the other fathers of that council, and the gist of their whole discourse is—the constant tradition and teaching of the Church, the sacred deposit of doctrine, has always been that Christ is divine. That Christ himself taught; that the apostles taught; for that the countless army of martyrs died; that the Church has always taught. If then Christ is divine, how can Arius assert, argued the fathers of the Nicene council, that Christ is not 'consubstantialis' with the Father? For if not consubstantial, then He must have another and a different nature from the Father. If another, then not a divine, nature—for there cannot be two divine natures. If Christ had not a *divine* nature, he was in no sense of the word divine. Hence the council declared 'anathema' to any one who would assert that the Son was not consubstantial with the Father. Hence, too, the terrible war which the Arians waged against the word 'consubstantial.' That word was a clincher. It admitted no cavilling. The Arians were willing to give a Pacific Ocean of high-sounding titles to the Son. For they were all susceptible of interpretation which taught that the Son of God is not divine. But the word, consubstantial, admitted of no such interpretation. For if consubstantial to the Father, then the Son had one and the same nature with the Father, whose nature was the divine—and consequently the Son had a divine nature. This, therefore, was a fuller, more explicit teaching of a doctrine which had been held from the beginning. But not a new doctrine brought about by the force of numbers, as you have assserted, and which was to be foisted upon an unwilling world.

"I might go through with all the doctrinal decisions of the various councils, and demonstrate this uniform conduct of the Church. For brevity's sake, however, I will examine the famous infallibility question.

"The council of the Vatican, in 1870, published the decree: 'We declare the Roman Pontiff when he speaks, *ex-cathedra* possesses that infallibility promised by Christ to His Church, and therefore such definitions are of themselves, and not merely when they shall have received the consent of the Church, unalterable.' Now the decree itself gives us the cue to the history of the case. Louis XIV., King of France, not satisfied with having absorbed in himself all the powers of the French government (*l'état c'est moi*), yielded also to the temptation which has so often assaulted kings in every age, to dabble in theology. Hence was gotten up what was known as the Gallican party. They were Catholics—of course—for was not their patron—the king—his most Catholic Majesty? They acknowledged the Pope to be the vicar of Christ—the visible head of the Church—the one to preside in all the œcumenical councils—the supreme judge in questions of faith and morals—the successor to St. Peter's place and rights and prerogatives for the government of Christ's kingdom on earth—the one for whose faith Christ had prayed that it should never fail—the one who had received the command to strengthen in the faith all his brethren—the divinely appointed shepherd to feed, not only all the lambs, but the sheep also. Well, the unsophisticated reader will say : What more do you desire? But with all their grand titles the Gallicans foisted in one little clause. That little clause was the following: The decrees of the Pope had first to be accepted by all the bishops of the Catholic world before they had the legitimate binding force in conscience. How nicely did this little clause destroy the high-sounding titles given to the Pope. The cunning subtlety of the Gallicans reminds us of the serpentine spirit of the Arians. Christ, said the Arians, was the Son of God, Light of light, begotten before all ages, etc., etc., but then you see he was not consubstantial with the Father. The Pope, said the Gallicans, is the head of the Church, the supreme judge, the shepherd to rule the lambs and the sheep—but then, you see, before his decisions as supreme judge, and regulations for the flock, are binding, the community must accept his decisions, the sheep must endorse the arrangements of the shepherd. Hence the decree of the Vatican Council was necessary, and hence, too, it was worded : ' The definitions of the Roman Pontiffs are of themselves, and not merely when they shall have received the consent of the Church, unalterable.' For that reason many of the fathers of the Vatican considered it unnecessary to pass the above decree. For if the Pope is truly the vicar of Christ, as all believe, does it not seem superfluous to say that his decrees are not to be reformed by the bishops of the Church at large? Nor was this decision of the Vatican council a new doctrine brought about by mere discussions of the learned, as you suppose; a mere new doctrine that the unfortunate world had not dreamed of before, but now was compelled to believe under pain of damnation. Or rather, was it not just like the Nicene and other cases? Before the council of Nice, Christ was called the Son of God, worshipped, adored, and honored with every divine honor. When the Council of Nice issued its decree asserting against Arius that Christ was consubstantial with the Father, this was a broader explanation of an old doctrine—but not a new one. Before the Vatican, had not the Church taught that the Pope was the successor of St. Peter, was the visible head of the Church; had not the Popes decided question after question; had they not presided in œcumenical councils? And if, for a moment, doubt of all this arise, we need but refer to the writings of that Corypheus of the opposition to the Vatican Council, Dr. Doellinger. What, therefore, was this much calumniated and misrepresented decree, but a clearer exposition of what had always been the teaching of the Church—a putting down a sophistry which, if admitted, destroyed her doctrine concerning the Pope.' The judge

[1] In this connection the following, from pp. 182, 183 of *Plain Reasons Against Joining the Church of Rome*, by Richard Frederick Littledale, London and New York, 1880, is interesting:

" It may serve to show what divergence there was quite lately on this on the bench does not make a new law; but the judge must be there to decide what is the law, when ignorance or the sophistry of unprincipled men would put interpretations which would destroy the law. Christ has established a corporate body, duly organized, under one visible head, and has given it the commission to teach all nations. It must evidently be able to teach when, in the course of ages, factions and bad men, as it is to be expected, may bring up their quibbles, their sophisms, which would tend to corrupt that sacred deposit of doctrine entrusted by Christ to her to be taught to the world. And that this corporate body has done, from the days of the apostles down to the present time. It has received the commission to teach, not politics, not the physical sciences, but 'whatsoever I [Jesus Christ] have commanded you'; in other words, to impart to all nations those doctrines which it has pleased God to reveal to the world. While these truths are many, and sufficient for us in this life, eternity will, no doubt, reveal countless others to our eyes when we see Him face to face who is infinite perfection—when we see God just as He is. . . . [This omission is explained farther on, and is of purely personal matter, not affecting the discussion on either side.]

head (Infallibility) from the now current teaching, to cite a question and answer from an anti-Protestant work, Keenan's *Controversial Catechism*. This book received the approval and license of Archbishop Hughes, of New York, and the editions published here (London) bear the formal approbation of the four Roman Catholic Bishops in Scotland, dated 1846 and 1853.

"'Q. Must not Catholics believe the Pope himself to be infallible?'

"'A. *This is a Protestant invention; it is no article of the Catholic Faith:* no decision of his can bind, on pain of heresy, unless it be received and enforced by the teaching body—that is, by the bishops of the Church.'

"Since the Vatican decrees, this question and answer have been quietly dropped out of the volume by a clever re-arrangement of the type, but pains have been taken to make it seem the *very same edition*, nay, the very same thousand of that edition, and no hint of any change is given."

"To your charge then that her doctrines have arisen by the discussions of men, and what has not been known in one age has by the mere force of numerical majorities been made new articles of faith, you have my answer.

"In your first paper you had asserted that what had been held as a sacred truth in one age she had rejected as error in another, and *vice versa*. I challenged you to show one instance of such conduct on her part. In your second paper, unable to accept the challenge, you back down from that proposition, and ask me to accept your new charge, which is: 'She [the Church] failed to recognize as truth in one age what she afterwards propounded as a dogma.' Does the definition made at Nice of 'consubstantial' offer any proof that she had hitherto failed to recognize the truth that Christ was divine? Does the definition of the Vatican council that the decree of the sovereign Pontiff was unalterable, offer any proof that she failed to recognize the Pope as the head of the Church, the supreme judge on earth, the vicar of Christ, etc.? So far from this, by the councils of Nice, Ephesus, Chalcedon, Rome, Constantinople, and all the way down to the council of Trent and the Vatican they are and have been recognized. What the fathers then taught she still teaches.

"You conclude by kindly insinuating that we *blindly* believe in the Pope and councils. I have shown you that ours is not a blind belief in any man or men. You say that 'I have preferred to do my own thinking.' Now, as a matter of fact, all this boast which, with the modern infidels, you make about 'rejecting authority,' and doing your 'own thinking,' is both unfounded and irrational. It is utterly unfounded, for you and all of us, in the daily concerns of life even, believe many things on the authority of others, and let others do the thinking for us. The Catholic Church does not ask us to suppress or reject reason in order to be a member of her Church. Quite the contrary. She has ever produced such master-minds as a St. Augustine, a John Chrysostom, an Anselm, a Thomas Aquinas, a Bossuet, a Fenelon, and in our own days she can point to a Bronson, John H. Newman, Manning, and other illustrious children. It is just my intellect which tells me there is a God. In accepting this truth I am only uniting with the great intellects of every age—aye, with the voice of all the human family. It is not suppressing my intellect, but following its luminous rays, when I again acknowledge that with regard to the things of God, whom I have never seen—with regard to the things of the next world, which I have never visited—my intellect cannot be expected to tell me much. It is by following my intellect, therefore, that I conclude that if we are to have in this world a knowledge of God, and the things of eternity, God must by some means make known to us the knowledge of Himself, and the things of the other world. My own intellect tells me that man, by the mere efforts of his own intellect, can never have a knowledge of God and eternity sufficient for his spiritual wants. Now God sent Jesus Christ to teach us the truths of God and the hidden realities of eternity. Not a blind acquiescence in others' opinions, but the calm exercise of my reasoning faculties, the honorable searching of the historical evidence, prove a demonstration to my intellect, and myriads of other greater intellects than mine ever will be, that Jesus Christ was a messenger from God, that not only he did what no other man ever did, but that he did what a mere man could not do, or attempt to do. Having established the fact that Christ was the messenger sent into this world by God to teach us and instruct us, it is my intellect which tells me that I must accept as truths all that he will ask me to believe. But to convey his doctrines to all ages, he duly organized a corporate body of men who were to hand down from age to age, and spread abroad to all men, these his doctrines. Were Jesus Christ a mere man, then this corporate body might yield like other human institutions, might be broken to pieces in the shock of ages, and might fail to convey his genuine doctrines to the world. But as I said before, the abundant testimony at hand shows me that Jesus Christ is God. He therefore can do what a mere man cannot do. I know, therefore, that there is truth in his doctrines and stability in his works. This corporate body has been entrusted with the duty of enlightening the world with truth by the same God who commanded the sun to shed its life-giving rays upon us. We may as little fear the one to fail us as the other. This truth is made doubly certain by His assurance, ' I am with *you* all days, even till the end of the world. They that hear you *hear me*.' It is, therefore, my own intellect which tells me that this corporate body, instituted by God, and in which He says that He ever dwells, guiding, preserving, animating it, should be listened to in telling me Christ's doctrines. Because God has set it up to shine the moral truth upon the world, and because God is ever with it to enable it to do so, my intellect accepts unhesitatingly its blessed light.

"You may ' prefer to do your own thinking '—but how much will your own thinking alone teach you about God, or the next world? Or what certainty will your own thinking give you of that infinite Being whom you have never seen, and never will see in this life? Or what knowledge will your own thinking give you of the things of eternity? Why, about as much knowledge as a man would acquire of China, who, never having visited China, and being too strong-minded to trust to the authority of travellers' books concerning China, would lock himself up in his room, and, perched on a high chair, would prefer to do his own thinking about China! And even you do not do your own thinking; for even in religion you have been allowing others to do a great deal of thinking for you. Unfortunately, instead of the grand old doctors of the Church, it is such fellows as Viscount Amberly and Voltaire whose thinking you have adopted! As a gentleman of culture and possessing much leisure you may be tempted to try your own thinking. But how many even in our own age of cultivation are capable to rely on their, solely on their, own thinking in matters of religion? And God help them if they did! You, even, do not rely on your own thinking for medicine, mechanics, jurisprudence, and many other sciences which I might mention. And, strange, you single out the highest, and consequently the most profound, of sciences wherein to laugh at authority, and say that you will believe only what you acquire by your own thinking.

"And all this free-thinking that has so deeply your sympathy, what is it leading to? Is it to greater peace, happiness, law, order, and true enlightenment? Let the socialism and communism, unknown in ages of faith, answer. Let the socialism and communism of that eminently rationalistic and anti-Catholic government of Prussia answer. In fact it is just the truly cultivated intellect of our age which is paying homage to the Catholic Church as never before. The splendid literary achievements of a Voigt, Gfrörer, Huebner, Roscoe, Strickland, and other Protestants have wiped away the filthy calumnies of Voltaire and his gang, and drawn the admiration of genius upon that glorious teaching corporate body established by Jesus Christ; there stands that corporate teaching body—the Catholic Church—doing now what it was founded to do nineteen centuries ago. Macaulay, bigoted Protestant as he was, has in his famous essay grandly depicted her triumphs over the effects of time and fearful persecutions. She has faithfully taught the same doctrines. The decisions of her councils were merely the anathemas against the impudent denial of her doctrines, as in the case of the image breakers of the East; or they were the fuller declarations of her doctrines made necessary by the sophism of artful men, as in the 'consubstantialis' of Nice, and the 'unalterable' of the Vatican council. Bold, bad men, like Leo the Isaurian—and other crowned tyrants—have tried by brute force to destroy her doctrines; the artful Arius, the Gallicans, and others have sought the same by their sophisms. The Catholic Church has met the one and the other kind of enemy with the anathema that defended and explained the doctrines entrusted to her ever faithful custody. Just the cultivated intellect of the age has, I say again, done the Catholic Church an homage unparalleled in the history of the world. For amid the decay and wreck of other systems, philosophical and religious, there she stands, the city on the mountain—the house built on the rock, more numerous, more widespread, more intensely united than ever. The persecutions of a Bismarck and Victor Emmanuel have confessedly resulted in their outrageous loss and her glorious gain. The cultivated intellect of our age has paid her another homage. Great Britain, the United States, France, Germany, are the countries which our age is constantly holding up as the models of intellectual refinement and culture. Now just in these countries has the Church met with a success that seems marvellous. Who, a hundred years ago, would have been so rash as to predict that instead of a few lowly chapels where in fear and trembling a handful of priests and laity were keeping alive the faith in England, Scotland, and Wales, we would now have hundreds of grand churches and the full hierarchy of bishops! Who would have been so rash as to predict the wonderful number of converts in Great Britain, and their high rank and brilliant intellects. Who, journeying one hundred years ago through New England and the other parts of our present Union, could have predicted that in less than a century the Catholic Church would be by far the most numerous body of Christians in the Republic! And she who then had not one bishop within the limits of our borders would in so short a space of time have nearly seventy bishops and would cover the land with her churches, colleges, and other institutions. And America has rivalled Great Britain in the number and in the distinguished qualities of the converts who have acknowleded her truth. Let any one compare the condition of the Church in France at the present hour with the condition one century ago, and he will acknowledge how great are the strides which she has made in that truly wonderful country. Now let us cast a glance at Germany, the acknowledged home of all modern freethinking, and of the wildest socialistic ideas—never before has the Church put forth such valor—never before has she shown such an illustrious martyr-clergy, and a people so devoted with genuine German heartiness to the glorious old Church! Prince von Bismarck and Kaiser William in the hour of the grandest triumph recorded in history, and standing in reality at the head of Europe, began their attack with fearful cunning and force against the Church. Seven long years has the attack raged.[1] Hundreds of the pastors of the flock have been imprisoned and banished. And now who is the winner and who is the loser? Steady as Alexander's bristling phalanx stands the unconquered Church; wider, far wider, has she extended her lines; closer than Cæsar's legions, in battle array, stand her compact forces. On the other hand, how is it with the German Empire? An exhausted treasury, a discontented people, and a divided empire, a lost popularity, and, above all, the pandemonium of socialism and communism, looming up to its fright, make the Boulevard 'Unter den Linden' unsafe for the Emperor William and his henchman Bismarck.

"I have simply hinted here at the fact. But the pen of the future historian will show that in our age deistic and infidel writers have added nothing to the rule of law, peace, and happiness, but on the contrary are building up the lawlessness of socialism and communism in Europe and America; while just in the nineteenth century cultivated intellect has rendered the Catholic Church the highest homage."

Such is the whole argument on the side of the Church; at least it is all the Bishop has ever given me, it seems to include all that could be urged in that connection, and I know of no other.

I give my reply, again changing the pronouns, and dropping the epistolary form.

Before discussing the answer to my argument deduced from the history of the œcumenical councils, I consider

[1] This was written some twelve years ago.

the remark which so exercised the Bishop that he refers to it more than once.

After having shown the contradictory actions of various of these councils and which he has not pretended to deny, I said, as already stated, that I knew he would say that some of these councils were good and some bad, and that the good have always agreed. He replied in a portion of his letter which, being purely personal, I have omitted, that he "has never said and never will say any such thing," and wished to know why I put such a "silly assertion" in his mouth, and then wondered why he should utter so "foolish" a defence.

My reasons for attributing such a defence to the Bishop were these: I have heard others use that defence; I have understood that there was a list in the Vatican of such councils as were considered binding; that a number of councils considered valid by the Roman Church were considered invalid by the Greek Church, and *vice versa;* that therefore the Roman Church considered some of the councils good and some bad—that is, some valid and some invalid. I assumed that the Bishop would hold the same views as did his Church: the more especially as his first paper was to the effect, as I understood it, that there was no disagreement between the councils; so that I was in a measure forced to conclude that in his opinion, and the opinion of the Church, the valid, or good, councils all agreed. If the Bishop would admit that the councils recognized as valid by the Church of Rome have disagreed and differed, the one from the other, I would withdraw that portion of my remarks which would make him say that the good councils have always agreed. Otherwise it must stand. It will be observed that I did not pretend to say *why* the Bishop would claim that some were good and some bad; I only declared my belief that he would assert such to be the case. It was a little prophecy, the reasons for making which I have just given. Let us see how it has been fulfilled.

Referring to the argument which has just been given we find that the Bishop, after so fully and clearly explaining the organization of the Catholic Church, says: " Had you remembered this you [I] would not have said 'I suppose the 600 bishops at Rimini as apt . . . to be right as 150 bishops at Constantinople.' For the enactments of the 600 bishops at Rimini were all rejected by the head of Christ's kingdom on earth—the successor of St. Peter —the Bishop of Rome."

Here is one œcumenical council pronounced bad by him.

After further explanation of the Church's organization, the Bishop says: " Hence when you ask: 'how shall we tell the true from the false councils,' you need not have added the nonsense, 'I know that you will say some of these councils were good and some were bad, and the good have always agreed.' I will say no such foolishness. It was perfectly gratuitous in you [me] to place such assertions in my mouth. For like every true Catholic I will say that only those councils are good whose decrees have met the sanction of the vicar of Christ, the visible head of the Church. Hence Rimini, and many others which you copy from Voltaire, have always been rejected by Catholics because they have been rejected by the head of the Church."

If this is not saying that some of these councils (cited by me) are good and some bad, then I do not understand English: and these extracts are full, not garbled. As to the *reasons* why I thought he would set up such defence, and pronounce some of the councils valid and others invalid, I had said nothing. He denied more than once that he ever had said or ever would say such "foolishness" (the word is his own) and then said it, giving his reasons. And unless he would say that I have misconstrued his views, and that he believes that the councils which he does consider good have disagreed among themselves, which of course is not to be expected, I must insist that my little prophecy has been more exactly and literally fulfilled, as I meant it, and as I understand my native tongue, than any he can point to in Holy Writ; and his condemnation of the predicted explanation as "foolish" is his condemnation of his actual defence.

And I enter so fully into this seemingly trivial matter because it illustrates the theological system of argument —bold and re-iterated denial in the face of even the most apparent facts.

The Bishop has been especially severe on Voltaire. He has hit so often, so hard, and in such vulnerable points, that I cannot blame any Churchman, whether Catholic or Protestant, for not loving him. But they should remember that if we wish to know the truth about ourselves we should consult our enemies. But I doubt if the Church wishes to hear the truth about herself: certainly she did not like it formerly. As the Bishop suggests, I would not care to go to B. F. Butler and Thaddeus Stevens as my sole authorities for facts as to the late Confederacy; but if they stated publicly as fact any disagreeable thing about our people, I would not content myself with saying that the statements were incorrect, nor in branding them as "liars," as the Bishop does Voltaire, but I would disprove the facts first, if I could, and then I might use such terms as the circumstances and my taste warranted. I have no doubt but that both of the persons alluded to have made inaccurate statements about the Confederacy, perhaps unintentionally, possibly designedly. But the statements would be true or false as the facts were, and not because of the men who made them. If they have made any statements which have been published and brought to the attention of those affected by them, and they have not been disproved, any one has the right to treat such statements as true. I do not believe that Voltaire was either untrustworthy or bad. There are two accounts of him, one making him both great and good, and the other, the Church's, making him all that is vile. But the Church hated him, and resolved to destroy him as far as she could, body, soul, and reputation; and when the Church has an object to attain she is not wont to be particular as to either her epithets or her statements.

The Bishop says, as a reproach, that Voltaire's constant expression was "*écrasez l'infame*," meaning the Church. Not polite, certainly; too vigorous to be strictly parliamentary; but when we take into consideration that he knew all about her in her then condition, the character of her priesthood at that time, her persecution and abuse of him, and that he was raised a Christian and therefore probably a good hater, can we blame him? Another "infidel," now living, R. G. Ingersoll, in his oration on Paine, says:

"But the Church is as unforgiving as ever, and still wonders why any infidel should be wicked enough to endeavor to destroy her power.

"I will tell the Church why.

"You have imprisoned the human mind; you have been the enemy of liberty; you have burned us at the stake—wasted us with slow fires—torn our flesh with iron; you have covered us with chains—treated us as outcasts; you have filled the world with fear; you have taken our wives and children from our arms; you have confiscated our property; you have denied us the right to testify in courts of justice ; you have branded us with infamy ; you have torn out our tongues; you have refused us burial. In the name of your religion you have robbed us of every right ; and after having inflicted upon us every evil that can be inflicted in this world, you have fallen upon your knees, and, with clasped hands, implored your God to torment us for ever.

"Can you wonder that we hate your doctrines—that we despise your creeds—that we feel proud to know that we are beyond your power—that we are free in spite of you—that we can express our honest thought, and that the whole world is grandly rising into the blessed light?

"Can you wonder that we point with pride to the fact that Infidelity has ever been found battling for the rights of man, for the liberty of conscience, and for the happiness of all ? Can you wonder that we are proud to know that we have always been disciples of Reason, and soldiers of Freedom ; that we have denounced tyranny and superstition, and kept our hands unstained with human blood ? "

So speaks Ingersoll ; to the same effect wrote Voltaire ; and, if history be true, both were justified in their statements; and the only blame I can attach to Voltaire for his energetic war-cry is its lack of courtesy.

But Voltaire was a brave man, as is shown by his outspoken, fearless writings at a time very different from our own, and such are not usually liars. He may have been occasionally inaccurate, may have, under excitement, exaggerated, may have been misled ; but I do not believe he ever intentionally misrepresented ; I think he was willing to leave the monopoly of that weapon to the Church, which could plead high authority for the practice, as we shall see when we compare the ethics of the Pagans, the Jews, and the Church—Prop. IV. Certainly the Bishop has not established any misrepresentation in what I have cited on his authority.

The Bishop cites the *American Encyclopedia* as declaring Voltaire " utterly untrustworthy as an historian." If he were, that would only show that we should not rely on any facts related by him alone; his stating a fact which was well established by other writers would hardly be claimed as destroying it; and, as we shall presently see, the facts which I have cited from him, and which are denied by the Bishop, are all of that character. But the Bishop seems to rather overstate what the *American Encyclopedia* says. What I find there is this: "his histories are sprightly, entertaining, but not authentic." It does not say in what; it probably means in his anecdotes and incidents of a personal nature; it is altogether unlikely that he would have published any important facts as history without their being authentic, for they could so easily be disproved, and I know of hardly any historian writing of affairs which are at all near the time of the writer who is not claimed by those whose interests or inclinations run counter to his statements to be unreliable. Nor do I think he could be the vile wretch depicted by the Church whose last words were (on the authority of the same article, quoted by the Bishop), "I die worshipping God, loving my friends, not hating my enemies, but detesting superstition";—evidently not yet reconciled with the Church.

The Bishop in very general terms calls Voltaire a "liar," but directly denies only three of his many statements cited by me. The denial is in these words: "When again, copying from the worthless statements of Voltaire, you say dogmas of transubstantiation and confession were first announced at the council of Lateran in 1215, you must thank such a guide for leading you into a most palpable untruth. Into a falsehood equally absurd has Voltaire led you when you assert 'in 842 another grand council at Constantinople . . . the adoration of images was solemnly established.' But I have not the time to follow all the crude ideas and infinitely false assertions contained in Voltaire's account and quoted by you."

Here again, in general terms, the whole account is declared to contain many untruths, but as only three instances are specifically pointed out by the Bishop it is fair to assume that they (transubstantiation, confession, adoration of images) are the most glaring falsehoods.

I had warned him that the facts stated by Voltaire were also stated by other authors, and that I used Voltaire for convenience only; but the indignation aroused by the hated name seems to have caused the Bishop to overlook that fact.

I now consult, on these three points, other, and to the Church perhaps less objectionable authorities: and first I quote from the *American Encyclopedia*, whose article on Voltaire the Bishop called " very moderate and impartial," as to transubstantiation, title " Lord's Supper."

" The first great eucharistic controversy was called forth by a book of Paschasius Radbertus in 831 (De Corpore et Sanguine Domini) in which he advanced the doctrine that the substance of the consecrated bread and wine in the eucharist was changed into the very body of Christ which was born of the Virgin. This was declared to be an act of creation by almighty power, though invisible to any but an eye of faith. He was especially opposed by Ratramnus, a monk of Corbie, who adhered to the view that in the Lord's supper there is a communion of the earthly with the heavenly. The controversy was brought before the highest authorities, when Berangarius, Archdeacon of Angers, maintained that there was a change in the sacramental elements only in a figurative sense."

The article then shows how this controversy lasted until it was finally decided when " the 4th council of Lateran, in 1215, declared transubstantiation an article of faith." Thus this authority confirms the statement made by Voltaire.

Next, as to confession, I quote the *Encyclopædia Britannica*, 9th edition, an universally recognized authority, title "Confession."

"Passages from the fathers, such as St. Cyprian, St. Basil, St. Gregory of Nyssa, and others, recommending the practice (confession) have to be confronted with the small prominence given to it in the works of St. Augustine, and the strong declarations of St. Chrysostom on the sufficiency of confession to God ; but the practice gradually became more common, especially in the west, and more a matter of rule and precept, until at length, in the fourth Lateran Council, held under Pope Innocent III. in 1215, it was enjoined upon all members of the Church of Rome once a year, by the famous 21st canon, beginning with the words, '*omnis utriusque sexus fidelis.*'"

Which also confirms Voltaire.

And in support of my position as to the councils, generally, I quote from the same book, title "Council :" "These prevailing practices were approved or reprehended, and the dim persuasions of the few or the many were sharpened into dogmatic statement binding on all."

Third, about the establishment of the adoration of images by the council of Constantinople in 842. The articles bearing on the subject are too long for quotation here. But I refer to *Chambers's Encyclopedia*, titles "Iconoclasts," and "Image Worship," and the *Dictionary of Sects, Heresies*, etc., by J. H. Blunt.

The undoubted facts seem to be simply these. For a long time no pictures or images were allowed in the churches, but by degrees they were introduced. Then some objected to the practice, and such, the "Iconoclasts," as they were called, gained such strength and influence that those who favored the practice concentrated their strength and at the second council of Nice, convoked by Irene in the name of her son Constantine, the adoration of images was decreed. This was in 787. In 794 Charlemagne convoked the council of Frankfort, as cited by me, and that council condemned the action of the second council of Nice so far as it related to images. But the Pope explained that there was a mistake in translating the proceedings of the council of Nice, which were in Greek, into Latin, and that the adoration to be given to images was *doulcia*, and not *latreia*—that is to say, was of a different sort from that given to God, and therefore was not idolatry. This was, of course, eminently satisfactory, and at the council of 842 the adoration (*doulcia*) of images was firmly established; and of course no Roman Catholic ever gives to the images the same sort of adoration that he gives to God, for, since the explanation of the Pope, even the most superstitious and ignorant now fully comprehend the precise difference between *douleia* and *latreia*, though the learned translator of the proceedings of the council seemingly did not; and their image-worship in no manner partakes of the nature of idolatry—if we would believe the Church.

Thus the only three statements which the Bishop distinctly brands as false are fully corroborated and sustained by the authorities now cited; and if Voltaire is untrustworthy in his statements of fact—as to these instances—so are many others who have not hitherto had that reputation; and the evidence seems strong enough to call for a better refutation than a mere denial, a mere plea of not guilty, unsustained by proof; but I strongly suspect that the Church will not admit the truth of any history, secular or ecclesiastical, which does not bear her own imprimatur, unless the narrated facts coincide with her views.

The explanations of the " consubstantialis " and Papal infallibility dogmas, given by the Bishop with so much detail and clearness, are not only interesting, but are, in this controversy, exceedingly valuable; because, on his own showing, a majority vote explained, interpreted, broadened, enlarged, contrary to the wishes, views, and belief of the minority; and the majority sometimes voting under instructions from the Pope, were therefore not necessarily nor probably voting always in accordance with their own opinions.[1]

Some tenet of the Church, some text of Scripture, had come to have different interpretations put upon it. The bishops met; if they were allowed to discuss the matter at all some said the tenet or text meant one thing, some said it meant another, the majority declared *its* interpretation to be the true one, the one that always was right, and, to prevent future misunderstandings, the tenet or text was enlarged, broadened, changed, re-explained, or re-defined, to suit the views of the majority; and if the majority had happened to think the other way, the broadening would have been in the other direction. And then to clinch the matter, and settle the question beyond all cavil, the doctrine with its new interpretation, certainly with its new wording, is made a dogma; and when the majority declared anything to be a dogma which was not a dogma before, but only a practice or belief, it put a new obstacle in the road to heaven and forced the minority to clamber over it; which is just what I was contending for, and the Church's own argument establishes my theory.

But an argument based on history alone is comparatively worthless, for to destroy the argument it is only necessary to deny the history; and when two histories

---

[1] See *ante*, p. 83, where the Bishop says: "For that reason the successors of St. Peter have often, in assembling bishops, written to them directing and ordering them the manner in which they should treat subjects which were to be broached in the councils."

have been written from two different standpoints recounting events happening many centuries ago, it is difficult sometimes to establish which is correct, especially to the satisfaction of those who hold opposite views. So after giving an historical sketch of the councils I made an argument based on the necessities of the case. The only reply to this argument is an indirect one deducible from the assertion that the Church was organized and constituted by Jesus—that is to say, by God. This point is fully argued, and, I trust, fully met, in Prop. IV., in discussing the divinity of Jesus. So I merely here call attention to the fact that as I use the history of the councils as one of the arguments against the divinity of Jesus, any argument based solely on the assumption of that divinity is entirely without force; for it assumes, as a starting-point, the very point at issue: the same old argument in a circle—the Church is infallible because Jesus, who is God, organized, and promised to be with it all days; and we know that Jesus is God, because an infallible Church tells us so.

As to the Bishop's remark that I had been unable to accept his challenge to prove the proposition contained in my first paper, and had "backed down" from that position and offered another proposition, I have only to say that my learned friend is mistaken. The proposition which I changed was his way of putting it, and I simply preferred to formulate my own propositions; and I put it in the form I did to make it conform nearer to my original statement and to more fully meet what I anticipated (correctly, as it turned out) would be his explanation. But the facts cited by me not only support the proposition as modified by me, they sustain the proposition as formulated by him in his challenge.

The argument by which the Bishop attempts to show

that "rejecting all authority," and "doing one's own thinking" is "unfounded and irrational," is so obviously erroneous that I give it only a passing notice. Either he did not understand my position, or he cannot rid himself of the clerical habit of using utterly illogical arguments. Of course, I "believe many things on the authority of others" in every-day life,—when I know the persons, and the statements are not unreasonable; but I also disbelieve much of what I hear. And I also allow "others to do the thinking for" me to a certain extent; that is, if their thoughts as expressed by them, their arguments, convince my mind, I adopt them. I let any one who will think for me and give me the benefit of his thoughts; but I decide for myself.

It is a little instructive to hear the Bishop just after speaking so regretfully of the past and gone "ages of faith," as compared with the present condition of the world, refer to the great advances which Roman Catholicism is making at the present day. In those "ages of faith," as he calls it, "dark ages" as others put it, Europe was all Roman Catholic; but advancing thought so triumphantly combated the Church, driving her from stronghold after stronghold, that now it is a matter of boast that she is seemingly regaining a little of her lost power. But this need not comfort her. She has been so improved by her conflict and contact with the spirit of truth that she is no longer a semblance of her former arrogant self, and has become politic and tolerant, using sophistry where she once used force, fawning where she was wont to command. Besides, old beliefs, under the pressure of free thought, are becoming unsettled, and, as a consequence, men shift from one faith to another. But the end is coming, very slowly, perhaps, but very surely. The Church must live and flourish for a long time yet: so long as ignorance and superstition exist in this world, so long will the Church hold her own. And by ignorance I mean theological ignorance. A man may be deservedly eminent in any of the learned professions of law, medicine, and divinity, and yet profoundly ignorant of anything theological beyond the Christian creed. Very few scientists now hold to the creeds of the Church, and even on those who are not scientists her grasp is weakening. I know personally numbers of people who are nominal Christians, Catholic or Protestant, and who believe very little more of their Church's creed than I do. They conform from habit, from pride, for respectability, for fear of public opinion; but they have admitted, in strict confidence, that in their souls they reject much that is taught by the Church: and here is another evidence of the decadence of the Roman Church. She seeks new converts, and so long as she is not understood she will get them; but while she is seeking to extend her own peculiar faith among those of other denominations, many born and bred in the fold believe but from the teeth outwards.

The Bishop's question: "All this free-thinking that has so deeply your [my] sympathy, what is it leading to; is it to greater peace, happiness, law, order, and true enlightenment?" I answer, most emphatically, yes; and refer to my remarks in discussing the influence of the Church on civilization, Proposition I. (*a*). The Bishop says: "Let the socialism and communism, unknown in the ages of faith, answer."

Just after the third Napoleon's *coup d'état*, *Punch* published a cartoon representing a woman, labelled "France," bound and chained, hand and foot, lying at the feet of a soldier who held a bayonet to her breast; underneath was the legend, "France is tranquil." So in the "ages of faith" was Europe tranquil—but it was the tranquillity of the dove in the talons of the hawk, of the lamb in the clutches of the lion—it was the tranquillity of death; and if it had not been for free thought she would never have known an awakening. The socialism, communism, nihilism, and other revolutionary "isms" of the day are but the reactions of the human mind so long held down by the unyielding, unpitying, iron despotism of superstition, ignorance, intolerance, and tyranny. Light is dawning on the benighted mind, and it is blinded by the unaccustomed glare; hope has come to the despairing heart, and it strives to realize its flattering tale; what wonder that with the example of their despots, State and Church, before them, men, bewildered by such novel mental conditions, and just beginning to realize their strength and to know their rights, should use force to repel aggression, organized secrecy to combat organized power, violence to resist tyranny, assassination to terrorize their foes. True, this is all wrong and deeply to be deplored, but the people are not alone to blame. Improperly educated, ignorant—except where by their own exertions they have picked up just enough knowledge to be dangerous to, and mislead, them; instead of being permitted to urge their vagaries in the open air where they could be met and combated and their fallacies refuted, they have been forced to hold their peace in public, and have had to meet and discuss in darkness and secrecy. No wonder that pernicious ideas, like noxious weeds, should grow apace under such conditions. The Church has taught the gospel of might, her pupils are putting her precepts into practice. She has used force to attain her ends, they are but following her example. She has sown the wind, the whirlwind is being harvested.

But time will correct all this. Truth, now that the Church has lost her temporal power, is free to combat error, and truth will ultimately prevail; but so long as authority, of itself alone, without the consent of the governed, whether it be authority of State or authority of Church, shall seek to oppress mankind, just so long will men rebel, and in rebelling advance the cause of liberty and truth.

THE ARGUMENT.

PROPOSITION IV.

IV. Jesus of Nazareth was not God, nor the son, in the sense of offspring, of God; he never claimed to be either, nor did others claim it for him until long after his death; and during his life he never sought or received divine honors.

He taught no new ethics; and the ethics of many of the "Pagans" were superior to those of the Jews, and equal to those of the Church.

I am aware that there are many, very many passages in the Bible which are cited to prove the opposite of this proposition; and that many better and wiser men than I believe firmly in the divinity of Jesus Christ. But this is to be expected. All of the New Testament was written long after the death of Jesus, and such passages were evidently inserted in the interest of the new sect that was struggling to attract the attention and win the sympathy of mankind; and are the embodiment of such of the current traditions and superstitions as concurred with the opinions, or met the views, of the compiler or writer. And such persons as I have spoken of believe as they do partly from habit, partly from an indisposition to interpret, study, and reason for themselves; partly because they have accustomed themselves to allow others to think for them on this subject, but principally because they start out in life with the idea, drawn in with their mother's milk, that the Bible is a sacred book emanating from God Himself, and not to be examined or scrutinized except with the determination to believe anything and everything, no matter how contradictory or unreasonable it may be.

I will be as brief in my discussion of this subject as its importance, and the necessity of stating my arguments clearly, will permit.

If I should undertake to examine the five Gâthâs of Zoroaster[1] (or any other of the world's many sacred books) to determine if they are, as many millions believe, of Divine origin or authority, it will hardly be denied by any one that it would be my duty, before accepting them as such, and becoming a Parsee, to examine carefully and critically the internal evidence of the book itself, as well as its surrounding history, to compare its majestic truths with its obvious myths, and to weigh the whole well and thoroughly by the aid of all the powers of mind with which I am endowed; that if I must use my reason and think deeply before undertaking an ordinary business scheme which might affect my whole present life, so much the more should I think, and study, and hesitate before I took a step which would affect my future life through all eternity.

I see no reason why I should not pursue the same course with reference to the Christian Bible. The Gâthâs are as sacred to the Parsee as the Bible to the Christian, and for the same reason—and no other: they have been taught as children to so regard them. Therefore I inves-

---

[1] These Gâthâs are a portion of the Zend-avesta, the Parsee scriptures, and are spoken of as "of Zoroaster" in the text, not to indicate that they were composed by him (though Dr. Haug thinks portions were), but because they are the most important portions of the scriptures of the faith of which he may be considered, if not the founder, the greatest teacher and prophet.

tigate the sacred book of my own race as I do the sacred books of other races, many of them older, and teaching very similar ethics.

Looking, then, at the Bible as a book to be studied as any other book, I am struck with the very flagrant contradictions put into the mouth of Jesus by those who wrote of him after his death. He, so far as it appears, taught orally entirely, writing nothing, certainly nothing permanent; so that we are compelled to rely on the reports of others, and where these reports are contradictory, as both cannot be true, we must endeavor to determine which is entitled to our credence. I cannot believe that Jesus would say such very contradictory things, for instance, as "I and my father are one," and "My father is greater than I"; or to his disciples "Go and preach the gospel to every creature," while saying of himself "I am not sent but unto the lost sheep of the house of Israel." Hence we must examine the evidence under the same rules and tests that we employ in ordinary legal or critical investigations.

There are recognized in law two classes of statements, *representations* and *admissions*. Statements made in one's own favor, for the purpose of advancing one's interests, are called representations, and are of themselves alone entitled to very little weight; statements against one's interests are called admissions, and, while they should be closely scanned and cautiously received, are, if clearly established, of overwhelming weight. This is not an arbitrary rule, but is the result of long experience, and is founded upon an accurate knowledge of human nature. While one may be tempted to represent himself in a more favorable light than he is justly entitled to, he is not at all apt seriously and deliberately to admit that he is not what he claims to be, unless the admission be true. Such is universal experience, such is universal law. The seeming exceptions are only seeming; as where one confesses to a crime of which he is innocent, to save the life, liberty, or reputation of another whom he loves more than himself. In such case the statements, while apparently admissions as against the seeming interest of the one making them, really are not such, but are representations made to further his actual intentions.

Hence, when the question is as to who and what Jesus was, and it is claimed that he was God, his *admissions* that he was not, are entitled to more weight than his *representations* that he was, even if he ever made any such representations, which I do not believe. And I do not believe it, apart from any question as to the authorship, date, and validity of the books of the New Testament, because I think Jesus was too pure, too honest, too earnest, in his efforts to teach his fellows the truth that was in him to play fast and loose, to be double-tongued, or to try to perplex or deceive. Therefore, while his admirers might falsely attribute to him many things and sayings tending to elevate him higher than he really was, or wished to be, they would never invent and put into his mouth words which plainly mean the reverse of what they claim for him. Hence, when they say that he admitted that he was not God, it may be safely believed that he did so admit; but when they say that he also claimed that he was God, it may be most capitally doubted, for it is much easier to believe that they would, in endeavoring to further their own ends, manufacture testimony unskilfully, than that Jesus would teach one thing to-day and the contrary to-morrow.

I therefore cite such passages of Scripture as occur in

the course of my argument on this point of the divinity of Jesus as *admissions*, and, for the reasons just given, unundoubtedly authentic, and good evidence against the doctrine that Jesus is, or ever claimed to be, God.

And it will be no answer to say that these contradictory statements are proof that the gospels were honestly written as otherwise these contradictions would never have been allowed to appear, because it is not so much a question of honesty as of correctness, and my position is that those which represent Jesus as he really was—an inspired teacher and reformer—were the original statements of the gospels, or the traditions on which the gospels are founded, and that the other class of statements representing him in a different and higher position were the result of exaggeration, accidental or intentional —natural or fraudulent,—of his followers, and were injected into the previous accounts without those who did it realizing, as it was realized later, the irreconcilable contradictions—those contradictions only becoming really glaring as we elevated our conception of God.

Jesus said, Matt. xv., 24: "I am not sent but unto the lost sheep of the house of Israel." Does this mean that the great God of the universe cared for none of His creatures except those who have been called His "chosen people?" Or does the "house of Israel" include all the earth? Or did not Jesus merely mean to tell them that he was a Jew working for the reformation and advancement of his own people?

The evangelists Luke and Matthew, in their desire to prove that Jesus was the Messiah looked for by the Jews, and who, the prophecy said, was to be of the line of David, proceed to give genealogies to show Jesus to be descended from David through Joseph, while still claiming that no blood of Joseph was in his veins,—a strange way to prove kinship. And in these genealogies it is a curious and pregnant fact that while the two evangelists agree in making Joseph the father of Jesus, they each give him a different paternal grandfather. And from David to Jesus, through Joseph, Matthew makes twenty-eight generations, while Luke makes forty-three, being a difference of fifteen generations, amounting to, say, 400 to 450 years; certainly a rather startling discrepancy to occur in inspired writings. But perhaps these evangelists were not inspired on this particular subject.

At any rate, as they claim Jesus as the son of David, through Joseph, and as this could not be unless Jesus was the physical, natural, son of Joseph (as his contemporaries believed), this admission is stronger than the implication conveyed in the statement in Matthew that Joseph was the " husband of Mary, of whom was born Jesus "; or the statement in Luke, in parentheses (and which looks very much like an interpolation), as follows: " Jesus being (as was supposed) the son of Joseph."

Besides, Luke traces his genealogy through David to Adam " which was the son of God "; and yet I believe that it is held that Adam was the son of God only figuratively, as the true believers are called the "children of God," though where the same expression is used of Jesus it is claimed that it must be taken literally.

Again, if Jesus was God, and his disciples knew it, it seems strange that they never worshipped him as such; yet I know of no passage of Scripture that shows that they ever worshipped him as God, or that he ever desired, expected, or received divine honors.

I have said that Jesus' contemporaries believed him to

be the son of Joseph, and the natural brother of his four brothers and two (at least) sisters. The parenthesis of Luke above quoted "as was supposed" would show that such was the case; but we have more.

That his neighbors and fellow-townsmen so regarded him, and had so regarded him for more than thirty years, is shown by Matt. xiii., 55, 56: "Is not this the carpenter's son? is not his mother called Mary? and his brethren, James, and Joses, and Simon, and Judas? And his sisters, are they not with us?"

And again, Mark vi., 3: "Is not this the carpenter, the son of Mary, the brother of James, and Joses, and of Juda and Simon, and are not his sisters here with us?" By which, also, it would seem that Jesus had grown up and worked at his father's trade at home.

Again, Luke iv., 32: "And they said, Is not this Joseph's son?" And John vi., 42: "And they said, Is not this Jesus, the son of Joseph, whose father and mother we know?"

So it is certain that his immediate fellow-citizens did not believe in him either as God, or as the son of God; further, his brothers did not believe in him—John vii., 5.

Strange that with all the wonders of the "immaculate conception," the visits of angels, and what, if all we read be true, their mother must have told them, his very brothers did not believe in him; and yet the apostle admits it.

But, stranger still, the probabilities are strong that even his mother, Mary, did not believe in him.

"While yet he talked to the people, behold his mother and brethren stood without desiring to speak with him. Then one said unto him, Behold thy mother and thy brethren stand without desiring to speak with thee. But he answered and said unto him that told him, Who is my mother? and who are my brethren? And he stretched forth his hand towards his disciples and said, Behold my mother and my brethren, for whosoever shall do the will of my Father which is in heaven, the same is my brother, and sister, and mother."—Matt. xii., 46-50; Mark iii., 31-35.

It is true Luke says (viii., 19) that they could not get at him for the press, but as he, as well as the other apostles, represents them as standing outside, and some one calling his attention to them, the fact of Mary's being outside with her unbelieving sons (for their being Jesus' brothers and Joseph's sons would show them to be either Mary's sons or step-sons, I care not which) striving to interrupt him while he was preaching, and that Jesus would have nothing to do with them, seems to point very strongly towards Mary's unbelief also. And this view is strengthened by the fact that although the names of some of his female followers are given, his mother is not named among them. It is true that John represents her, at the last, as at the crucifixion, at the foot of the cross, but if she was there, the other evangelists either did not know of it or thought it not worth mentioning. But her presence on such an occasion was natural, without its being necessary to suppose her a believer in the extraordinary views now held of her son.

Further, Jesus said, speaking of himself: "A prophet is not without honor but in his own country, and among his own kin, and in his own house."—Mark vi., 4. And he lived at Capernaum, and not with his family.—Matt. iv., 13. And he did not or could not perform his miracles at Nazareth because of the unbelief of the people: "And he did not many mighty works there because of their unbelief." —Matt. xiii., 58. "And he could there do no mighty work, save that he laid his hands on a few sick folk, and healed them. And he marvelled because of their unbelief."—Mark vi., 5, 6.

Does it not seem strange that God could be affected or influenced by, or should marvel at, men's belief or unbelief? Does God's ability to perform mighty works depend more on the mental condition of the beholders than on His own powers? Surely such an idea is absurd.

Again, Jesus himself declares that he is inferior to God in knowledge: "But of that day and that hour knoweth no man, no, not the angels which are in heaven, neither the son, but the Father"—Mark xiii., 32; in power: "But to sit on my right hand and on my left hand is not mine to give, but it shall be given to them for whom it is prepared"—Mark x., 40; in virtue: "And Jesus said unto him, Why callest thou me good? There is none good but one, that is God"—Mark x., 18.

And, finally, his cry on the cross: "My God, my God, why hast Thou forsaken me?" Mark xv., 34, declares in the most emphatic manner, and at a time when, if ever, all striving for effect, all false pretensions would cease, and the truth rise to the surface, that he is not the same with God.

All of this, with many other passages and circumstances,—such, for instance, as his prayer in the garden of Gethsemane, that the cup, if possible, might pass from his lips, but "not as *I* will, but as *Thou* wilt"; and numerous other instances,—would seem to indicate that if Jesus was God, or the son, in the sense of offspring, of God, co-eternal and consubstantial, co-equal and divine, he himself was ignorant of the fact; for we have no right to assume that on such an important subject as who and what he was, he would knowingly mislead the very people he had come to save.

And this argument is based entirely upon the internal evidence of the Gospels without reference *aliunde*, and without appealing to natural reason, which would seem to abhor the idea that the great Almighty God, Ruler of the entire universe, could or would engender a physical son to be borne and born, in a purely human way, by and of a woman, His own handiwork, upon this speck of matter which we call earth.

I do not care to discuss, at least at this time, the theories devised to explain and reconcile the contradictions and admissions just given. As I have said, I cannot believe that Jesus would utter contradictions, and I accept in its literal sense the text which is consistent with his character and with common-sense, and reject the other as being a pure invention, or a figure of speech. For, had they really been said as reported, though the theories of the Church may explain away, in the minds of learned theologians, these seeming contradictions so that they are no longer contradictions to them, at the time they were uttered, and to the common people to whom they were said, they would have been as contradictory and as confusing and misleading as they are to the mass of men now.

Nor do I care to discuss the questions as to how much, if any, of the accounts in the Gospels are original with the evangelists, or interpolated by later writers, nor how much of that which is original may be incorrectly reported owing to the desire to prove a point, and the inexactness consequent upon reducing to writing events and words seen and heard long before. These matters will be touched on, to some extent, in my Concluding Remarks.

The foregoing is about what I wrote to my friend, the Bishop, in my first attempt to show him why I could not agree with his Church in its doctrine as to Jesus; and I closed that branch of my letter with the following beautiful tribute to Jesus from *An Analysis of Religious Belief*, by Viscount Amberly. After speaking of Jesus being called the " Man of Sorrow," and showing that the term was not particularly appropriate to him, he says, page 368:

"While, then, I see no proof of the peculiar sorrow ascribed to him on the strength of a prophecy, I freely admit that he had the melancholy which belongs to a sympathetic heart. His words of regret over Jerusalem are unsurpassed in their beauty. At this closing period of his career we may indeed detect the sadness of disappointment, and in the bitter cry that was wrung from him at the end, 'My God, my God, why hast Thou forsaken me?' we look down for a moment into an abyss of misery which it is painful to contemplate: physical suffering and a shaken faith, the agonies of unaccomplished purposes, and the still more fearful agony of desertion by the loving Father in whom he had put his trust.

But Jesus, though he knew it not, had done his work. Nay, he had done more than he himself had intended. After-ages saw in him—what he saw only in his God—an ideal to be worshipped, and a power to be addressed in prayer. We, who are free from this exaggeration of reverence, may yet continue to pay him the high and unquestioned honor which his unflinching devotion to his duty, his gentle regard for the weak and suffering, his uncorrupted purity of mind, and his self-sacrificing love so abundantly deserve."

I give the Bishop's reply textually, merely correcting some palpable verbal errors of his amanuensis, because if any of it were omitted it might be thought that the omitted part was important.

The quotation from Amberly seems to have had anything but a soothing effect, and he comments on it, before replying to my argument on the divinity of Jesus, in the following words:

"Your quotation from Viscount Amberly is taken, you say, from page 368 of his book. Christ is called by the prophet: the man of sorrows and acquainted with infirmity.—Is. ch. liii.

"The learned Viscount can see no claim that Jesus has to this prophetic title. He can only see the 'melancholy of a sympathetic heart.' Christ was dragged before different tribunals, in each of which every form of law and justice was outraged in His person; uncondemned, He was struck in the face in open court. He was blindfolded; they gave Him blows, and spat in His face. Innocent, He was rejected as more worthy of death than a thief and murderer. The judge in open court declared Him innocent, and yet condemned Him to the cruel and shameful scourging. He was given over to an entire cohort of soldiers who treated him as they pleased. Stripped naked, He was crowned as a mock king; clad in a purple rag, and sceptre in hand, He was plunged into a sea of taunts and scoffs. Dragged through the streets of the capital city, between two thieves, He was brought to the place of public execution, and there put to the most shameful death ever invented by man. Naked on a gibbet which insultingly bore a mock title of His royalty, He was, with unheard of barbarism, insulted in His dying moments. And yet with all this before Him, and much more which I have not put down, the Viscount Amberly cannot see any claim of Christ to be the prophetic 'man of sorrows.' Were the Viscount Amberly's physical sight as dull as his mental vision then truly his would be a hopeless case of blindness.

"Having stripped Christ of His touching title of 'man of sorrows,' the Viscount smears over Him some balderdash about 'melancholy of a sympathetic heart.' But Viscount Amberly would lower Christ still more. He dares assert that Christ died with a 'shaken faith—the agonies of unaccomplished purposes.'

"Christ naked to the gaze of an indecent mob is not so

much humiliated as these words would make Him. His mission was not a failure. That mission was to teach the world;—Before Christ we find everywhere the most shocking paganism in religion; we find woman a slave; the child, when allowed to be born, often used for the most hideous purposes; and a slavery terrible to read of. Now, if there is anything clear, it is that Christ, so far from having a 'shaken faith' or sorrowing over unaccomplished purposes, was perfectly conscious of the success of His great mission to this world. Christ had taught as no one had ever taught. He had preached those beautiful truths which had made paganism flee. The last act in the drama of His wonderful career had come. His own all-atoning sacrifice so often predicted by Him was to commence that night. The immortal one for sinners, the just for the unjust, was to suffer. And like a lamb that openeth not his mouth, He was led to the slaughter. Instead of dying with 'a shaken faith—the agonies of unaccomplished purposes,'—Christ says that night, addressing the Father: 'I have accomplished the work which Thou didst give me that I should do.'[1] Instead of a 'shaken faith,' He says: 'Do not fear, I have conquered the world.' And when, hanging upon the cross, and about to die, instead of the 'agonies of unaccomplished purposes,' it is He who tells us with His latest breath: 'consummatum est'—it is consummated.

"The greatest of works was accomplished by Christ. Socrates, Plato, Aristotle, and other great men of Antiquity, shocked at the paganism of their countrymen, endeavored to teach the truth about God, and a pure morality. But their teachings, while containing some truths, were all

[1] Another illustration of the fact that he was not God, but merely God's faithful servant.—W. D. H.

deeply alloyed with many grave mistakes. They were failures, not only as teachers, but they had not the power to make the multitude accept their teachings. As a modern writer has sarcastically said, they 'could not persuade those who lived in the same street with them.' A mere handful of followers was their only success. Not so Jesus Christ. His pure and sublime teachings, unalloyed by error, have been the admiration of the greatest geniuses. Where His doctrines—where Christianity—has been accepted, polytheism has disappeared; woman has ceased to be the ignoble being that she was, and still is among nations that have Him not; the child has been protected; slavery, with its countless abuses, has disappeared, and just those nations have attained a perfection in just laws, true liberties, and in all the arts and sciences, unrivalled in the history of mankind. Compare China, Turkey, Africa, with the Christian nations of Europe and America, and all that I have asserted is abundantly proved. Christ taught not only by His doctrine, but these doctrines were illustrated by His own most brilliant example. And nowhere does even Christ preach sublimer truths than during His blessed sufferings and death. Every age has endorsed the saying of that stupendous genius of Hippo: 'Signum illud, ubi fixa erant membra morientis, etiam cathedra fuerit magistri docentis.' And what name on earth has been so tenderly loved by all the pure and gifted ornaments of our race as the name of Jesus? To countless myriads of the most enlightened men and noblest of women the name of Jesus has been like sweetest strains of angelic music, or as strong wine firing the heart to heroic deeds and every virtue. And yet with all this as clear as the noontide, your deistic Viscount represents Christ as a failure, and as avowing His utter failure at the very moment when He was asserting His grandest victory over the world, sin, and hell. Surely to put any truth into the Viscount's skull, it would require a surgical operation.

"You deny the divinity of Jesus Christ. Your arguments are, in the main, the following, viz.: [1]

"1st. Such passages of the Bible which could not be attributed to one who is God—as 'The Father is greater than I,' etc.

"2d. The disciples 'never worshipped Him'—and it does not appear that 'He ever desired, expected, or received divine honors.'

"3d. That His contemporaries and His relatives did not believe Him to be God.

"4th. The 'probabilities are strong that even His mother, Mary, did not believe in Him.'

"Permit me to say, that the whole of your first argument shows that your mind, so honest, has not as yet learned that cardinal doctrine of Christianity—the Incarnation. Without the doctrine of the Incarnation, I entirely agree with you that the Gospels would represent Christ as saying of Himself contradictory things.

"You endeavor to escape the dilemma—God or impostor —by saying that those passages of the Bible referring to Christ as God are interpolations. We could not have recourse to such a subterfuge. For the passages of the Bible showing Christ to be God, are not a few fugitive pieces scattered here and there through the New Testament, and which we might have supposed to have crept in by interpolation; but, on the contrary, tear out these texts and we will be obliged to destroy an immense part

---

[1] These were not my arguments, but merely some of the corroborative points.—W. D. H.

of the Gospels. We need not, however, have recourse to this subterfuge; for the doctrine of the Incarnation not only shows that Christ did not utter contradictory statements, but that without such statements we would have only a one-sided view of Christ. Christ is not man only —nor God only. The Christian doctrine of the Incarnation is that the Word, the second person of the adorable Trinity, the Son of God—who is consubstantial with the Father—and who was with God—and who is God—and by whom all things were made—assumed human nature in its entirety. The Holy Ghost formed in the spotless womb of the ever Virgin Mary a human body and a human soul. In this human body and human soul from the first instant of its creation, the Son of God thus assumed our human nature. While preserving His own divine nature entire and undiminished, He took a human body and a human soul with their infirmities and weaknesses—sin only excepted. Thus Christ was a divine person with a human nature. Two distinct natures—the human and divine—were united in one personality—*i. e.*, the person of the Son of God. In this each nature retained all of its respective attributes and laws. Christ therefore possessing each nature in its entirety, possessed the attributes of each nature. To illustrate this union of two distinct natures in one person, we can refer, in a qualified sense, to man. For our body is a material substance like the animals—while the soul is a spirit and immaterial. Like the animals our body suffers hunger, thirst, etc. But united to this gross material substance there is the soul. The soul is a spirit, and therefore of a nature entirely different from the body. The soul can reason and think. It can soar to the loftiest heights of philosophy and theology, and contemplate God Himself.

It will not be satisfied with the lower sensual cravings of the body—but seeks higher spiritual pleasures. It finds its delight in knowledge, the sciences, and in the pursuit of learning. It has its own fair realm of pleasures, sufferings, and ambition, to which the body—our animal nature—is an utter stranger. Yet these two natures, so entirely different from one another, are intimately united by laws mysterious. The operations of the two natures go on daily; and each person speaks indifferently of the operations of each nature. Every one says: *I* hunger, *I* think, though it is the body, the material substance, which hungers in its craving for food, and not the soul; and it is the soul which thinks, our animal nature, flesh and blood, being incapable of reflection. In thus speaking we do not utter contradictory statements, for we have only one personality with two different natures. Now in Christ there are two distinct natures united in one person, each with its proper laws and operations. The entire human nature and the divine are united in one personality. We say of Christ that He slept, and we say of Him that He is the ever-vigilant. We do not contradict ourselves. For Christ's human body slept, while His divine nature knows no such weakness. Christ, therefore, speaks indifferently of the operations and laws of each nature. 'I thirst,' said Christ, 'and before Abraham was made, I am.' Christ certainly could say: 'I and my Father are one,' when speaking of His divine nature. For no one would be so foolish as to think that Christians supposed the finite body, the material flesh and blood, of Jesus Christ to be anything with the Infinite Spirit, God the Father. And when He in human flesh and blood said that He was going to the Father, 'for the Father is greater than I,' the whole context showed that He was speaking of His human nature. For there can be no talk of the divine nature going from one place to another, since it is everywhere. But the human nature of Christ, like any other human body and soul, is not everywhere, and must leave one place to go to another. And therefore when He said that He was going to the Father, 'for the Father is greater than I,' He spoke in His human nature, of which it must be truly said that it went from one place to another, and was inferior to God the Father.[1] All these texts serve only to prove that Christ had a true, real human nature, a body exactly like ours, capable of suffering, and a soul like ours, subject to all the emotions of our human soul, and which suffered from all the griefs, the agonies, the abandonments of God's sensible presence, and the other sorrows that souls have endured in this world.

"The Bible gives a true history and representation of Christ. Now it would be only a one-sided view of Christ did the Gospels represent Him as a man only, or as God only. But the workings of each nature give us the true view of Christ; therefore your first argument against Christ's divinity, based upon texts of the Bible which show Him to be a man, falls to the ground. For Christ was truly man. He was also truly God. The divine nature was really united to a real human nature. Hence Christ calls Himself the son of man—and also the Son of God. A correct history of Christ must therefore represent to us scenes in Him which were merely human, and attributes which belong only to God. And this the Gos-

[1] If God is everywhere—if Christ was God—why should his human nature wish to go to the Father? How could his human nature go to the Father? Where would it find Him any more distinctly than where it then was? Was not the Father with it there and then? Was not Christ that Father —W. D. H.

pels do. Therefore those texts which you suppose to be contradictory, are not only not contradictory, but are necessary to show us that Christ had really two distinct natures united in one person. Indeed there have been many heretics who deny that Christ had really a body of flesh and blood. They asserted that He had a body only in appearance. And, strange to say, the first heresies against the doctrine of the Incarnation nearly all deny that Christ had really a body and soul—while they did not doubt for a moment that He was God. Consequently your first argument amounts to nothing, and only betrays a forgetfulness of the grand, fundamental doctrine of Christianity, the Incarnation.

"Your next argument to prove that Christ is not divine is, that 'it does not appear that Christ ever desired, expected, or received divine honors,' and 'the disciples never worshipped Him.' You say that a great deal of what you have written you owe to Viscount Amberly's book. I had suspected that you had trusted too much to that worthless book. Had you trusted to your own good judgment and followed reliable authors, you would have seen the overwhelming proof that Christ really did expect to receive divine honors, and that the disciples believed Him to be God and worshipped Him as such.

"First of all, Christ claims for Himself the *same* honors as those paid to the Father: 'That *all men* may honor the Son as they honor the Father'—John v. Now we worship the Father by faith, hope, and charity—and Christ asked the faith, hope, and charity which the creature can give to God only. I will now make this evident. Christ claims that faith: 'He that believeth in the Son hath life everlasting, but he that believeth not the Son, shall not see life, but the wrath of God abideth on him'—John iii.,

36. 'He that believeth in Him is not judged. But he that doth not believe is already judged, because he believeth not in the name of the only begotten Son of God' —John iii., 18. ' Jesus said to him, Dost thou believe in the Son of God? and he said, I believe, Lord. And falling down he adored Him '—John ix., 35. Christ claims thus the faith which the creature can give only to one who is God. But He also claims the hope and charity due to God alone, and holds out promises which God alone can make. ' If any man love me, he will keep my word, and my Father will love him, and *we* will come to him, and will make our abode with him'—John xiv., 23. What man can claim a love which will be rewarded by the possession of God the Father? And who else but a God can promise to come with the Father and dwell in the soul, not of one, but of all men who will love him ? ' He that loveth father or mother more than me, and he that loveth son or daughter more than me, is not worthy of me.' —Matt. x., 37.

" Every one that hath left house, or brethren, or sisters, or father, or mother, or wife, or children for my name's sake shall receive an hundred-fold, and shall possess life everlasting '—Matt. xix., 29. Christ repeatedly declares that on the judgment day He will judge all men; in Matt. xxv., 32, He gives the very sentence which as supreme Judge of the living and the dead He will pass upon the good and the wicked. The giving of life—an attribute of God—Christ claims repeatedly, ' For as the Father raiseth up the dead and giveth life, so the Son giveth life to whom He will'—John v., 21. ' Every one who seeth the Son and believeth in him may have life everlasting, and I will raise him up in the last day'—John vi., 40. ' And *I* give them life everlasting; and they shall not perish forever—and no man shall pluck them out of my hand'—John x., 28. 'All my things are thine [Father's] and thine are mine'—John xvii., 10. 'For what things soever He the [Father] doeth, these the son doth in like manner'—John v., 19. 'I am the resurrection and the life. He that believeth in me although he be dead shall live, and every one that liveth and believeth in me shall not die forever'—John xi., 25. 'He knew *all men* . . . He knew what was in men'—John ii. Christ says: 'I am the light of the world. He who followeth me, walketh not in darkness, but shall have the light of life'—John viii. All these here claimed by Christ are beyond the slightest doubt divine attributes, and in demanding of men to recognize in Him, and believe Him to be endowed with, such attributes, Christ claimed, in the highest sense of the word, divine honors.

"Your assertion that Christ never was adored by His disciples is equally reversed by the facts of history. 'And they [the disciples] adored Him'—Matt. xxviii. St. Thomas exclaimed: '*Dominus meus et Deus meus.*' '*O Κύριος μου καί ὁ Θεός μου,*' John xx. My Lord and my God. I have quoted the Latin and the Greek text to show that this is not an exclamation, for then it would be in the vocative case; but as in both languages the nominative case is used, St. Thomas adored Jesus as his Lord and God when using the above-quoted expression. Christ not only did not rebuke St. Thomas for giving Him divine honors, but gently rebuked him for being so tardy in yielding to His divinity. As other evidences that Christ was worshipped by His disciples, I will quote you a few more texts. 'I believe, Lord, and falling down he adored him'—John ix. 'Neither is there *salvation* in any other name under heaven given to men whereby we must be saved '—Acts iv. 'Thou hast the words of eternal life. And we have known and have believed that Thou art the Christ, the Son of God '—John vi. 'Thou art Christ the Son of the living God '—Matt. xvi. That St. John believed Christ to be God, I simply refer you to the first chapter of St. John's Gospel. The entire chapter is a demonstration that Christ was God. St. Paul everywhere in his epistles shows his belief that Christ is God. A few quotations will suffice to make good this assertion. 'For in Him [Christ] dwelleth all the fulness of the Godhead corporally '—Col. ii. 'When He bringeth the firstbegotten into the world he saith, And let all the angels of God adore him [Christ]. And of the angels indeed he saith: He that maketh his angels spirits. But to the son: Thy throne, O God, is for ever and ever '—Heb. i. 'Of whom is Christ according to the flesh, who is over all things, God blessed forever '—Rom. ix. I might bring many, very many other texts from the Gospels and writings of Christ's disciples, but these will suffice to show, beyond the shadow of a doubt that His disciples believed Christ to be God and adored Him as such.

"Your next argument against the divinity of Christ is, that His contemporaries did not believe Him to be God. If you say that *some* of Christ's contemporaries did not believe in Him, I consent. But if you mean to assert that *all* of Christ's contemporaries did not believe in Him, you are asserting what is absolutely false. Christ did not all at once hold up His divinity to the astonished gaze of an unexpecting world. But as the sun rises not with the full splendor of meridian brilliancy, but with a certain gradation and progressive increase of light from dawn till noon, —so with the Sun of justice. He remained hidden and retired under Joseph's roof, His sacred humanity growing in the natural way, like any other human body, from infancy to childhood, and from youth to its full bloom in manhood. He kept the great purpose of His mortal career concealed all this time under the veil of His seclusion in Nazareth. That wonderful wisdom spoke not; His mighty powers were hidden under the apparent weakness of His human nature. During the period of His hidden life of thirty years He quietly attended the Church services, and not a sermon fell from His silent lips to tell of the lore of wisdom that lay concealed under that quiet exterior. There were doubtless the sick, the infirm, and the dying during that long period. But nothing was done by Him to manifest the power which He possessed. But all this is no argument against His possessing the powers. The rank weeds and grass had flourished and withered for ages, and the savage Indian and the Spaniard and American had roamed and chased over the fields of California, and little was dreamed of the mines of gold that lay hid beneath. But the hour came when to the eyes of an astonished world was revealed the huge mine of gold. Christ lived in retirement under His foster-father's roof. Little did the ignorant villagers of boorish Galilee dream of the wonderful treasure hidden away in Nazareth. He concealed His divinity, and He appeared to their eyes as only the carpenter's son. But when He would reveal that He was the Son of God, it was in other towns and in other places than the home of His hidden life that the golden eloquence and prodigious miracles were displayed as proofs of His claims. That therefore *some* of the people of Galilee would not believe Him to be the Son of God is of no consequence for us. For we would not believe Him to be the Son of God had we no other proof than that the ignorant peasants of Galilee believed it.

And we will not reject His claim to be the Son of God, because, forsooth, they refused to admit it. What we wish to know is, Did Christ claim to be the Son of God? And that Christ seriously made that claim, the proof is simply overwhelming. For we read in John x. that the Jews took up stones wherewith to stone Him—and why? 'Because thou, being a man, makest thyself God.' And in John v., 'Hereupon, therefore, the Jews sought the more to kill him, because he did not only break the sabbath, but also said God was his Father, making himself equal to God.' That the disciples of Christ fully admitted His claim to be the Son of God is beyond all doubt, as I have shown above. Now they surely were His contemporaries, and certainly in a better condition, being the daily witnesses of His teachings and miracles, to know what Christ claimed, and the justice of that claim. But besides the testimony of the disciples and of the Jewish people that Christ really claimed to be the Son of God, we have the judicial proceedings against Christ—His trial and condemnation. In open court witness after witness charged Him with claiming to be the Son of God. At length the judge officially interrogates Him. And when amid the solemnities of the trial Christ declares Himself to be the Son of God, the entire court and assembled witnesses united in declaring Him guilty of blasphemy, and, consequently, according to their law, deserving of death. When, again, Christ was taken into the court over which presided the Roman governor, the legal accusation brought against Him was that He claimed to be the Son of God. Your training as a lawyer will doubtless teach you that the legal proceedings of two courts of justice are certainly ample proof that the contemporaries of Christ knew that He claimed to be the

Son of God. That many of His contemporaries, while acknowledging that Christ claimed to be the Son of God, still refused to believe in Him, is no proof against His divinity. There are many atheists who deny God's very existence; but it is not proof that God does not exist. You asserted that Christ did not claim to be divine, and that His contemporaries knew nothing of the claim. I have shown you that there is overwhelming proof that Christ claimed to be God, and demanded divine honors; that the disciples—surely His contemporaries—admitted His claim, and gave Him divine honors; and that the Jewish people and the courts of the land fully acknowledged that Christ claimed to be the Son of God.

" Now as to your remarks about Christ's relatives; your words are as follows : 'Strange that with all the wonders of the immaculate conception, the visits of angels, and what, if all we read be true, their mother must have told them, his very brothers did not believe in him.' This is a medley indeed. What has the conception of the Blessed Virgin Mary to do with Christ's Incarnation? And will you please tell me what was the necessity, physical or moral, which acted so irresistibly on Mary that she 'must have told them.' Far from your view, the Gospels portray Mary as quietly keeping everything in her own heart. They tell us that she very prudently said nothing, even to her spouse St. Joseph, of the miraculous conception of Christ in her womb. Her silence exposed her to suspicions the most galling to a chaste woman's heart. Where, then, is your proof for asserting that Mary must have told all this to others? That the brothers and sisters of Jesus were not brothers and sisters to Him in the narrow sense of our English words, can easily be shown. That the ever Blessed Mary was a Virgin having no other child than the miraculously born Jesus, has been the constant teaching of all Christians from the commencement. The title of 'the Virgin' has been given her in all ages; the writings of all history are here to prove this; and therefore perfectly unknown to any age the high honor of being the carnal son or daughter of the Blessed Virgin. The Bible was not written in English, but was written in the Hebrew and Greek. We must therefore consult the '*modus loquendi*' of the Bible to ascertain its definite meaning. Any one translating from the German would, on coming across the word 'Vetter,' or 'Gebruder,' or 'Geschwester,' be obliged to consult the context of the book. For these words mean brother, sister; and also a much wider relationship is just as often expressed by them, and which can be determined only by the context. And this is exactly the peculiarity of the Bible in using these words. In Genesis, chap. xi. and xii., we are shown that Lot is the son of Abraham's brother; yet in the next chapter, verse 8, Abraham says to Lot, ' fratres enim sumus '—for we are brothers. Again, Paralipomenon, chap. xv., we again see the word 'fratres,' brothers and sisters, used evidently in the sense of relatives. 'Wiel et fratres ejus centum viginti '—Wiel and his one hundred and twenty brothers; and so repeatedly in this chapter is the word thus used. In Job xlii.: ' Venerunt autem adeum omnes fratres sui et universæ sorores suæ,'—and there came to Job all his brothers and all his sisters. When, therefore, the brethren of Christ are spoken of in the Bible, the well known idiom of Bible language implies thereby 'kinsfolk' —relatives—and not the brothers of Christ as in our language, and such has always been thus taught in all ages from Hegessippus, Origen, and other Christian writers of the very first days of Christianity down to our own. And even of those who are called the brothers of Christ, it is the Bible itself which shows us that they were not his brothers in the English sense of the word. For the Apostle James the less is called by pre-eminence the brother of the Lord, but is always styled the son of Alpheus whose wife was Mary—the sister of Christ's mother—Matt. xxvii., Mark xv. That many of Christ's relatives according to the flesh believed in Him we know for a certainty from the fact that Judas, Thaddeus, James, and others were his most devout disciples. That some of Christ's kinsfolk may not have believed in Him, counts for less than nothing in an argument against Christ. It can only be adduced as a proof of their stupidity or malice—and nothing else. All your talk, therefore, about the unbelieving sons and daughters of Mary is wanting in point.

"Your last argument against the divinity of Christ is expressed in the following words: 'But, stranger still, the probabilities are strong that even his mother, Mary, did not believe in him.' You must permit me to say that I believe that you have here quoted from Viscount Amberly's book. It is his researches (!) and not your own honest study of the question which have made you fall into such a charge. For where is the logical proof for 'the strong probabilities' of Mary's unbelief? The only fact for such an assertion you base on a scene related in the life of Christ. Our blessed Lord was one day preaching to large crowds. His mother came and desired to speak to Him. Is there anything surprising or unnatural in that? A son might be intensely engaged in the grave duties of his official position, on the bench or in the Church. His mother, not knowing all the circumstances as he does, might, listening only to a mother's love, desire to speak to him when it would be inconvenient. The mother's desire would surprise no one, and the refusal of the son to interrupt the grave business of his office to converse with his mother, would only be expected by sensible men. Christ is preaching, and his mother comes and desires to speak to him—and therefore 'the probabilities are strong that even his mother, Mary, did not believe in him' ! ! ! Hence I say that just here you must be quoting again from Viscount Amberly's book; it is so like his style. Your own honorable mind, accustomed to reasoning, would never have led you into such conclusions. Moreover, it is so in keeping with the noble Viscount to make such brazen assertions while coolly ignoring the overwhelming proofs of just the reverse. For the proofs of Mary's faith are beyond all cavil. In chap. i., Luke, we are told that the archangel Gabriel appeared to the ever blessed Mary. This great archangel tells her that she is to conceive in a most miraculous manner. She, a virgin who never 'knew man,' was to bring forth a son. This son was to be the long-expected Messiah, the 'Emmanuel,' who, as she knew, is so often called by the prophets to be divine; and who, Gabriel himself tells her, 'will be called the son of the Most High,'—and 'who will reign for ever in the house of Jacob.' She certainly could not doubt an angel's word—and therefore when she saw in her miraculous pregnancy the fulfilment of the angelic promise, she had the most absolute proof that she was the favored mother of the Messiah God. St. Elizabeth, on the occasion of the Blessed Mary's visit, exclaimed under inspiration of the Holy Ghost, 'Whence is this to me that the mother of my Lord should come to me?' Here though her son is called divine by one who speaks under the influence of the Holy Ghost, Mary does not decline the high title given her, but on the contrary, in that sublime canticle, the Magnificat, confesses her faith, and gives thanks to God for the great things which He has done for her. She also makes the astounding prophecy, whose boldness is only surpassed by its wonderful fulfilment : ' For behold from henceforth all generations shall call me blessed.' For truly in all generations the modest Virgin of insignificant Galilee has been blessed by poets, orators, sculptors, artists, and peoples of every tongue, as never woman had been praised.

" Thus from the very first moments of the Incarnation there is every proof that the Blessed Mary believed in Him. The apparition of the angels at His birth, the visit of the Magi who prostrated themselves and adored Him, the great things which the holy old man Simeon and Anna said of him in the Temple, would alone have been sufficient to make her believe that her son was God.

" In speaking of Mary's presence at the foot of Christ's gibbet, you say : ' Her presence on such an occasion was natural, without its being necessary to suppose her a believer in the extraordinary views now held of her son.' I confess that I am astounded to see that you look upon the presence of Mary at the foot of the bloody cross as something very 'natural.' I have read something of history ; but I must avow that in all the history of modern Europe and America, I have never yet met a case where a mother voluntarily stood on the gibbet while her son was put to the cruel and bloody death. 'T is true history is full of heartrending farewell scenes between the victim and his relations—but even these did not take place at the scaffold itself. Perhaps Viscount Amberly can get up some for the occasion. Strange, if the presence of the mother at the bloody gibbet was but ' natural,' history cannot produce other examples. If you would put the question to a mother, would she stand at the gibbet of her son—it would be but natural for her to reply that it is hard enough for a woman's tender heart to witness the execution of any criminal, but from the gibbet on which is hanging the bloody body of her only son, it would be but natural for the tender, dear mother to remain away. The presence, therefore, of the Blessed Mary at the fearful execution of her son, while not a conclusive proof of her belief in Him—for we don't need it in the abundance of other proof,—offers a strong probability that she, with woman's fidelity, still clung to Him as God, when men had crucified Him for asserting it.

"You conclude your attack on the divinity of Christ with the following remarks: 'And this argument is based entirely on the internal evidence of the Gospels without reference *aliunde*, and without appealing to natural reason which would seem to abhor the idea that the great Almighty God, Ruler of the entire Universe, could or would engender a physical son to be borne and born, in a purely human way, by and of a woman, His own handiwork, upon this speck of matter which we call earth.' I have said before, it is a pity that you do not seek for knowledge from purer sources. This definition of the Incarnation you have, I presume, drawn from such worthless authors as Viscount Amberly; for no Christian writer on Catholic theology ever got off such nonsense. Your definition of faith was ludicrous enough [see Prop. I. *(a)*, note], but the above definition of the Incarnation goes infinitely beyond it for absurdity—is what might be called the sublimely absurd! You wish to know how could God engender 'a physical son'—born in a purely human way 'of a woman.' A physical son, *i. e.*, a son having a mere human body and soul, and engendered by God 'in a purely human way, by and of a woman'—is merely a horrible caricature of the doctrine of the Incarnation. A son, to be the son of his father, must have the same nature as his father. When therefore you talk of God, the Infinite Spirit, ENGENDERING 'a physical son, of a woman,' you are guilty of a 'contradictio in terminis.' We have not the right to exact a profound knowledge of theology in laymen—though many illustrious names of laymen both living and dead could be mentioned who acquired a vast and deep knowledge of that sublimest of sciences. But natural reason would seem to abhor the idea that a gentleman, loving books and study, should entertain such utter misconception of the Incarnation—the very fundamental doctrine of all Christianity.

"The testimony of the Holy Gospels shows beyond all doubt that Christ claimed to be the Son of God. I have shown that such was the belief of Christ's contemporaries, the apostles and disciples. Now I might show how their successors in age after age down to our own time have believed the same. For we have the writings of a Clement, a Justin, an Origen, a Tertullian, an Irenæus, and other writers who lived in the very first ages of Christianity. I might prove Him to be the Son of God from the exact fulfilment of His prophecies. I might establish it from the foundation and perpetuity of His wonderful works—but to do all this would require me to write a volume. And, moreover, our controversy has been upon the fact —Did Christ claim to be the Son of God?—Do the Scriptures represent Him to be the Son of God?"

Such is the reply and argument of the Bishop. I have given it in full, omitting nothing for the reason already stated, even where the argument seems based on a misconception of my position, which is the case in several instances.

I now give my answer to his argument, departing very slightly from the reply sent to him, and which has remained unanswered.

The Bishop is, perhaps not unnaturally, quite indignant with Viscount Amberly for saying that he saw " no proof of the peculiar sorrow ascribed to him [Jesus] on the strength of a prophecy," and to show that the Viscount is wrong, he cites all the sufferings and indignities undergone by Jesus towards the last. But the Viscount spoke of his whole career, including the last. He thinks, apparently (and I see nothing in the facts cited by the Bishop to show the contrary), that Jesus suffered in no extraordinary way during his life until his arrest ; and though he suffered much then, it does not appear that he suffered more than any one else ever had, and if others had suffered as much as, not to say more than, he had, he could not properly be considered as deserving the " touching title " of the " man of sorrows " : —that is, he had no peculiar and especial claim to it. And it seems to me that there can be no doubt that, before as well as since Jesus, men have suffered as much as he did, mentally and physically, and equally unjustly, and without having the consciousness which (on the Church's theory) he must have had, that he was God, and his sufferings were but the necessary details of his own plan to save mankind.

The sufferings of Jesus are trivial as compared with the tortures inflicted by the Holy Inquisition, and I hardly think that the Christians of that age, when the Church was supreme, cruel as they were, were more merciless, or more ingenious in devising tortures, than their predecessors, the religious fanatics of the East. So I think that the Viscount, admitting all the suffering which the Bishop claims that Jesus underwent, was fully justified in concluding that he had not suffered more than any other, and was therefore, so far as he could see, not entitled to any title which implied that he had; and I think that all who are free from what the Viscount calls "this exaggeration of reverence," will agree with him. It is the sacred halo which has been thrown around him by "after ages" which dazzles the eyes of man, and prevents so many from seeing what, when that halo is once removed, is so very obvious.

The Bishop says: "The Viscount smears over him some balderdash about 'melancholy of a sympathetic heart.' But Viscount Amberly would lower Christ still more. He dares assert that Christ died with 'a shaken faith—the agonies of unaccomplished purposes.' Christ naked to the gaze of an indecent mob, is not so much humiliated as these words would make him."

What means the cry from the cross, "My God, my God, why hast Thou forsaken me?"

To the ordinary mind, construing the sentence as if it were spoken by a mere man suffering for his faith—a martyr to what he believed to be his duty,—it would certainly seem to imply that he believed himself to be forsaken by God, or why ask God such a question? Was that a time for trifling? If he was forsaken by his God, then must his faith have been shaken, for the question shows that he did not expect to be forsaken, and that his expectation—his faith—was disappointed. If his being allowed to be sacrificed was the reason—and no other appears to be even suggested—why he thought he was forsaken by his God, then it is clear that it was his purpose to have lived longer, and that he did not consider his mission ended, and he must necessarily have considered his purposes unaccomplished. This is, of course, on the theory that Jesus was but man. If he was man, and man only, the above conclusions are irresistible. The only answer to it, as it seems to me, is the theory of the Incarnation. The Bishop's texts do not help the matter. Whatever may have been thought and said before that time—whether by Jesus, or by others, and attributed to him,—in that supreme moment, when all disguise or deception (if any ever existed) would be thrown aside, from the very depths of the man's soul comes the bitter, despairing cry that tells the whole story in a manner beyond the power of metaphysics or sophistry to explain away.

And even the Incarnation, if that horrible theory were true, would be of little or no help. If Jesus were God, his human mind, his human soul, would have been aware of the fact,—for he certainly was intelligent, and if he did not believe in himself how can we be expected to believe in him; and as the soul was immortal and sinless, the God-head eternal, deathless, and omnipresent, even the human part of Jesus could not have been guilty of the absurdity of asking such a question at such a time,—of considering himself as man forsaken by himself as God because his own previously arranged plan was being consummated as he wished it to be.

But to proceed: the Bishop says that Jesus' mission was not a failure; so does the Viscount. He says Jesus had done more than he himself knew or intended; here they diverge. The Bishop says, "that mission was to teach the world," and gives a picture of the outside world, and the effect of Jesus' teachings on it. I think the Bishop, of course, unintentionally, very seriously exaggerates both the condition of the outside world, and the beneficial effect to it of Jesus' teachings (as taught by the Church). The effect of the Church's teachings, which I suppose the Bishop and all other good Churchmen would consider the teachings of Jesus, has already been fully considered in discussing Prop. I., but we may now consider the condition of the outside world at the time of Jesus' coming, in connection with the Bishop's assertion that " Christ taught as no one had ever taught. He had preached those beautiful truths which had made paganism flee ": this being urged as one of the proofs of his Godhood.

It is much to be regretted that the Bishop did not specify some particular moral truth which Jesus taught, and which had not been taught before his coming, for I have been led to believe that he taught none such. And it would have been edifying, to say the least, to have learned what were the "beautiful truths" which "made paganism flee." Certainly not his ethics, for most of them, as beautiful as they really are, were old before he was born, and all, I think, had been taught before he came.

It will not do to compare the best of Christians with the worst of pagans; it would not be fair. There were many pagans false to the teachings of their religion, as there were, and still are, many Christians false to the moral teachings of Jesus; and the one system is no more to be judged by those who do not keep its commandments than is the other. We should compare the worst with the worst and the best with the best.

I believe the greatest moral teachings of Jesus were: " Thou shalt love the Lord thy God with all thy heart, and with all thy soul, and with all thy mind. This is the first and great commandment. And the second is like unto it. Thou shalt love thy neighbor as thyself. On these two commandments hang all the law and the prophets."—Matt. xxii., 37–40.

This should be, as Jesus evidently intended it, the whole of religion, for he says: "On these two commandments hang *all* the law and the prophets." All that could be taught by law-givers and prophets is summed up in that sublime utterance, and if this were all of Christianity it would be a grand religion indeed; and there would have been no need of a Church to act as depository of all those "sacred truths" which are either covered by these two commandments or useless; and, consequently, no necessity for pious frauds and forgeries to convince its friends, or useless wars and cruel tortures to punish its enemies, that the Church might flourish, and its hosts of bishops, priests, and deacons be sustained. And though this would have been very bad for the "corporate teaching body," humanity would have been greatly the gainer.

Then we have the "Golden Rule": "As ye would that men should do to you, do ye also to them likewise."—Luke vi., 31. This is, of course, included in the two great commandments, but it is so beautiful an illustration of it that I think the world is better off for its having been said.

But while these sayings are, as I believe, the embodiment of all true religion, and are probably the grandest ethical conceptions of the human mind in any age, they were not new. The same ideas seem to have prevailed among the heathen, or pagans, and consequently it was not these teachings which "made paganism flee." If paganism fled I should rather attribute its flight to the saying ascribed to Jesus, "I came not to send peace, but a sword" (Matt. x., 34), a singular utterance to be ascribed to the "Prince of Peace," and "Lamb of God who taketh away the sins of the world."

Jesus also taught the immortality of the soul, and the doctrine of future rewards and punishments in another life, neither of which seems to have been known to Moses. These also were pagan doctrines.

I now proceed, still discussing the second part of my proposition, and the Bishop's reply to it, to inquire into what the pagans really thought, that we may see if I am correct in saying that none of these doctrines, above set forth, were originally taught by Jesus, and if the Bishop is right in saying that Jesus "taught as no one had ever taught," and that the "beautiful truths" taught by him "made paganism flee."

As this is a matter of history in which we are necessarily dependent upon others, I must rely upon the facts as I glean them from those who are recognized as authorities. I quote (p. 39) from a little pamphlet by J. M. Peebles, entitled *Jesus: Myth, Man, or God*, and I quote him principally for the authorities which he cites, and to many of which I have not had access.

"Those intuitive truths and moral precepts that bubbled up from the sensitive soul, and dropped like pearls from the inspired lips, of Jesus, were the frequent enunciations of that common consciousness which relates to the universal Religions of the races. The immortality of the soul, taught in the Egyptian *Book of the Dead* and the Brahminical *Vedas*, shone with increased brightness in the matchless sayings of Pythagoras, and Socrates, Thales, Zeno, Plato, Anaximenes, Empedocles, Persian Magi and Indian Sages, long before the birth of the Asian Teacher Jesus. This will not be denied. On the other hand, if there is a doleful book in existence relating to immortality and the future life, it is the Old Testament, a part of the Christian Scriptures.

"Bishop Warburton, and other candid Church writers, admit the absence of all allusion to a future life in the Mosaic system. The Book of Job is a Drama. The oft quoted passage, 'I know that my Redeemer liveth,' etc., gives not a hint even of a future conscious existence. Rightly translated from the Septuagint it reads thus : 'For I know that he is eternal who is about to deliver me on earth, to restore this skin of mine which endures these things; for by the Lord these things have been done to me, of which I am conscious, to myself, which mine own eye hath seen, and not another, but all was fulfilled in my own bosom.' (Weymes, *Job and His Times*, chap. xiii.)

"Consider the following Bible texts :

"'The dead praise not the Lord.' David (Ps. cxv., 17).

"'They sleep with their fathers.' Moses (Deut. xxxi., 16).

"'Whose end is destruction.' Paul (Phil. iii., 19).

"'There is no work nor device nor knowledge in the grave.' (Eccl. ix., 10.)

"'For to him that is joined to all the living there is hope ; for a living dog is better than a dead lion. The dead know not anything, neither have they any more a reward, for the memory of them is forgotten. Also their love and their hatred is now perished.' (Eccl. ix., 4-6.)

"Isaiah evinces an equal destitution of faith in a future life and resurrection when he says : 'They are dead, they shall not live ; they are deceased, they shall not rise.' (Isa. xxvi., 14.)

"'As the cloud is consumed and vanisheth away, so he that goeth down to the grave shall come up no more.' (Job v.i., 9.)

"Job expresses his lack in future hope by such disconsolate expressions as : 'If I wait, the grave is mine house, I have made my bed in darkness. I have said to corruption, Thou art my father ; to the worm, Thou art my mother and my sister, and where is now my hope? As for my hope, who shall see it ?' (Job xvii., 13-15.) He inquires : 'If a man die, shall he live again ? Man giveth up the Ghost, and where is he ?' (Job xiv., 10-14.)

"'They shall be as though they had not been.' (Obadiah 16.)

"'For that which befalleth the sons of men befalleth the beasts ; even one thing befalleth them ; as the one dieth, so dieth the other,—yea, they have all one breath, so that a man hath no pre-eminence above a beast ; all go into one place ; all are of the dust, and all turn to dust again.' (Eccl. iii., 19, 20.)"

It may be claimed that these Biblical writers were speaking of the body alone, not of the soul. I think that is true; for they do not appear to have ever heard of a soul. Examine the five books ascribed to Moses, and I do not think a single instance can be found where either the immortality of the soul or the doctrine of future rewards and punishments can be fairly said to be taught. All the rewards and punishments promised or threatened by Moses are, so far as I have seen, temporal, of this world. The Old Testament is the foundation on which is built the New, and is, so to speak, the basement story of the Church. It is claimed to be the only revelation made by God to man prior to the coming of Jesus. Jesus taught the immortality of the soul, and the doctrine of future rewards and punishments. So did the pagans. How comes it that God concealed, or permitted Moses to conceal, these wonderful and all-important facts from His chosen people, and yet permitted them to be known to the pagans, His so-called enemies.

The Bishop has failed to answer this question. I will be grateful to any one who will.

Now for the pagans. I quote again from Dr. Peebles, p. 41.

In referring to Max Müller's third lecture before the Royal Institution upon the "Science of Religion," he says Müller placed them in order of time as "The Turanian, the Aryan, the Semitic."

"These primitive religions were ultimately reflected in the Sacred Books of the Chinese, Hindoos, and Hebrews. . . . They (the Turanians) also 'reverenced their ancestors, believed in the immortality of the soul, and in blissful reunions in heaven with those they had known upon earth.' Herodotus thinks the Egyptians 'were the first who distinctly taught that the soul of man is immortal.' That they believed in future rewards and punishments is testified by the paintings on the tombs, in which Osiris sits as judge, looking intently upon the balances weighing the 'quick and the dead.' Diogenes Laertius affirms that Thales taught that 'Divinity was infinite and the *souls of men* IMMORTAL.' Pythagoras, living in the sixth century before the modern era, believed in the divine existence and the immortality of the human soul. To this end the classical Millman declares that many of our Christian writers who repudiate this 'Heathen Philosopher' repeat his 'golden sentences' as if they were 'originally uttered by the more learned of the Christian Fathers, not knowing that those fathers enriched themselves at the expense of pagan thought.'

"Zoroaster, after speaking of Ormuzd, that God who is 'indestructible, eternal, indivisible, the celestial, and the dispenser of all-good,' adds, 'The soul, being a bright fire, by the power of the Father remains immortal, and is mistress of life.' (Euseb., *Præp. Evan.*, lib. i., 10.)

"Crito, asking Socrates, another 'Pagan Philosopher,' how he would be buried, the heaven-inspired philosopher smilingly answered: 'As you please, if only you can catch me—if I do not escape from you.' He further said: 'I cannot persuade Crito, my friends, that I am that Socrates who is now conversing with you, and who methodizes each part of the discourse; but he thinks I am he whom he will shortly behold dead, and asks how he should bury me. But that which I sometime since argued at length, that when I have drunk the poison I shall no longer remain with you, but shall depart to some happy state of the blessed, this I seem to have argued to him in vain; though I meant at the same time to comfort both you and myself.' After arguing that the soul, being invisible. is not separable into parts, but goes into the presence, at death, of a good and wise God, he asks, 'Does not the soul then, when in this state, depart to that which resembles itself, the *invisible*, the divine, immortal, and wise? And on its arrival there, is not its lot to be happy, free from error, ignorance, fears, wild passions, and all the other evils to which human nature is subject, and, as is said of the initiated, does it not in truth pass the rest of its time with the Gods? When, therefore, death approaches a man, the mortal part of him, as it appears, dies, but the immortal part departs safe and uncorrupted, having withdrawn itself from death.'

"'The soul, therefore,' he said, 'Cebes, is most certainly immortal and imperishable.'

"Cicero, born 106 B.C., teaches in one of his books, written just after his daughter's death, these beautiful truths:

"'The origin of the soul of man is not to be found upon earth, for there is nothing in the soul of a mixed or carnate nature, or that has any appearance of being made out of the earth. The powers of memory, understanding, and thought, imply that these principles must have been derived from God. . . . Do not consider yourself, but your body, to be mortal. For you are not the being which this corporeal figure evinces; but the mind of every man is the man, and not that form which may be delineated with a finger. Know, therefore, that you are a divine person. Since it is the divinity that has consciousness, sensation, memory, and foresight—that governs, regulates, and moves the body over which it has been appointed, just as the Supreme Deity rules this world; and, in like manner, as an Eternal God guides this world, which in some respect is perishable, so an Eternal spirit animates your frail body. The good man does not die, but departs, as the inextinguishable and immortal nature of his purified soul demonstrates, which goes from him into heaven, without that dissolution or corruption which death appears to induce.' (*Tuscul. Quæst.*, lib. I.)

"Christian writers who assert that these doctrines of the divine existence, the immortality of the soul, and the reward of virtue were derived from the 'chosen people'—the Jews—manifest an ignorance only excelled by their impudence. The Father-hood of God, enriching the Rig-Veda and the Talmud, was taught also by Homer, Hesiod, Philo, Horace, Seneca, Epictetus, in the Socrates of Xenophon, the Song of Cleanthes, and in the Hymn of Aratus, quoted by Paul in his appeal to the Athenians. The Rev. Dr. Collier (*Lec.*, xii., p. 499) makes Pythagoras to say: 'God is neither the object of sense, nor subject to passion, but . . . invisible and supremely intelligent. . . . All beings receive their light from Him. He is the light of Heaven—the *Father* of *all*.' The Brotherhood of Man, with the moral duties growing out of such humanitarian instruction, was taught by Diodorus, Menander, Zeno, Epictetus, Terence, the learned Philo-Judæus, and others, in these words: 'All men everywhere belong to one family.' 'No man is a stranger to me providing he be a good man, for we have all one and the same nature.' 'All men are our friends and fellow-citizens,—Greeks and barbarians drink from one and the same cup of brotherly love.' 'Will you not bear with your brother? He is born of the same divine seed that thou art. Wilt thou enslave those who are thy brothers by nature and the children of God?' asks Epictetus.

"Pythagoras, after enjoining trust in God, adds: 'Yield to mild words, and to deeds that are useful. Do not hate your friend for a trifling fault. Do nothing base, either with another, or in private; and, most of all, have a respect for yourself. Next practice uprightness both in deed and word. And accustom yourself to have a diet simple and non-luxurious. And guard against doing that which begets envy. Do not expend beyond what is reasonable, like a person ignorant of what is honorable. Nor be illiberal. Moderation in all things is best. And do those things which will not injure you: and calculate before the act: nor receive sleep upon your softened eyes before you have thrice gone over each act of the day, what have I passed by? What have I done? What necessary act has not been done by me? and, beginning from the first, go through them. And then, if you have acted improperly, reproach yourself; but if properly, be glad. So labor, so practice: these precepts it is meet for you to love. These will place you on the footsteps of divine virtue.' (*Greek Anth.*)

"No scholar at this day of historic research will assume the proposition that Jesus was the first to voice the 'Golden Rule.' It was a common proverb among Chinese, Syrian, and Grecian thinkers before the dawn of the Christian Era. These are the forms in which it was announced by Hillel, Isocrates, and Confucius:

"'Do not to another what thou wouldest not he should do to thee: this is the sum of the law.'

"'Thou wilt deserve to be honored if thou doest not thyself what thou blamest in others.'

"'What thou dost not wish done to thyself, do not do to others.'

"In the Rev. J. Williams' work upon the *Bards' Druidic Creed*, treating of the religion of the Ancient Britons, several hundred years before Christ, occur these Druid teachings:

"'Three things evince what God has done and will do: infinite power, infinite wisdom, and infinite love.'

"'The three divine qualities of man are liberality, love, and forgiveness of injuries.'

"'The three great laws of man's actions are, what they forbid in another, what they require from another, and what they care not how is done by others.'

"Monsignior Bigandet, Catholic Apostolic Bishop of Ava, in his *Life of Buddha*,[1] says: 'It must not be deemed rash to assert that most of the moral truths prescribed by the Gospels are to be met with in the Buddhist Scriptures,' while elsewheres this Roman prelate writes: 'In the particulars of the life of Buddha-Guatama, it is impossible not to feel reminded of many features of our Saviour's character and course.'

"Will anyone, assuming the superior title of 'Christian' . . . specifiy one—just one—'primal truth' that flashed upon the world for the first time through the instrumentality of Jesus Christ."

Again, on p. 46, occurs this quotation from the " candid yet soundly orthodox," Rev. J. B. Gross *Introduction to Heathen Religion.*

[1] *The Life or Legend of Gaudama, the Buddha of the Burmese*, etc., by the Rt. Rev. P. Bigandet, Rangoon, 1866.

"Perhaps on no subject within the ample reign of human knowledge have so many fallacious ideas been propagated as upon that of the gods and the worship of heathen antiquity. Nothing but a shameful ignorance, a pitiable prejudice, or the contemptible pride which denounces all investigations as a useless or a criminal labor, when it must be feared that they will result in the overthrow of pre-established systems of faith or the modification of long-cherished principles of science, can have thus misrepresented the theology of heathenism, and distorted—nay, caricatured—its forms of religious worship. It is time that posterity should raise its voice in vindication of violated truth, and that the present age should learn to recognize in the hoary past at least a little of that common-sense of which it boasts with as much self-complacency as if the prerogative of reason was the birth-right only of modern times."

And Max Müller, perhaps the best living authority on the subject, says there were none of the old religions which did not teach men "to do good and shun evil."

I have no apology to make for this long quotation, nor for the others which I have made, and will yet make, in the course of this discussion. My facts must necessarily be chiefly at second-hand, and it is but right to state my authority for them; and when I find my ideas better expressed than I can express them myself, it would be folly not to quote, giving proper credit to him whose labors I profit by, and unpardonable vanity to make excuses for substituting his researches and language for mine.

Now was the paganism which I have just detailed the paganism which fled from the teaching of Jesus? Is there any important thing in his ethical teachings not included in those I have cited? And further citations could be made almost *ad libitum*. What then were "the beautiful teachings" which made "paganism flee"? I know of none really from Jesus which could have that effect on any one. But there are many teachings of his so-called followers well calculated to make pagans, or any other conscience-possessing people, flee: as, for instance, the vindictive teachings of the Old and New Testaments carried out by Christians in persecutions for conscience' sake. The burning of heretics on the plea, as said to be stated by Mary of England—that "as the souls of heretics are hereafter to be eternally burning in hell, there can be nothing more proper than for me to imitate the divine vengeance by burning them on earth."

And why should not Christians hate and burn and persecute with the example before them of a God who is "angry every day" (Ps. vii., 11), and who had authorized His "chosen people" to kill their and His enemies, man, woman, and child, cattle and beasts, except such women as had not known man, and to debauch those; and who is supposed to have approved the sentiments of the cix. Psalm!

Or that other "beautiful teaching" of the early Christians as related by Mosheim in his *Ecclesiastical History*, vol. i., pp. 381, 382, as cited by Dr. Peebles, where he admits that early in the fourth century it was an almost universally adopted maxim "that it was an act of virtue to deceive and lie, when by such means the interests of the Church might be promoted," and "that pious frauds were approved of by the Christians as early as the time of Hermas."[1] And the learned Blunt is candid enough to admit that these Christian fathers justified their deception and falsehood by these, and other quotations from the scriptures: "O Lord, thou hast deceived me, and I was deceived (Jer. xx., 7). "I the Lord have deceived that prophet" (Ezek. xiv., 9). "God shall send them a strong delusion that they should believe a lie; that they all might be damned" (2 Thes. ii., 11, 12).

[1] The first quotation is literal. The second I do not find in words, as cited, in the edition of Mosheim which I have, but I find the substance.

The Bishop admits that "Socrates, Plato, Aristotle, and other great men of antiquity, shocked at the paganism of their countrymen, endeavored to teach the truth about God, and a pure morality."

Then, if paganism did not flee from their teachings, why should it flee from those of Jesus, which, ethically, were much the same as their "pure morality"? And if Jesus' teaching these truths be any evidence of his divinity, or inspiration, why were not these "great men of antiquity" also divine, or inspired? Where and how did they learn the truths they taught, and why may not the truths of Jesus have been discovered in the same way, or have been borrowed, without credit, from them?

And what are we to think of a God (or the only God, since while there are three there is but one) who comes on earth to save mankind, to teach them morality and truth, and who can convey no higher moral truths than those taught already, ages before he came, by uninspired pagan philosophers? But the Bishop adds that their truths were "all deeply alloyed with many grave mistakes." He does not point out the "grave mistakes," but I am satisfied from my general information on the subject, from the general tone of his arguments and of the other arguments which I have heard in this connection, that such mistakes were strictly with reference to what are now the dogmatic teachings of the Church as to Jesus and his status; or, in other words, their errors are not in their ethics, but in their divergence from modern dogmatism.

Thus the Incarnation, on which the Bishop lays great stress, is a dogma which is fatal to those who hear of, but do not, or cannot, believe it. These pagan philosophers did not teach that, certainly; but then I do not class that as a "moral truth," nor, so far as I can see, was it ever taught, or even hinted at, by Jesus; and even the sayings attributed to him which might be construed into an endorsement of the theory, are, to put them in their strongest light, but a very indirect support. The theory seems to have been an after-thought, an invention, to harmonize the palpable contradictions of the New Testament as to his doings and sayings; not an invention in the sense that it was manufactured for the purpose of deceiving, but a theory invented to, and believed because it was thought it did, harmonize conflicting statements both of which were accepted as equally true.

But even this "teaching" is not new. It is an old doctrine of many Eastern religions.

Read this quotation from the *Bhagavat-Gita*, as cited by Dr. Peebles:

"Chrishna of India preceded Jesus by hundreds of years. He was an incarnate God, and he had a favorite disciple, Arjuna, to whom he said: 'Although I am not in my nature subject to birth or decay, and am the Lord of all created beings; yet, having command over my own nature, I am made evident by my own powers, and as often as there is a decline of virtue, and an insurrection of vice and injustice in the world, I make myself evident; and thus I appear from age to age for the preservation of the just, the destruction of the wicked, and the establishment of virtue.'"

It is thought, from the very great similarity between Chrishna and Christ, that Christian theologians have borrowed much from the former; and the similarity between the Jewish and Hindoo religions has given rise to the suspicion that the Jewish is derived from the Hindoo. And my attention having been directed to the book by what turned out to be a rather inexact reference, I find in the preface, p. v., to the *History of Hindostan*, translated from the Persian by Lt.-Col. Alexander Dow, London, 1803, a statement that the Hindoos report that the son of Tura apostatized, and was banished by his father to the west, and fixed his residence in a country called Mohgod, and propagated the Jewish religion about 4887 years from the writing of the book. May there not be some connection between the Rajah Tura, whose son the Hindoos say founded the Jewish religion, and that Terah who dwelt beyond the flood, and was the father of Abraham, and served other gods? (Joshua xxiv. 2.)

There are many reasons for believing that the Jewish faith was borrowed from their surrounding neighbors, and their various taskmasters, and that their first conceptions of the immortality of the soul, a fact which seems to have been carefully concealed from them by their own God, was gained from the Egyptians (from whom they are said to have gotten their ceremony of circumcision), though the record does not so show. The ancient Jews appear to have been a gross and sensual people, incapable of æsthetic refinement or metaphysical culture, and this may account for the great difficulty they evidently had in getting to comprehend and believe such elevated doctrines as their conquerors first, and Jesus later, tried to teach them. And they are the only people with whom God vouchsafed to communicate! Well may Voltaire have exclaimed in his *Catéchisme Chinois* (*Dictionnaire Philosophique*, portatif, 1765, p. 115):

"Malheur à un peuple assez imbécile et assez barbare pour penser qu'il y a un Dieu pour sa seul province; c'est un blasphême. Quoi? la lumière du soleil éclaire tous les yeux, et la lumière de Dieu n'éclairerait qu'une petite et chétive nation dans un coin de ce globe! quelle horreur! et quelle sottise! La divinité parle au cœur de tous les hommes, et les liens de la charité doivent les unir d'un bout de l'univers à l'autre."

What a pity that such a thought should be only noble and not orthodox.

The Bishop says that these ancient philosophers had not " the power to make the multitude accept their teachings. As a modern writer has sarcastically said they ' could not persuade those who lived in the same street with them.' "

Does not this sarcasm come with very bad grace from one who must admit that Jesus, with omnipotent power to back him, could not persuade his own relatives, to say nothing of the rest of his fellow-citizens in the little village of Nazareth—" the ignorant villagers of boorish Galilee," as the Bishop calls them? Is not the point of the wit somewhat blunted when we remember that Jesus was forced, in his own bitter experience, to exclaim: "A prophet is not without honor but in his own country, and among his own kin, and in his own house"? And do not these great heathen philosophers deserve a little, just a little, credit for having thought out for themselves (for I do not suppose the Church will admit that they were inspired of God) and taught those wonderfully beautiful truths which are the only redeeming points of Christianity?

We have now reached the Bishop's reply to my argument against the divinity of Jesus drawn from the Bible itself. It will be observed that he makes no attempt to answer—in fact, in no way notices—the following points to which I specially called his attention:

1. That the Bible of the Christian should be studied in the same manner as the Bible of any other race.
2. The two genealogies of Jesus as given by Matthew and Luke.
3. That though it is distinctly stated of Adam that he was the son of God, we are expected to take that figuratively, but when the same statement is made of Jesus, we must take it literally.

4. The inability of Jesus to do any "mighty works" at his own home on account of the unbelief of the people.

5. The doctrine of admissions and representations.

This is to be regretted. I would have liked to have his views.

The Bishop does not fairly state, nor does he fairly meet, my argument on the contradictory sayings attributed to Jesus.

I began my argument by saying "that there are many, very many passages in the Bible which are cited to prove the opposite of" my views, and stated my belief that such passages were "inserted in the interest of the new sect that was struggling to attract the attention and gain the sympathy of mankind," the whole New Testament having been written long after the death of Jesus; and he meets my argument by quoting these very passages to convince me.

I had thought my position clearly defined. I will endeavor to state it still more distinctly. The Bible, in its present form, makes Jesus, in some portions of it, seem to claim divinity, and divine honors, for himself, and such portions, by themselves, would justify the position that the Book made him God: but in view of the facts that these portions do not stand by themselves, but are confronted by other portions which indicate just the contrary, and which are the older portions of the accounts; that the Gospels were written long after the death of Christ and his disciples, and the longer after his death a Gospel was written the stronger the passages in favor of his divinity became, as is very apparent in John; that these Gospels were certainly not written by any of the disciples, especially not by the men whose names they bear, and are, at best, but a selected compilation of various and varying traditions; that there have been, from time to time, various Gospels written, used for a while, and then rejected, one by one, until only four now remain as recognized by the Church as authentic; that as some, aye, most of the Gospels written have been decided by the Church to be unauthentic, it is not unlikely (unless the Church be infallible, which is one of the points which we endeavor to disprove) that some portions, at least, of the recognized accounts may be inexact; that the recent revision shows that such is clearly the case in many instances, thus strengthening the view that it may be incorrect in others where the evidence of the variation from truth was not so accessible; that these variations were not desired, but were made because necessary to make the translation true; that tradition is an unreliable foundation for history, as it cannot well fail to be warped by the beliefs and desires of its custodians; that in the earlier centuries there were conflicting views as to Jesus' status which are shown by the records, while those not recorded must have been innumerable;—I have concluded that, as a matter of fact, critically examining the various accounts in their entirety, that the texts supporting this claim of the Church are not genuine. They may be mistranslations, misconceptions, exaggerations not unnatural to an Oriental people, or what not. Not conveying the truth, I do not believe that Jesus said them, or authorized them, and I give him the benefit of the doubt. But even if he had said them, or authorized them, upon the principle of representations and admissions, already discussed, they would not be effective evidence in the face of the admissions to the contrary.

I do not consider this matter further, for to go into the argument to prove the assertions herein made as to the authenticity and date of the Gospels would take more time and space than I can well command, and would change the character of these papers from that of a free-and-easy, every-day matter-of-fact discussion to that of a rather stately argument whose necessarily dry details would drive from it the very persons whom I hope to reach. There are many books, however, which will give the information much better than I could, and I especially refer to *The Creed of Christendom*, by Wm. Rathbone Greg; *Supernatural Religion*, published anonymously, but now acknowledged by Prof. W. K. Clifford, F.R.S.; and *History of Christianity to the Year 200*, by C. B. Waite.

I had also stated that I did not care to discuss, at this time, the theories devised to explain and reconcile the contradictions and admissions which I had cited, and he launched the dogma of the Incarnation at me. I was anxious to have his reply to my argument on admissions and representations and their comparative value as evidence. I conclude, from his falling back on the Incarnation, a pure matter of faith, that reason afforded him no reply. Indeed, he seems to admit the correctness of my views and the force of my argument, and, practically, so far as my purposes are concerned, to give up the whole question when he says: "Without the doctrine of the Incarnation, I entirely agree with you that the Gospels would represent Christ as saying of himself contradictory things." I say that this is giving up the whole question so far as I am concerned, because it plainly and distinctly confesses that my argument admits of but one answer—the doctrine, or dogma, of the Incarnation, which is just what I anticipated; and that dogma was what I had in my mind when I said I did not care, at least at that time, to discuss the explanatory theories of the Church. And now I will state more fully why I have not cared to discuss it. Of course I was perfectly familiar with the doctrine, but I could not believe it. It is undoubtedly what the Bishop calls it "the cardinal doctrine of Christianity," the most important dogma of the Church, but my mind refuses to believe that God would have come on earth to found a Church, and omit to announce its cardinal doctrine, its fundamental article of faith; yet it seems to have been unknown to Jesus.

I am aware that the first and third Gospels contain certain statements as to the conception of Jesus by Mary, though the statements by no means agree; but even there it is not intimated that he ever heard of the stories.

According to Matthew, Joseph being espoused to Mary found her to be with child. Not liking that, but being a just man, he was disposed to put her away privily. But he had a dream, and was informed by an angel, while he slept, that Mary was with child by the Holy Ghost alone.

According to Luke, the angel appeared to Mary, and not in a dream, and before she had conceived, and told her what was to come to pass. No notice, according to this account, seems to have been given to Joseph, who apparently thought it was all right.

The second and fourth Gospels say nothing on the subject. As it was a matter of such vital importance, it seems strange that Mark and John should not also have at least mentioned it, even if they did not enter into details; for, since it is frequently urged that the discrepancies of the Gospels are valuable as showing the absence of collusion, they probably did not know that Matthew and Luke had told the story, even in such contradictory terms.

Now when I reflect that the entire evidence to establish this stupendous miracle is a dream of the husband *after* he had discovered his wife's condition, according to Matthew; or a prophetic vision of Mary in which the wonderful event was foretold; and the subsequent interview with her cousin Elizabeth, according to Luke, nothing being said by this last writer about what Joseph thought, or said, or did; that the other evangelists make no allusion to it, either not knowing of it, or considering it not worth mentioning, though they reproduce many less important matters; that Jesus himself, so far as I can discover, never made the slightest allusion to the miraculous circumstances of his birth, and never announced the doctrine, or fact, of the Incarnation; and that that doctrine—Incarnation—is common to nearly all the Eastern religions; I can but think that all this is an exceedingly small foundation upon which to build so large a creed; and must conclude that the dogma was an afterthought, for the purpose of reconciling, as I have already said, those very contradictions. And the Bishop's argument confirms my belief. It is ingenious, and shows exactly how the theory of the Incarnation, and the sub-theories, if I may so speak, of two natures, two wills, etc., originated; but nowhere does he show that the fact or the doctrine was announced or taught by Jesus; nor that Jesus ever taught that he sometimes spoke as God and sometimes as man. And if Jesus had so taught, and had specified which was which, instead of leaving it for his Church to find out, in after ages, by induction and other uncertain methods, it would have saved a great deal of trouble. The Bishop merely shows that the contradictions I point out can be explained in no other way; that this theory, as he claims, explains them fully; and that therefore this theory must be true. That because the body of an ordinary mortal contains a soul which is a separate entity, therefore there is no reason why Jesus' body, in addition to its soul, should not have contained a God also. To me this looks lik a *non-sequitur*, for the fact that all men have only two entities (body and soul) is rather an argument against any one man's having had three. And it suggests another difficulty in the way of my accepting the theory of the Incarnation, which is this: If, as the Bishop says, Jesus' body and soul were purely human, and these two were united with his Godhood, when he died, and rose from the dead, and ascended into heaven, what became of the soul? If the soul was like what the Church teaches us to believe of the usual human soul, it was inherently immortal: therefore the soul of Jesus, distinct from his Godhood, must either have been stripped of its immortality and annihilated, or must be existing still. If the soul can be so annihilated, we lose the assurance of immortality, for what has been done once may be done again, and immortality, instead of being a quality of the soul, is simply a revocable permission of the Deity; if still existing, it must exist as a part of God, or as distinct from Him: if distinct from Him, then there must be two Jesuses in heaven, Jesus the soul, and Jesus the God; if not distinct, if it is still a part of Him, then God the Son differs from God the Father and God the Holy Ghost in possessing, in addition to his eternal God-Spirit, an everlasting human soul.

I therefore think that the theory explains by asking us to throw aside experience and reject reason, and on no better grounds than the necessities of the Church.

The Bishop defines it, explains it, urges its reasonableness, pleads its necessity; but he fails to establish it either as a revelation, or as one of Jesus' original teachings. The most that can be said for it is that it is a deduction and has been voted to be true. This voting is a great thing—for the Church; it settles all difficulties satisfactorily—to the faithful; but my views of church-established dogmas have been already fully given, with my reasons. Hence I must continue to think that this "cardinal doctrine" rests, as before said, on nothing more substantial than the exigencies of the Church, and that it was never imagined, because not needed, until long after Jesus had passed away.

And another reason why I did not, and do not, care to argue it, is that, until the verity of the New Testament is established; until it is shown to be a divinely inspired record; until the divinity of Jesus is proven, or, at least, rendered probable, it were a waste of time to discuss what may, or may not, be logically deducible from its, or his, teachings.

At the close of my opening argument I said: "If Jesus were God, and his disciples knew it, it seems strange that they never worshipped him as such, and I know of no passage of Scripture that shows that they ever worshipped him as God, or that he ever desired, expected, or received divine honors." This the Bishop attempts to disprove. Let us see with what success.

He quotes a number of texts of the class which I have to some extent discussed, in which Jesus is made to appear as claiming to be the son of God, and even to possess divine attributes and powers. These are some of the contradictory texts to which I have applied the doctrine of admissions and representations some time since. But even these do not say that he either "desired, expected, or received divine honors." The Bishop uses them to make deductions from. I think so important a matter, had it been true, would have been so written down, not inferentially, but distinctly. And the undisputed facts all show that I am right; and that during his life Jesus walked, talked, eat, drank, slept, rejoiced, and grieved with his disciples, as one of them, though their recognized chief; and that he received no more consideration from them than any other teacher believed to be inspired would have received from his disciples and followers; and Jesus nowhere tells them to treat him differently.

Let us examine the texts.

The first is John v., 23. "That all men may honor the Son even as they honor the Father." The Bishop leaves out the word "even," but with or without this word the text clearly means nothing more or less than that inasmuch as men honor the Father, therefore they should also honor the Son; but not necessarily worship him, not, at least, in the same manner as God. This is made clear by the 41st verse of the same chapter, where he says, "I receive not honor from men." Here the complaint is not that he is not worshipped, but not honored, —not believed,—as the following verses show. And it makes Jesus himself a witness to the fact that he was not, at that very time, receiving divine worship. I hardly think the Bishop's first quotation a happy one for the Church.

The next, John iii., 18 and 36, are simply on the importance of belief in the Son of God, a subject which has already received full consideration; they make no reference to worship, or divine honors, desired or extended, during his life.

The next, John ix., 35, 37, 38, is the case of the blind man whose sight is restored. "Jesus said to him, Dost thou believe in the Son of God? . . . and he said I believe, Lord. And falling down he adored him." The Protestant Bible says simply, "and he worshipped him."

And is this something on which to build an argument that Jesus sought or received divine honors? If the account be true, it is only an instance of an ignorant and superstitious man, who, being relieved from a terrible infirmity, very naturally is disposed to worship the one who cured him. Such adoration is common in the East to the present day, where a little " baksheesh " judiciously distributed will bring titles, and methods of expression of gratitude, which to the Occidental ear and eye are remarkably near to the ordinary idea of divine worship, but it does not really mean that he who gives it thinks he is worshipping his God, or that he worships in the same way as he would his God. Nor does the text indicate that Jesus expected or desired this man to do even what he did; and if he had supposed that the man was giving him that adoration which belongs to God alone, Jesus would most certainly have rebuked him, as when he remonstrated with the man who merely called him " Good Master," Mark x., 18. And that Jesus spoke of himself figuratively as the son of God in this case, as well as in all others, is shown by what the same writer represents him as saying, just before his ascension: " I ascend unto my Father, and your Father; and to my God and your God " (John xx., 17). Here Jesus, after the resurrection, is represented as stating the relations between God and himself to be the same as between God and his (Jesus') disciples. And let me, parenthetically, in this connection, quote what Peter said of him (Acts ii., 22): " Ye men of Israel, hear these words: Jesus of Nazareth, a *man* approved of God among you by miracles and wonders and signs, which *God* did by him in the midst of you, as ye yourselves also know." Peter, at that time, although the infallible head of an infallible Church (if the doctrine of infallibility is not a new one), did not apparently have any knowledge of, or, if he did, much respect for, the "cardinal doctrine" of the Incarnation. A *man* approved of God by the miracles which *God* worked through him! And this after his death and resurrection.

But to resume. All the other texts quoted by the Bishop have absolutely nothing to do with the assertion which he is endeavoring to combat, unless it be Matt. xxviii., 17, and John xx., 28. The other texts, if they show anything, only show, like those already referred to, that he claimed divine powers and attributes, and detailed the advantages of believing in him, but again nothing is said as to desiring or receiving divine honors. And this is a pregnant point; it passes belief that if Jesus went about telling the multitude, including his disciples, that he was master of life and death, and could determine the future status of each soul, and was *believed*, he would have been treated like any other man who was a teacher, a leader, a prophet.

Now for the two texts which I have just referred to. They are: "And when they saw him they worshipped him; but some doubted," Matt. xxviii., 17 (though the Bishop omits these last three words "but some doubted"); and the text which is evidently considered the crowning quotation of all, for it is given in Latin, Greek, and English: "And Thomas answered and said unto him, My Lord and my God," John xx., 28. These two instances are said to have occurred *after* the resurrection, and hence are hardly evidence of what the disciples did before, while Jesus was living with them, which is the period I wrote about. Jesus living is, to a certain extent, an historical personage; Jesus resurrected is utterly and entirely scriptural, and his resurrection is attested only by the Gospels.

or, to anticipate a quotation which I shall shortly make in this connection, the only testimony of his resurrection is the testimony of the only persons on earth whose interest it was to misrepresent the facts. But taking the account as it is, these texts support my view. My assertion was that the *disciples* never worshipped him, meaning, as the context clearly shows, during his life, and the Bishop's reply is, in substance, that after his death, on one occasion, *some* of the disciples worshipped his apparition (because some doubted), and that on another occasion his apparition was worshipped by one disciple, Thomas. Or, in plain English, if there be any truth in the story, which, as we shall see presently, is, to put it mildly, very doubtful, these men, knowing that Jesus was dead, when they saw him before them thought they saw a ghost, and did what they seemingly never did before, worshipped—frightened, perhaps, into prayer.

And another conclusion is to be drawn from these accounts, in favor of my views. If the disciples had worshipped Jesus during his life, had considered him as God, they would not have been so very doubtful about the result of the crucifixion, would not have found it so hard to believe that their immortal and eternal God still lived.

Upon the subject of the resurrection I quote, at length, and without comment, from the admirable work of Viscount Amberly, from which I have derived so much valuable aid already, p. 273.

" Comparing now the several narratives of the resurrection with one another, we find this general result. In Mark Jesus is said to have appeared three times:
1. To Mary Magdalene.
2. To two disciples.
3. To the disciples at meat.

" Two such appearances only are recorded in Matthew :
1. To the women.
2. To the eleven in Galilee.
" In Luke he appears :
1. To Cleopas and his companions.
2. To Peter.
3. To the eleven and others.
" In the two last chapters of John the appearances amount to four :
1. To Mary Magdalene.
2. To the disciples without Thomas.
3. To the disciples with Thomas.
4. To several disciples on the Tiberias Lake.
" Paul extends them to six :
1. To Peter.
2. To the twelve.
3. To more than 500.
4. To James.
5. To all the apostles.
6. To Paul.

" Upon this most momentous question, then, every one of the Christian writers is at variance with every other. Nor is this all, for two of the number bring the earthly career of Jesus to its final close in a manner so extraordinary that we cannot imagine the occurrence of such an event, of necessity so notorious and impressive, to have been believed by the other biographers, and yet to have been passed over by them without a word of notice or allusion. Can it be for a moment supposed that two out of the four Evangelists had heard of the ascension of Christ—that the most wonderful termination of a wonderful life—and either forgot to mention or deliberately omitted it? And may it not be assumed that Paul, while detailing the several occasions in which Christ had been seen after his crucifixion, must needs, had he known of it, have included this, perhaps the most striking of all, in his list?"

I also submit the following from *Doubts of Infidels*, by LeBrun, being a letter addressed to the clergy by " a weak Christian." I quote the conclusion, as to the Resurrection :

" The malevolence and incredulity of our adversaries the unbelievers are visible in nothing so much as the criticism they make on the resurrection. They complain, and with some degree of reason, that this most miraculous event, instead of possessing that extraordinary and uncommonly clear evidence which its incredible nature requires, bears, on the contrary, every mark of a forgery. Instead of reappearing to all the world, that the world might believe, he is said to have appeared to his disciples, who were the only men on earth whose evidence could be exceptionable in this case,—men who, already engaged in the attempt of forming a sect or party, could be by no means disinterested in their report,—the only men on earth who could be suspected of forgery in the present instance. These are the men, say our enemies, who were to preach Jesus Christ to the world, and to find arguments to support the fact; which Christ might have *incontrovertibly* established. But the generation was unworthy of that condescension, we reply, which they wickedly paraphrase thus: 'God, who desireth not the death of a sinner, left them in their sins that they might die. God who spared not His beloved son, but gave him to the bitterness of death that sinners *might be saved*, chose, nevertheless, to deprive mankind of the proper *evidence* of the resurrection, because the *Jews* of that age were sinners.' Mercy is the character of the first act; but how shall we characterize the latter? Is the God of the *Christians* inconsistent with himself? Did the great and merciful Being act thus? Did He inspire four men to write accounts of the *resurrection* which disagree in almost every circumstance? Does His divine truth bear the semblance of forgery and invention that we may show our faith and reliance on Him by making sacrifice of our reason, and believing by an act, not of the understanding, but of the will? But why, O thou Supreme Governor! why hast Thou given us reason if reason be the accursed thing which we ought to cast from us? Or, rather, is not reason the first and only revelation from Thee? And are not those enthusiasts accursed, who, promulgating vile systems unworthy of Thee, find their purposes are not to be accomplished till they have first deprived us of Thy best gift? These, Reverend Sirs, are the reflections of infidels and unbelievers,—reflections which our truly Christian zeal and detestation would have prevented us from repeating, if we had not been supported by a pleasing anticipation of the glorious and satisfactory manner in which they will be answered, explained, and overthrown by you to the entire satisfaction and conviction of us weak Christians. Not by persecutions, pains, penalties, fines, and imprisonment; otherwise the unbelievers will then sneeringly say that you are incapable of answering them, or, what is more unfortunate, that they are really unanswerable."

I resume the argument.

The Bishop says that my " next argument against the divinity of Christ is—that His contemporaries did not believe him to be God. If you say that *some* of Christ's contemporaries did not believe in Him, I consent. But if you mean to assert that *all* of Christ's contemporaries did not believe in Him, you are asserting what is absolutely false."

I am afraid the Bishop let his indignation get the better of him at this point, and inadvertently fell into the old orthodox habit of eking out argument by epithets. I therefore overlook the outburst; I do not think he meant to be—what he was.

The idea which I desired to convey is this. In my opinion, no one of whom we have any record ever believed Jesus to be God Almighty, or the offspring of God Almighty, during his (Jesus') life. And I cited Luke iii., 23: "And Jesus himself began to be about thirty years of age, being (as was supposed) the son of Joseph, which was the son of Heli." Luke does not limit or qualify his remark. He does not say, "as was supposed by some," but he makes the broad assertion that it "was supposed" that he was the son of Joseph. And certainly if it was "supposed" that he was the son of Joseph, it was not supposed that he was the son of God, literally, or that he was God. Then I cited various texts, which I need not here repeat, to show that the villagers thought he was the natural, legitimate son of Joseph and Mary. And I have never heard of, nor has the Bishop pointed out, any of them who thought otherwise. I also alluded to the fact that his very "brothers" did not believe in him, and considering that "brothers" meant "brothers," and not merely "relatives," from the fact that they evidently lived in the house with him (for he speaks of being without honor in his own house), thought it strange they should not believe notwithstanding what their mother (step-mother, possibly) must have told them about his miraculous origin. I supposed that she must have told them because her condition was such, at the time Joseph married her, that it had to be accounted for, and if they were older brothers, by a former wife (as some think), the explanation, in justice to their father and his bride, should have been extended to them; and if they were the sons of Joseph by Mary after Jesus' birth, which is very possible, not to say probable,[1] it seemed to me but natural that their mother, if she so believed, should have told them that their eldest brother was their God, and, in support of her somewhat startling assertion, have at least alluded to the facts of the Incarnation.

These inferences seem to me to be not only justifiable, but almost necessary; and if they are correct, then my statement, which seems to have so excited the good Bishop, must be true. And what does he advance to disprove it? He admits that for the first thirty years of his life " little did the ignorant villagers of boorish Galilee dream of the wonderful treasure hidden away in Nazareth. He concealed his divinity, and he appeared to their eyes as only the carpenter's son "; so that if any one knew better he must have been taken into his confidence by Jesus before he was ready to act; and I am referred to no such confidant.

---

[1] Matthew i., 25, says, speaking of Joseph remaining away from Mary at first, " And knew her not until she had brought forth her first-born son," thereby implying that after the birth of Jesus she became the wife, according to the flesh, of Joseph and bore him other sons; and Luke also says, ii., 7, " and brought forth her first-born son " (and it would seem, from the text in Matthew, whether she again became a mother or not, that she lost her right to the continued title of " virgin "); and I cannot see why there should be such an impossibility in her having had other children, or how such fact, if it existed, could detract from her honor; in fact to be a barren wife was not formerly considered to be an honor.

At this point the Bishop utterly begs the question, and proceeds to cite texts to show that Jesus claimed to be the son of God, a point which I have already discussed, but he neglects to show who, if any, believed him. Then he gets back to the question by saying, "that the disciples of Christ fully admitted his claim to be the son of God is beyond all doubt—as I have shown. Now they surely were his contemporaries." They certainly were his contemporaries, and had better opportunities to judge of him than had others. The difficulty is not there. It is in the Bishop's thinking that he has proved that they believed him to have been the physical son of God, and God himself, while I think he has proved nothing of the sort. This has been discussed while arguing the question of Jesus' receiving divine honors on earth; and we there saw that even after it was "consummated" some of the disciples doubted. The texts now cited do not justify the Bishop's assertion, nor do I find him more fortunate in his reference to the "legal proceedings of two courts of justice": for while he uses them to show that Jesus claimed to be the son of God, the facts cited seem to establish the point that nobody believed him; that, on the contrary, they thought him guilty of blasphemy. Then after stating that the legal accusation brought against him was that he claimed to be the son of God, he adds: "your [my] training as a lawyer will doubtless teach you that the legal proceedings of two courts of justice are certainly ample proof that the contemporaries of Christ knew that he claimed to be the son of God."

My training as a lawyer shows me two difficulties here which the Bishop's training as a priest caused him to overlook. One is that before the record of a court is proof of anything, it must be established as a record—not as a report made by some unknown, or unauthorized, person, but as the official record, so recognized by the judge, and properly authenticated ; and as the only record of the alleged proceedings is the account given by the evangelists, the trustworthiness of which account I am attacking, the " proceedings " in the form in which they are presented do not possess any extraordinary degree of value in my eyes ; they have yet to be established.

The other difficulty is that he produces these proceedings to show that the contemporaries of Jesus knew that he claimed to be the son of God, while the point which he was trying to combat, at this time, is not that they did not know that he so claimed, but that, even if he did, they did not believe him. The point is (and I am surprised that the Bishop forgot it, for it seems to have annoyed him more than any other), did his contemporaries *believe in him ?* And these " proceedings," if the record were established and admitted in evidence, would be my witness, not the Church's, on this point. It is true that I elsewhere maintain that Jesus did not claim to be God, nor the son, in the sense of offspring, of God ; and these proceedings do not show the contrary even of that. If admitted, they would only show that he claimed to be, not God, but the son of God, whether figuratively or literally they do not say, leaving that point to be determined by other evidence.

I fear the Bishop may be correct in accusing me of inaccurate use of Roman Catholic technology in speaking of the Immaculate Conception. But what I meant was the immaculate conception *by* the Virgin Mary *of* Jesus—not the immaculate conception of the Virgin Mary : the old, original, not the recent, one. I trust my "medley," though I think it was more seeming than real, is cleared up.

I have already answered the Bishop's question as to why Mary should have told the brethren of Jesus about the wonders of his birth, and I have given some authority for supposing them to be the sons of Mary. The Bishop's attention had not, at the time he wrote his argument, been called to the statements of Matthew and Luke as to Jesus being her first-born son: he, as a learned priest, undoubtedly knew of the texts, and my not having called his attention to them could only have affected the argument by causing him to suppose that I did not know of them, and that as I had not cited them he need not answer them; but if I had, I suppose his reply would have been the same: "That the ever blessed Mary was a Virgin, having no other child than the miraculously born Jesus, has been the constant teaching of all Christians from the commencement." This either proves nothing or proves too much. The miraculous birth of Gautama-Buddha, and his Incarnation, have been constantly taught from centuries before the birth of Jesus until now, and are believed by priests so highly educated and so intelligent that very few Christian missionaries can cope with them in argument. But does that prove the story true? If it does in the one case, why not in the other?

He says, "the title of 'the Virgin' has been given her in all ages; the writings of all history are here to prove this." Can we find her so called by others than Christian writers? Did they know more about it than we do? Is not all they know from the Bible, and the Church, and does their calling her so prove any more than the Bible or the Church does? Does it add any force whatever to the argument?

As to the argument that Jesus' "brothers" were not his brothers, but more distant relatives, I have only this to say. In any view of the word, the use made of it in this place, and in this way, indicates that it was intended to convey the idea of blood relations who lived with him, and who went about as companions of his mother; and speaking of brothers and sisters as a means of identification (are not his brothers so and so, and his father and mother Joseph and Mary, and do we not know them, and his sisters), and the surprise implied in the statement that they did not believe in him either (or if not surprise, the complaint), would show that the word was more probably used in its nearer, rather than in its remoter sense. Its being used in a remoter sense seems to me to have no more authority in this connection than the other view, if so much; but it has the advantage of explaining away a very ugly difficulty as to Mary's continued virginity; and that is the only advantage it has; for relatives as intimate with the family, and as much cherished as they evidently were, would answer the other purposes of my argument just as well as if they had been real brothers and sisters.

Now, as to his mother's belief, I do not care to add much to what I have already said. I have expressed myself very moderately. I have not said it was positive, I only said the "probabilities are strong." I have stated the facts and drawn my deductions. The Bishop thinks it but natural that Mary, "not knowing all the circumstances as he does," should wish to speak to him and should not hesitate to interrupt him when he was preaching. I am again constrained to differ from him. I think that if she believed her son to be God Almighty—her own Creator, since he made all things—she would have taken it for granted that he knew what he was doing, and would not have attempted to interfere with him in any manner. Nor would she, in my opinion, if she did undertake to interrupt her God while he was preaching, have taken his unbelieving "relatives" with her. Under such a belief the whole transaction would have been very singular, very unnatural, very improbable. But when we consider that the Pharisees were taking counsel how they might destroy him (Matt. xii., 14), and he was therefore making enemies as well as friends, the enemies being by far the more powerful; when we remember that his friends, just before, were out seeking to "lay hold on him," saying, "He is beside himself" (Mark iii., 21), the conclusion seems well-nigh irresistible that his mother and brothers called him to them for the purpose of checking him in a course which they feared would, as it did, result in his destruction. And if this view be correct,—and I see no escape from it,—his mother, not probably, but surely, did not believe he was her God.[1]

I must notice, very briefly, some other points made by the Bishop. He considers the Angel's visitation to Mary as evidence of Mary's belief in her son as God, gravely asserting that "She certainly could not doubt an Angel's word." I trust I may be pardoned for suggesting that Mary herself was to herself better authority as to this particular matter than even an Archangel; and as my argument, as a whole, is intended throughout to disprove that, among other myths, I hardly think my mind, "accustomed to reasoning," would have laid much stress on it even if it had been new to me. Pretty much the same story is told in too many religions, very much older than the Christian, for it to have any very wonderfully con-

---

[1] See also Luke ii., 46-50, where, when Jesus spoke to them about his "Father's business," they did not understand what he meant.

vincing powers. The Bishop has fallen into an error common with the clergy. I attack a certain doctrine founded on a Biblical story, and endeavor to show from the innate defects of the doctrine, and the palpable inconsistencies and absurdities of the story, that the doctrine cannot be true, and he cites to me the disputed story as sufficient evidence to establish the doubted doctrine. Verily, it looks as if, to enter the kingdom of Heaven through the door of the Church, it is necessary to become as a little child, not only in faith, but in argument.

When I said that I did not believe that Jesus was God, nor the son, in the sense of offspring, of God, it was, of course, included that I did not believe in the Incarnation, or any of the myths which are supposed to sustain that theory. And I think there is enough in the Bible in the way of contradictions and absurdities to prove my view correct; and when I finish my comments on the Bishop's argument I shall point out some of them under Prop. VI.

As to the wonderful prophecy ascribed to the Virgin Mary, contained in her little speech to Elizabeth, and its fulfilment; if the Bishop can derive any comfort from its being believed, and therefore fulfilled, by those who have never known any better, I am not disposed to interfere with him. Only I do not think he ought to adduce it as evidence of anything except the wonderful character of Christian faith that halts at nothing—not even the sacrifice of the intellect.

The Bishop is quite indignant and somewhat eloquent at my saying that Mary's presence at the cross was "natural without its being necessary to suppose her a believer in the extraordinary views now held of her son." I think the Bishop misconstrues my meaning. I certainly did not mean to say that it was "natural" for a mother to desire to behold the execution of her son; but only that if she did go to the last act of the tragedy it was a natural result of the disposition of that particular mother to stand by, and be ready to do what she could for her child when he was in his last extremity and deserted by every one else, even at the cost of any personal suffering of her own. The Bishop thinks her presence " offers a strong probability that she with woman's fidelity still clung to him as God, when men had crucified him for asserting it." So he evidently thinks it natural enough for " woman's fidelity " to make her do what would be unnatural if prompted by a mother's love. Does he think it would be less harrowing to see her son crucified because he was also her God, than if he had not borne that dual relation to her? Does a doubted God appeal more deeply to a mother's heart than a deserted son?

The Bishop is particularly severe on what he calls my " sublimely absurd " definition, and " horrible caricature," of the Incarnation. My remarks were that natural reason " would seem to abhor the idea that the Great Almighty God, Ruler of the entire universe, could or would engender a physical son to be borne and born, in a purely human way, by and of a woman, His own handiwork, upon this speck of matter which we call earth." I did not attempt to define; I merely meant to speak of the event as it must have occurred if it occurred at all.

The given facts are plainly these. Mary, a woman like other women, became with child; how, is not now the question. There can be no doubt but that—except the conception—everything went on naturally and in the usual course. The subject is a delicate one, and I do not care to go into details. But even if the conception were miraculous, and I suppose the Incarnation theory claims no more, all the rest of the affair is to me simply horrible to think about—and even the Book says she had to be purified after it was all over—in connection with my ideal of God. The story is essentially the invention of a coarse, unæsthetic people. The Greek idea of springing fully grown, armed, and equipped from the brain of Jove, is far more poetic, fully as natural, and certainly far less repulsive.

The term "physical son" seems to worry the Bishop. If Jesus' body was a human body, it was a physical body, and if he, with such body, was a son, he was a physical son; and if a physical son of God is an absurdity (which I most devoutly believe), so is the Incarnation, even though it be, as it is, the "fundamental doctrine of all Christianity"—that is, of all dogmatic Christianity.

I think I have shown incontrovertible reasons for believing that Jesus of Nazareth was not God, nor the son, in the sense of offspring, of God; that he never claimed to be either, nor did others claim it for him until long after his death; that during his life he never sought or received divine honors; that he taught no new ethics; and that the ethics of many of the "pagans" were superior to those of the Jews, and equal to those of the Church.

It seems to me that the only point on which there can be any doubt whatever, is whether Jesus ever represented himself as divine, either as God or as the son of God. I think the facts, in view of all the surrounding circumstances, clearly indicate that he did not; for myself I feel no doubts on the subject. But had he made such claims, their only effect would have been that we would then be forced to regard him as a fanatic, under an insane delusion, or as an impostor. But, thank God, we are not reduced to that strait: the preponderance of the evidence is overwhelmingly in favor of his innocence, and we can, from the depths of our souls, exclaim with Renan (*Jésus*, a condensation of *La Vie de Jésus*, by Ernest Renan, Paris, 1864):

"En tout cas, Jésus ne sera pas surpassé. Son culte se rajeunira sans cesse ; sa légende provoquera des plus beaux yeux des larmes sans fin ; ses souffrances attendriront les meilleurs coeurs : tous les siècles proclameront qu'entre les fils des hommes, il n'en est pas né de plus grand que Jésus."

THE ARGUMENT.

PROPOSITION V.

V. If Jesus of Nazareth was God, he could not have been betrayed, and Judas Iscariot was but a helpless instrument in the hands of Omnipotence; if Judas was a traitor, Jesus was not God; and the doctrine of free-will does not relieve us from the dilemma, for the attempt to reconcile free-will with the attributes of God results only in attacking His absolute supremacy.

Although this is the proposition which started our discussion, I think it more naturally comes in at this point.

I had heard the Bishop preach a sermon in the course of which Judas Iscariot received a very large amount of vituperation, and was held up to the execration of the world; I subsequently read an article from the Bishop's pen upon the same subject and to the same effect; I knew that he held and taught the doctrine that Jesus was God; and the evident inconsistency of the two positions occurred to me so forcibly that I wrote him a paper on the subject, and thus began what turned out to be to me, and I hope to many others, an interesting and instructive argument.

It may be well to mention, in view of the nature of the discussion, that in the course of the article referred to the Bishop says that the character of Judas is so well in accord with the prevailing ideas of the age, that he would not be surprised to hear of the erection of a statue in his commemoration.

After commenting very freely on the enormity of the crime of Judas, as viewed from his standpoint, he says, (in the same article) " supposing even that Jesus Christ was not God," and goes on to show how base, even in that view, Judas was.

If Jesus were a messenger of God—or a prophet—or an inspired teacher—or anything else, except God, he was betrayed by one whom he had selected as a friend, who held a responsible office among the apostles, and who was always treated by Jesus with the utmost kindness. And when Jesus (viewing him as a man only) sought to avoid arrest and punishment and withdrew, with that object, to a retired place, it was certainly most infamous in Judas to betray him, and especially to betray him in the manner narrated. Therefore, in this view of the matter, I have no hesitation in agreeing with the Bishop, and saying that Judas was, and is, without excuse, and deserves any amount of unpitying abuse and execration.

But many people think (and I am afraid the Bishop is one of them) that if it is so horrible to betray a mere man, it is much more so to betray one's God. But I think that is because they have not thought very fully on the subject, having found it easier to accept ready-made views, than to think out such things for themselves; or, more probably still, never having thought about it at all.

If Jesus was God, as is claimed by most of the Churches, Protestant as well as Roman Catholic, then the entire aspect of the affair changes. He was then omnipotent and omniscient; he had come into the world according to his own pre-arranged plan of salvation. By that plan he was to be born of the Virgin Mary; to be betrayed by a disciple of his own choosing, chosen for that purpose; and that disciple was to be Judas, who must have been created for that purpose, and his whole course pre-arranged; otherwise the scheme of salvation was undertaken and carried on without any clearly arranged plan.

If this be so, Judas was necessarily a helpless instrument in the hands of God, and could no more control his actions than he could have controlled his birth, or his selection for the purpose; and in this view he is entitled to our commiseration, our pity, not our abuse. It was punishment enough to have to play such a rôle.

Is this view correct? Was he a helpless instrument? Could he have controlled his actions? Did he possess free-will? This may, I think, be easily settled. If he was a free agent, capable of doing what he wished, then the whole of God's scheme of salvation was in imminent danger of miscarrying through failure to find a betrayer; for it will hardly be contended that Jesus did not try, by words and example (and if he were God, to *try* would seem to imply necessarily to *succeed*), to make all of his disciples good men: which might have resulted, if he were a free agent, in Judas' repentance and failure to betray; and the same difficulty might have occurred with all, especially if they believed their exhorter to be God, and therefore infallibly right, and so a betrayer might have failed him at the last moment. And a betrayer was certainly necessary, for, apart from the fact that I cannot believe that Jesus would descend to any unnecessary clap-trap, Jesus was clearly avoiding arrest. That this is so is shown by his going to a retired place to which Judas had to guide his enemies; and by his praying that, if possible, the cup might pass from him.

Being God, and omnipotent, it would be absurd to suppose that Judas could betray him before he was ready to be betrayed; and being omniscient, he must have known when he selected him that Judas would betray him. And, being God, he must have been, in the selection of a betrayer, in the avoiding arrest, and in the betrayal itself, but carrying out the details of his own plan.

Nor do we get out of this difficulty by saying that Judas was a wicked man, and was chosen for that reason, but could have changed his life, reformed, and refused to betray. He was chosen to betray, if Jesus was an omnipotent God, and, being omniscient, he must have chosen him because he knew he could not change. To suppose him able to change is to suppose the creature to be able to thwart the creator; for, as I have said, if Judas had reformed, so might any other selected in his place, and Jesus be thus left without a betrayer.

So, either Judas was restrained by omnipotent power from being a better man, and forced to do as he did, and hence not a free-agent; and being created, as he was, by an omnipotent power, which must have foreseen what he was to be selected to do, he is elevated from a merely base man to be one of the essential instruments of salvation; or, events can happen otherwise than as God wills, and any of His schemes (for this is said to be His most glorious) may be thwarted by His own creatures, who by an inexplicable contradiction are predestined free agents!

And this is not an attempt to measure the ways of God by human reason in any offensive sense. If there is anything which makes us " in the image of God," it is the gift of reason. As I have more than once said, all that is above and beyond our reason is proper subject-matter for faith; but that which is below our reason must be utterly unworthy of God. That He should be omnipotent and omniscient—that He should exist at all—is beyond our comprehension, and therefore may be believed, and cannot be disproved; but that, being all-powerful and all-knowing, events can happen which He did not wish, and did not foresee, is too palpable a contradiction, even to our limited apprehensions, not to be rejected as absurd.

I have heard but one answer: "The subject is too sacred for discussion." If this be so, as so many good people maintain; if we must yield our reason to the dictum of the Church; if belief in such absurdities be necessary to salvation, I can well understand why one must become as a little child to enter the kingdom of heaven.

At this point occur the remarks which brought on the discussion of dogmas and councils, and which being given there need not be repeated here. (See Prop. III.)

To return to Judas. What I have written seems to me to indicate, not that Judas was a good man, or deserving of eulogy or marble; but that of two things one. Either he was a wicked wretch, as he is so often described, in which case Jesus must have been man, and man only, since "to betray" carries with it necessarily the idea of an attempt on Jesus' part to escape from what he saw was imminent, and being disappointed in his efforts, ideas inconsistent with the very fundamental idea of God; or, he was merely an instrument in the hands of God; and whether chosen because he had been created wicked, or created wicked because he was to be chosen, equally entitled to be left to the mercy of his God.

To which the Bishop replied:

"The first charge which you make in your document is 'Jesus was clearly avoiding arrest.' I do not know where the grounds for such an accusation can be obtained except from the infidel works of Strauss, Renan, etc. The Gospel accounts tell just the opposite. They tell us that our Divine Saviour frequently foretold that He would be delivered into the hands of His enemies, be scourged, and put to death. He consequently not only expected it, but when Peter, in a moment of mistaken zeal, asserted that such a doom was not to be the fate of his beloved Master, Christ severely rebuked him. When at length the eventful evening came, instead of flight, all was calm expectation that His hour had arrived. On the day of His arrest He came from Bethany to Jerusalem where He knew that the highest officers of the State were, and that they were seeking an opportunity to arrest Him. Is this the conduct of a man seeking to avoid arrest? Calmly He celebrated the feast of the Paschal Lamb, and while doing so told the Apostles that the hour was at hand when they would all abandon Him (John xvi., 31); that Peter would that very night deny Him thrice; that 'this night' (hac nocte) the shepherd was to be struck and the sheep dispersed (Mark xiv.). He appointed Galilee as the place where He would meet them after His resurrection from the dead. Having celebrated the Passover, He retired, knowing His hour to be at hand, to a place for prayer. The place to which He went was one to which He was accustomed to go (Luke xxiii.). 'And Judas also knew the place, because Jesus had often resorted thither with His disciples' (John xviii.). Does a fugitive from the officers of the law waste valuable hours in prayer? Does he go to the place of his old habitual haunts, and well known to the very leader of the party seeking to arrest him?

"The next argument adduced to prove that Jesus avoided arrest is that 'He prayed that if possible the cup might pass away.' But you forget to state that to these words Jesus immediately added the prayer: 'but not what I will, but what Thou wilt.' As the martyr when brought face to face with the gibbet on which his limbs are to be racked, and on which he is to be put to a cruel death, will naturally feel his entire being recoil at the hideous torments prepared for him, so the innocent humanity of Jesus. The hour had come for the fearful torturing and unparalleled humiliations. His highly sensitive body naturally recoiled; but in adding the grand words of resignation, 'not my will but Thine be done,' Jesus, like every true martyr, far from seeking to evade, offered himself to, the awful sacrifice. His prayer, therefore, is only an additional proof that He did not seek to avoid arrest.

"You do not acknowledge Jesus to be God. The Catholic Church teaches that He was God, 'by whom all things were made, and without Him nothing was made'—St. John. And He — God — 'was made flesh, and dwelt among us.' Either Christ was really God clothed in flesh and blood, or He was merely a man. If He was merely a man, He must be looked upon as one guilty of enormous falsehood. For what more enormous falsehood can be conceived than for a man to claim that he is God? And this is what Jesus claimed. 'Abraham, your father, rejoiced that he might see my day. He saw it and was glad. And the Jews therefore said unto him: Thou art not yet fifty years, and hast thou seen Abraham? Jesus said to them: Truly, truly, I say to you, before Abraham was made, I am'—John viii. It needs no comment to make it evident that such language could not be used by a mere man without his being guilty of falsehood. Were I to say: Before Christopher Columbus was made, I am, people would justly pronounce me to be either a knave or a fool. And yet Christopher Columbus has lived only about three centuries before my time. Abraham had lived nearly two thousand years before the mortal career of Christ. If He was a mere man then He was guilty of an enormous falsehood. But He was not only man, He was the Jehovah—and He calls Himself by that sublime appellation given of Himself by Moses: 'I am who I am.' Therefore before Abraham was made, "I am"; before the world was made, 'I am'; for all eternity, 'I am.'

"In the discussion with the Jews recorded in 10th John, Christ was challenged by them to say who He was. His reply is: 'I and the Father are one.' This raised a storm of abuse from the Jewish audience who accused Christ of uttering blasphemy, and took up stones to hurl at Him. Were you, or any other man, to go out into the streets of one of our large cities, and, gathering around you a multitude of people, gravely inform them that you and God the Father are one, they would either justly accuse you of blasphemy and prepare to let fly at you; or, what is more likely to happen from an American audience, they would unanimously vote you a candidate for the lunatic asylum.

"Christ, having been arrested, was brought before the High Priest. The High Priest had his legitimate tribunal. He was its presiding judge. In open court, the judge asked Christ if He was the Son of the living God; Jesus unhesitatingly answers: 'I am'—(Mark xiv.). The High Priest then immediately adjudged Jesus deserving death. "What further need have we of witnesses? Behold now ye have heard the blasphemy'—(Mark xiv.). Consequently if Christ were a mere man, then truly He had blasphemed; if He had blasphemed, then He could legally be condemned to death. And in reality it was on this charge that Pilate condemned Jesus to death. 'We have a law, and according to the law he ought to die, because he made himself the son of God.' Consequently, if you believe that Jesus was merely a man, you must acknowledge that the accusation of blasphemy was sustained. If the charge of blasphemy could be sustained, then indeed Jesus had violated a law whose penalty was death, and therefore the death inflicted on Christ was legally a just one There is no half way. Christ either was 'the Word who was with God, and who was God'—or a mere man. If a mere man, He was guilty of an *infinite* falsehood in claiming for Himself a divine nature. Consequently, instead of being a messenger from God and an inspired prophet, He would have been an impostor.

"I will now make a few remarks in regard to your views upon Judas, etc. The Holy Bible tells us that God foresees all things. You must not, however, confuse ideas. Because things so happen, God foresees them as such; but not because God foresees them as such do they so happen. His foreseeing them does not influence the event of affairs. Were you, looking from a window of your house, to see a man stealthily creeping over the wall of a yard in order to plunder, you would, unperceived by him, notice his actions and his preparations to steal. But what connection has your seeing all that he is about to do with the bad fellow's actions? His own bad will is the cause of the action which he is about to do, and not your seeing it. His action comes from his own free-will, not influenced in the slightest by your seeing what he is about to do. You see what he is about to do, because he is actually about to do it. What an absurdity it would be to say that the man in question is about to clamber over the wall and plunder because you look down and perceive what he will do! And yet it is just such nonsense one is guilty of in daring to make God's foresight responsible for our actions. God looks upon this world and sees what actions men are about to perform; and because God sees what I am about to do, therefore, it is said, I am predestined to do it! We indignantly ask: What connection has God's sight of your action with your action? How is your action influenced by His knowledge? Your action evidently comes from the determination of your own will, and not from the knowledge of God. Because your will has decided upon this action therefore God foresees it; and it would be the very height of absurdity to assert that you *must* act thus because God foresees how you *will* act. Every man is conscious that he has a free-will. That free will is eminently in our own power. Tyrants may bind our limbs, scourge the body, mutilate and defile that body, but never can they make me, against my will, to sin. A stronger man than I might bind me; and violently placing a pistol in my hand, force my hand, unable to resist, to fire that pistol and thus slay a man; but no tribunal, human or divine, would call this action of mine a murder. And why? Because the superior force of another moved my hand, and not my own free-will. Hence we say that there was no such thing as Judas being created and forced to betray Christ. Judas was a man. If a man, then he had a free-will. For who ever heard of a man who had no free-will? If he had a free will, then just as you and I can steal or not, murder or not, blaspheme God or not, for we have free-wills, so also could Judas. To say that God created Judas without a free-will, is, without a shadow of proof, to declare that Judas was some kind of a nondescript brute, but not a rational being. To say that God created and forced Judas to execute the dirty act, is to make the thrice Holy God as much the really guilty one as the man who would ravish a helpless and resisting virgin.

"But you object, 'if Judas was a free agent capable of doing what he wished, then the whole of God's scheme of salvation was in imminent danger of miscarrying.' You forget. The betrayal of Jesus by Judas did not accomplish our salvation; nor was it at all necessary to it. How then have we been redeemed? By the death of Jesus. Will you say that God had only one way by which this sacrifice of Christ might have been accomplished? Why, a man of ordinary wisdom will find a dozen ways of accomplishing a desired end. You will, doubtless, concede as much to Him who possesses infinite wisdom. A skilful general looking down from a lofty eminence sees the plans, and tricks, and ambuscades which the enemy is preparing. Is it not justly regarded as the very apex of military skill if the general will accomplish the defeat of the enemy by the very plans, tricks, and ambuscades which he had prepared? A skilful pleader considers it the acme of brilliancy if he can take up the very line of his opponent's reasoning, and hurl back argument after argument of it for his opponent's crushing defeat. I trust you will admit as much to Uncreated Wisdom Himself. God has made us all free. I may use that freedom to keep God's commandments; and I may use it to steal, murder, and violate His law. But God, like the skilful general, takes the very machinations of His enemies and uses them to further His own plans. Hence it is said so often in the Holy Bible, 'omnia serviunt Tibi'—'all things serve Thee.' As a skilful physician uses the bloodthirsty leech, ay, even the most deadly poisons, for accomplishing his own charitable purposes—so the infinitely wise God takes those sinners who, by the act of their own free-will have become such, and uses them for attaining His end, the salvation. Judas was called to the glorious dignity of the Apostolate by the same God-man who called Peter, John, and Andrew. Just as I and any other bishop might betray the cause of God, and the fault would be all our own, so Judas was a traitor to the still higher dignity of the apostolate; and the fault is all his own, and not God's. That God made use of Judas' treacherous act in accomplishing His own designs, we do but see His wisdom herein imitated by the skilful general, wise advocate, and charitable physician. Evidently the infinite wisdom of God had at hand countless ways for bringing about the sacrifice of Jesus Christ, by which alone the world has been redeemed. To say, therefore, that had not Judas sinned, 'God's plan of salvation would have been in imminent danger of miscarrying'—is evidently, on the part of a finite intellect, to forget. This simple exposition shows that we are not placed in the dilemma of denying either the divinity of Christ, or a free-will to Judas."

Then follows the Bishop's challenge, in response to my remarks about dogmas, which has already been given (Prop. III.), and which closes his first paper.

The first point to which the Bishop addresses himself is my statement that "Jesus was clearly avoiding arrest," and he cites me to the Gospel accounts to prove the contrary. I must confess I hardly expected that what seemed so very obvious a fact would be seriously controverted. I would have supposed that the fact would have been admitted and explained, on the theory of the dual nature, by saying that the God was ready and willing for the sacrifice, but that the man was weak, and trying to postpone.

Be that as it may, however, the very word "betray" tells the whole story whatever the Apostles, and those who may have added to their statements, may have written since the happening of the event.

The assertion is that Judas *betrayed* Jesus. *Webster's Dictionary* (quarto, title "Betray") gives the definitions, which are sustained by the derivation of the word, by common consent, and, I think, by the sense in which the Bishop uses the word when he attaches guilt to it:

> I. To deliver into the hands of an enemy, by treachery, or fraud, in violation of a trust.
> II. To violate by fraud or unfaithfulness.
> III. To violate confidence by *disclosing a secret*, or that which was intrusted.
> IV. To disclose, to permit to appear, what is intended to be kept secret.

Under these definitions, so far, Judas, if he *betrayed* Jesus, must have delivered him to his enemies when Jesus trusted that he would not, or there could have been no violation of a trust; or he must have disclosed that which Jesus desired, or intended, should be kept secret.

> V. To mislead or expose to inconvenience not foreseen.

If Jesus foresaw (and not to foresee is to be not God), he was not *betrayed* under this definition.

> VI. To show; to disclose; to indicate what is not obvious at first view, or would otherwise be concealed.

In this sense to betray carries no idea of guilt.

> VII. To fail, or deceive.

If Judas failed Jesus, Jesus was deceived. Can God be deceived? If not, then he (if God) was not *betrayed* under this definition.

Finally, if the above definition be correct, and Jesus was "betrayed" in that sense, he was *avoiding* arrest, not necessarily flying to remote distances, but going to a place where he thought he would be safe, only to be disappointed through the treachery of Judas; in which case the portions of the Gospel on which the Bishop relies must be mistranslations, subsequent additions, or otherwise inexact. Or, if they be correct, let us cease saying that Judas " betrayed " Jesus, and seek some other word which will not carry such inconvenient ideas with it.

It may be claimed, however, and with great truth, as the intention is the essence of a crime, that although Jesus knew what Judas was about to do, and hence was not " betrayed " under the definitions given above, yet if Judas *intended* to betray, his crime was complete even though foreseen by Jesus. This I admit. But this view strengthens the other branch of the dilemma—that is, that, if Jesus was God, Judas was a mere instrument in the hands of a superior and irresistible power. For, as God is omnipotent and omniscient, it follows, necessarily, that He knew when He selected Judas as His disciple, exactly what he (Judas) would do. And as no one who agrees with the Church, or admires Jesus as I do, would for a moment believe him guilty of employing unnecessary theatrical effects, it must be conclusively presumed that the drama of the betrayal was performed for a purpose, and that purpose a necessary one. And as, surely, God would never have undertaken any scheme unless it was the best possible, and it was evidently a part of his scheme that he should be delivered up by Judas, he would never have adopted a plan which depended on what he foresaw Judas *might* do, but only on what he knew he *would* do; and if he knew he would do it, he knew he could not change, on account of the power of God exerted, directly, or indirectly through the disposition and character which God had created him with, on his mind. And Judas must have been a necessary and helpless actor in the drama without reference to his individual thoughts or intentions.

I cite two passages in point from *An Analysis of Religious Belief*, by Viscount Amberly, the first from p. 214:

"The efforts of the Chief Priests to bring about his destruction are described in two of our Gospels as the direct result of his proceedings about the temple, the impression he had made on the multitude being a further inducement (Matt. xi., 18, Luke xix., 48). Aware of the indignation he had excited, Jesus, soon after these events, retired into some private place, known only to his more intimate friends. So, at least, I understand the story of the betrayal. Either Judas never betrayed him at all, or he was lurking in concealment somewhere in the neighborhood of Jerusalem. That the conduct attributed to Judas should be a pure invention appears to me so improbable, more especially when the history of the election of a new apostle is taken into account, that I am forced to choose the latter alternative. The representation of the Gospels that Jesus went on teaching in public to the end of his career, and yet that Judas received a bribe for his betrayal, is self-contradictory. The facts appear to be that Jesus ate the Passover at Jerusalem with his disciples, and that immediately after it, conscious of growing danger, he retired to some hidden spot where he had lived before, and where friends alone were admitted to his company. Judas informed the authorities of the temple where this spot was. They thereupon apprehended Jesus, and brought him before the Sanhedrim for trial."

The second is from p. 259, where, after giving the several and varying accounts of the Last Supper, it is said:

"The improbability of these stories is obvious. In the three first, Judas is pointed out to all the eleven as a man who is about to give up their leader to punishment, and probable death, yet no step was taken or even suggested, by any of them to either impede the false disciple in his movements, or to save Jesus by flight or concealment. The announcement is taken as quietly as if it were an every-day occurrence that was referred to.

"John's narrative avoids this difficulty by supposing the intimation that Judas was the man, to be conveyed by a private signal understood only by Peter and the disciple next to Jesus. These two may have felt it necessary to keep the secret, but why could they not understand the words of Jesus to Judas, or why not enquire whether they had reference to his treachery, which had just before been so plainly intimated? That Jesus, with his keen vision, may have divined the proceedings of Judas, is quite possible; that he could have spoken of them in this open way without exciting more attention, is hardly credible."

The Bishop says that in adducing Jesus' prayer that, if possible, the cup might pass from him, as another evidence that he was avoiding arrest, I " forgot to state that to these words Jesus immediately added, 'but not what I will but what thou wilt.'" These added words do not affect the point at issue; and were not cited because unnecessary to my then purpose. Had I been seeking, at that particular time and in that particular argument, to show that Jesus was not God, those words would have been appropriate (as we have seen when discussing the divinity of Jesus), for they very plainly show that Jesus did not consider himself and God as one, as he uses very different pronouns to distinguish the one from the other, and distinctly asserts that he has one will, and God another, and that they were antagonistic, but that, like the true devotee he was, having but one object in life—to do what his Father wished—(I use the word "Father" in its spiritual application, as I believe Jesus did)—he was ready to submit his will to his God's, and meet a martyr's fate if such were really God's will; but, at the same time, in the absence of any precise knowledge of what that will was, he would keep out of the way as far as he could: for if he had had precise information as to the fact that it was God's decree that he should suffer as he did (and if he were God he would have known definitely), Jesus was not the man to beg off.

As to the Bishop's assertion that Jesus was either God, or an impostor, I have already considered the point, and need only say here that the Bishop does not seem to realize that there may be a third proposition—he may have had thrust upon him, since his death, honors which he not only never coveted, but which, had he foreseen them, he would have been prompt to reject.

The next branch of the Bishop's argument may be summarized thus: God foresees things because they so happen, they do not so happen because He foresees them. I must not confuse ideas. If I from my window saw a thief preparing to steal, my seeing would have nothing to do with his theft, and, so, God's seeing, or foreseeing, events has no effect on them. That to suppose otherwise is "nonsense." That all men have free-will, and every man is conscious of it. That Judas was a man and, therefore, had free-will. That the betrayal was not necessary to our salvation, because we are redeemed by the death of Jesus, which God could have brought about in any of a variety of ways. Then follows a comparison of God to a skilful general who uses the machinations of his enemies to forward his own plans; to a skilful pleader who uses the argument of his opponent for his opponent's defeat. That as the physician will use deadly poisons to accomplish his charitable purposes, so God uses the wilful sins of men as a means to attain His ends; and he concludes that therefore it is unnecessary to deny either the divinity of Jesus, or the free-will of Judas.

Is not this argument a most remarkable one? Yet it is, I believe, one which all Christian Churchmen use.

One of the leading objections which I have to dogmatic Christianity is that it tends to humanize God, to deify man; that it, for that purpose, seizes upon some one attribute, or text, or set of texts, from which to deduce a creed utterly inconsistent with other attributes, or texts, and then strains faith and stifles reason in its efforts to reconcile its own inconsistencies.

Thus, when the Bishop compares God to the general, the pleader, the physician, is he not humanizing God? When he says, in substance, that I would not be responsible for what I saw from my window, and, similarly, that God is not responsible for what He sees from heaven, is not this still further humanizing Him? bringing Him, by a comparison, down to the level of man? If he possessed vision and prevision *alone*, the argument would be good: but to Him are attributed also omniscience and omnipotence, and that entirely alters the case. Had I made the thief and given him, by creation, the disposition to do wrong stronger than the disposition to do right, and, in addition, had the power, by the mere exercise of my will, to prevent the theft which I knew he was about to commit, and I did not, by all laws, human and divine, I would be *particeps criminis*, and as guilty as he; and, morally, this would be equally true if I had had nothing to do with his character and disposition, but merely saw him about to commit a crime, and could have prevented it by the mere exercise of volition, without danger, trouble, or inconvenience to myself.

And if the Bishop's simile is a good one, the legitimate conclusion is that God would be also.

We are taught that God is omnipresent, omnipotent, omniscient; that without Him nothing exists, or can exist; that He created man; that He made man's soul, man's mind, man's will; but the Church says He emancipated the will, and the Bishop says every man knows it. I think not, and I have given my reasons in full elsewhere, together with the Church's argument (Prop. II.). But, right or wrong, the Church insists that every man has free-will, is a free agent, is, in this one particular, independent of his God; that, by this royal attribute, man can thwart God's plans, grieve God's heart. Is not this elevating man at the cost of lowering God? And, as if this were not enough, we must pull God still farther down to our level, try to make him in our image—an exaggerated man,—attribute to Him anger, hate, jealousy, fickleness, repentance, favoritism, nearly all of the faults and weaknesses of poor humanity, and seek to justify ourselves by saying, on the authority of the Jewish Bible, that God has so portrayed Himself.

The Bishop expresses some indignation at the idea that God's foresight should make Him responsible for man's acts (and I had taken no such position, but argued as to *all* His attributes at once); I think I may be pardoned if I feel somewhat indignant at having the crude ideas of a semi-barbarous race, as to the attributes of divinity, offered to a comparatively enlightened civilization as the measure of a God.

And this is why I characterize the argument as remarkable; for it can never cease to be a matter of surprise to me that the Church will persist in making arguments which, if carried to their logical conclusions, cannot fail to deprive God of His absolute supremacy.

I give the Bishop's final reply:

"In your first paper you asserted that 'Jesus was clearly avoiding arrest.' I denied the assertion, and brought the history of Christ's arrest to prove that He did not avoid arrest, but freely permitted it. In your last paper you say: 'I must confess I hardly expected that what seemed so very obvious a fact would be seriously controverted.' This may all be strange to you. But if it is 'so very obvious a fact,' is it not still stranger that the millions of Christians forming the most enlightened peoples that have ever trod the world do now believe, and always have believed, as I do on this subject? Although it is 'so very obvious a fact,' yet the historical facts in the case establish so unanswerably that Christ did not flee from or shun arrest, but permitted Himself to be given over to the power of His enemies, that you fall back upon a novel line of argument. For you assert that the definition of the word 'betray,' as given by Webster necessarily implies that Christ avoided arrest. Consequently the historical facts bearing on the case are either interpolations, or 'let us cease saying that Judas betrayed Jesus, and seek some other word.' There are many words in language whose definitions necessarily imply correlative ideas. We cannot say that a man is a widower without implying the idea that his wife is dead. If we say of a man that he is a husband, we necessarily imply that he has a wife. We speak of an altar, sacrifice is necessarily implied. Do you wish to say that the idea of avoiding, shunning, and fleeing from the danger is necessarily implied in the use of the word 'betray'? So, even as one speaks to me of a widow, the idea of a husband deceased is necessarily implied. It would destroy the definition of 'widow' were she one whose husband is still living. Do you seriously wish to assert that so soon as one tells me of a betrayal, the idea of a victim avoiding arrest and trying to escape is necessarily implied? Do you wish to say that we cannot think of a betrayal without at the same time thinking of the victim's avoiding and fleeing the betrayal? In that case the victim who would be delivered up while asleep or intoxicated would not be betrayed—because it can be established that being under the influence of sleep or liquor the victim was not avoiding and fleeing from arrest, and therefore there is no betrayal. Your appeal to Webster is particularly unfortunate. First of all there is nothing in his definition from top to bottom which makes the idea of the victim's fleeing arrest essentially connected with the notion of betrayal. Secondly, you quote Webster as defining betray to be: 'To deliver into the hands of an enemy . . . in violation of *a* trust.' In the edition of Webster (unabridged) of 1855 and in the one of 1877 the reading is in 'violation of trust.' There is evidently a great difference between 'violation of trust'—and 'violation of a trust.' The native-born who would mislead his fatherland, the child who would sell his parent, or the disciple who would deliver his master, would violate trust. For such mutual relations imply trust, though a specific trust has not been confided by one party to the other.

"And this constituted the act of Judas a betrayal in the dictionary definition of the word. For he being a disciple of Jesus was guilty of a 'violation of trust,' to deliver his own master into the hands of his enemies so faithlessly. Hence Webster (edition 1877) says: 'To deliver into the hands of an enemy by treachery or fraud in violation of trust; to give up treacherously or faithlessly;—" Jesus said unto them, the Son of Man shall be betrayed into the hands of men."'

"Thus Webster—the very authority to which you appeal—from the force of historical facts—quotes, in the moment of defining the requisites to constitute a 'betrayal,' our case of Judas as one having all the elements of a true betrayal. Hence, sir, I said that your reference to *Webster's Dictionary* is particularly unfortunate for your cause.

"You have made several quotations from the work of

Viscount Amberly. You speak of it in terms of unqualified praise.

"I do not wish to wound your feelings, but judging from the choice flowers of his work which you have culled and wreathed into your second paper to me, I pronounce it to be an utterly unreliable book—unworthy of a gentleman's consideration. For you quote the Viscount as saying: 'The representation of the Gospel that Jesus went on teaching in public to the very end of his career, and yet that Judas received a bribe for his betrayal, is self-contradictory.'

"The Viscount here garbles the 'representations of the Gospels.' The Gospels represent Jesus as being exceedingly popular with the masses of the people. Their love, admiration, and devotion, they frequently expressed. On one occasion, many, very many, of them wished to force Jesus, in spite of Himself, to be their king.[1] The triumphal entry of Christ into Jerusalem, when they strewed the way with palm branches and their very garments, and made the air resonant with their loud canticles in His honor, proves this. But Jesus, intensely loved by the majority of the people, was intensely hated by the Chief Priests and the generality of the Scribes and Pharisees, whose hypocrisy and other vices He severely rebuked. This being the case, what is more natural than to suppose that if the Chief Priests, etc., attempted to seize upon Jesus while addressing the immense throng that ordinarily listened with intense pleasure to his beautiful discourses, there would be a riot, bloodshed, and finally a failure of

---

[1] If this be true, then very evidently these people did not look upon Jesus as God, for they sought to honor him, and even such ignorant barbarians could hardly have supposed it would be a promotion to make the God of the Universe the king of a tribe.—W. D. H.

their attempt? What more natural than their desire to seek some occasion of seizing him by fraud and treachery, and when the crowds of delighted people would not be about? And this is just the account given by the Gospels. 'And the Chief Priests and the Scribes sought how they might by some wile lay hold on him and kill him. But they said, Not on the festival day lest there should be a tumult among the people'—Mark xiv. 'Then were gathered together the Chief Priests and ancients of the people into the Court of the High Priest who was called Caiaphas, and they consulted together that by subtilty they might apprehend Jesus and put him to death'—Matt. xxvi. 'And the Chief Priests and the Scribes sought how they might put Jesus to death, but they feared the people. . . . And he [Judas] sought an opportunity to betray him in the absence of the multitude'—Luke xxii. 'And they were glad and covenanted to give him money. And he promised'—Luke xxii. And this account Viscount Amberly calls 'self-contradictory'!

"You again quote Viscount Amberly as saying: 'In the three first [Gospels] Judas is pointed out to all the eleven as a man who is about to give up their master to punishment. . . . The announcement is taken as quietly as if it were an every-day occurrence that was referred to.' In this quotation Viscount Amberly asserts, first, that Judas is pointed out to all the eleven as the man about to perpetrate the vile deed; secondly, this announcement is taken by the rest as if an ordinary occurrence was declared to them. The Gospel account tells us something else altogether. It tells us that Christ said at the Last Supper in the clearest manner that: 1st; He was about to be betrayed: 2d; that a disciple would do the foul deed. Nowhere, however, does he mention the name of the traitor. He referred in such an obscure way to the person who would betray Him, that while the guilty conscience would make him understand, the others did not perceive to whom Christ had reference. 'And while they were eating: Amen, I say to you that one of you is about to betray me. And they being very much troubled began every one to say, Is it I, Lord? But he answering said—He that dippeth his hand in the dish, he shall betray me'—Matt. xxvi. 'And when they were at table and eating, Jesus saith: Amen, I say to you, One of you that eateth with me shall betray me. But they began to be sorrowful, and say to him one by one, Is it I? Who saith to them: One of the twelve who dippeth his hand with me in the dish shall betray me'—Mark xiv. 'But yet behold the hand of him who betrayeth me is with me on the table. And they began to inquire among themselves which of them it was that should do this thing'—Luke xxii. 'Amen, amen, I say to you that one of you shall betray me. The disciples therefore looked upon one another, doubting of whom he spoke. Now there was leaning on Jesus' bosom one of the disciples whom Jesus loved. Simon Peter beckoned therefore to him and said to him, Who is it of whom he speaketh? He therefore leaning on the breast of Jesus saith to him, Lord, who is it? And Jesus answered: he it is to whom I shall reach bread dipped. And when he had dipped the bread he gave it to Judas Iscariot, the son of Simon. And after the morsel Satan entered into him, and Jesus said to him: That which thou doest, do quickly. Now *no man* at table knew he had said this unto him,' etc.,—John xiii.

"I have quoted thus the Gospel account, the mere perusal of which will show the most superficial observer how utterly Viscount Amberly perverts and misstates this scene.

Judas is not, as Viscount Amberly asserts, clearly pointed out to the twelve as the one about to betray Christ. Not only Christ nowhere mentions his name, but the mere fact that each anxiously inquires to find out who was the guilty traitor, is ample refutation of Viscount Amberly's unwarranted assertion that 'Judas was pointed out to all the eleven as the man who is about to give up their master to punishment.' That Peter found it necessary to inquire of John and John had to inquire of Christ Himself, flings to the ground the brazen assertion of Viscount Amberly. His other charge is equally false: 'The announcement is taken as quietly as if it were an every-day occurrence.' For the Gospels tell us that no sooner did Christ announce that one of them was about to betray Him, than—'contristati sunt valde'—and they were saddened extremely!

"So much for the veracious Viscount Amberly's unfounded assertion that Christ pointed out Judas to ALL at table as the black-hearted traitor, and that the disciples took the announcement as quietly as an every-day occurrence."

The Bishop thinks it strange that I should consider the fact that Jesus was avoiding arrest as an obvious one, because so many "millions of Christians, forming the most enlightened people that have ever trod the world, do now believe, and always have believed, the contrary."

I have already noticed this class of argument, and can only here repeat that truth cannot be distinguished from error with any degree of certainty, by merely ascertaining the number of those who believe it. Minorities are as often right as majorities, and both may be wrong.

As a specimen of an equally illogical class of theological argument, I have given the Bishop's remarks upon what he ought to have known was a clerical error, my inserting "a" before "trust" in Webster's Definition I., of "betray"; and, for that purpose, have left the error in my argument.

The argument on my side is stronger with the article left out, as we will see. The Bishop's distinction between "violation of trust" and "violation of *a* trust," while true, is sophistically used; the distinction exists only literally, and not in the spirit. If the trust arises from an especial confidence in a particular instance, it would be "*a*" trust, and its violation would be a betrayal, because a violation of confidence reposed; if the trust arises from the relations, whether natural or assumed, between the parties, and is general, not special, that would be "trust" generally, and its violation would equally be a betrayal, because equally a violation of confidence reposed. Practically the letter makes no difference; I say that its absence would have suited me better because, as the Bishop admits, the relation existing between Jesus and Judas of itself implied trust, showed that Jesus relied on him, trusted him generally, and consequently it would have been unnecessary to establish any special trust in this specific instance. And if Jesus, on account of this relation of teacher and disciple (or whatever the Church may prefer to call it), trusted, in a general way, that he was safe from the treachery of Judas, his betrayal was at least as great a violation of trust as if such trust had been specially limited, less complete.

When the Church is reduced to such an argument as the Bishop has made on this point, and made seriously, it looks as if she were *in extremis*, or else in reality had sacrificed her intellect to her faith.

To have quoted Webster's illustration of the word, given under Definition I., and quoted by the Bishop with approval, would have been unfair. I believed the Bishop and his Church used the word in that sense; I knew that Protestants did. But I felt that I had no right to define his belief, and preferred that he should do that for himself; he, however, has now adopted the illustration and that acceptance of that use of the word is the end of the argument; for I do mean, seriously, to say that the word "betray," when used in this sense, that is, "to deliver up into the hands of an enemy by treachery or fraud, in violation of trust," does necessarily imply that the person or persons betrayed was or were avoiding arrest. The Bishop insists on making me say " fleeing." He is unfair. I had said very plainly "*avoiding* arrest, not necessarily flying to remote distances, but going to a place where he thought he would be safe, only to be disappointed through the treachery of Judas." When one is avoiding arrest and, thinking himself in a safe place, feels no anxiety, and so goes to sleep or becomes intoxicated, he is avoiding arrest, or rather trying to avoid arrest, just as much as when he was awake or sober, or as if he were in full flight. Avoiding arrest means simply taking any steps which it is expected or hoped will succeed in preventing capture, whether such steps be active flight or passive concealment.

Hence, if Jesus trusted—even in a general way only—that Judas would not betray him, and in that trust was disappointed, Judas was a traitor, and as I cannot conceive of a disappointed God, I must believe that Jesus was but man.

Or if everything happened just as Jesus, he being God, had appointed it to happen, then Judas did not "betray" him under the definition now being considered.

Now for Viscount Amberly. His book was the first of the kind I had ever read, and I read it several years ago, shortly after it first appeared, and have not since examined it. It may be that I have overestimated its value, but I think not. I think it is a clear, calm, dispassionate, eminently fair and able presentation of his views, and I believe it to be in the main unanswerable; and I have used many of his ideas besides sometimes quoting his words in this discussion. And although I have since read very many books upon the same subject, some of them of even greater ability,—*c. g.*, *The Creed of Christendom*, by Wm. Rathbone Greg, and *Supernatural Religion*, by Prof. W. K. Clifford,—the pleasant and favorable impression first produced on my mind by the Viscount's book has never been in the least effaced. And the Bishop most signally fails to impeach his statements, or answer his arguments, as we will now see.

The Viscount says that the Gospels represent Jesus as "teaching in public to the very end of his career." Even the Bishop admits that they do. The Viscount also says that they represent "that Judas received a bribe for his betrayal." The Bishop also admits that. The Viscount draws the conclusion that the statements are "self-contradictory," to which conclusion the Bishop demurs upon the ground that although teaching in public to the very end, the High Priests and their party were afraid to attempt a public arrest for fear of a tumult or a failure; and therefore bribed Judas to lead them where he would be comparatively alone and unprotected, and cites texts to sustain the point.

The testimony of the Bible is the testimony of interested witnesses, and consists of *ex parte* statements made in their own behalf, or in behalf of their cause; these witnesses have never been cross-examined, their antecedents and character are unknown, and, more than all, the evidence has been for hundreds of years exclusively in the hands of those in whose interest it was originally given, and they have had every facility for making such alterations, additions, or suppressions as might be thought desirable, and with no risk of being found out except through their own unskilfulness. Hence we are not obliged to take everything the Gospels say as being necessarily true, and then attempt to reconcile conflicting statements as best we may; we take them as we find them, and reconcile them when we can, and when we cannot, we try honestly and earnestly to decide which of the conflicting statements is true, and, having decided, we consider the other of the contradictory statements to be false.

Applying this principle, which I think is too palpably correct to need the support of an argument, we conclude that the wonderful popularity ascribed to Jesus in the texts quoted by the Bishop is a mistake; and the fact that when Pilate wanted to release him, the mob cried out against it, with the further fact that the high priests bribed Judas to guide them to him, is proof of it. It was among the lower orders that Jesus had his friends, but he seems to have had none who were willing to publicly take his part in the mob before Pilate; and if his teaching was so open and public as the Bishop thinks, then it were an absurdity to bribe any one to show his whereabouts, which would be notorious—for there would have been no need of concealment. And if Jesus was so well satisfied that his enemies were trying to capture him that he frequented, at night, private or secluded places where he could not be apprehended without a guide to lead the way to him (thus showing an indisposition—to put it mildly—to be arrested), it would have been a folly of which I am willing to acquit him to have appeared so openly in the midst of his numerous and powerful enemies, backed, as they were by the cohorts of Rome.

Undoubtedly Jesus had, as he deserved, a great many friends, but they were, as I have said, principally among the poor and humble, and they could not have been anything like a majority of the people, for the sect was a small one long after the death of Jesus. If Jesus had been "intensely loved by a majority of the people," as the Bishop says, where were they when Pilate wished to release him? They knew of the custom, and they knew that, being released by Pontius Pilate's order, the Roman soldiers would have protected him and them.

I think, therefore, that such texts as the Bishop alludes to are contradicted by the undisputed facts mentioned in other texts; that is, the *reports, rumors,* or *conclusions of the writer,* as set forth in some texts, are disproved by the *facts* set forth by the same writer in other texts.

Thus, they were afraid to arrest him during the feast lest there should be an uproar (Matt. xxvi., 5); but it was also at that same feast that a prisoner was to be released, and when Pilate tried to release Jesus, the very multitude which the high priests are represented as fearing, being persuaded by the priests (as the account says), cried for Barabbas, and they *all* cried Let him [Jesus] be crucified (Matt. xxvii., 15–22). Where were the "majority of the people," who were so devoted to Jesus, that this crowd, which seems to have been the one in which his friends were expected to be, was *unanimous* for his death? And on the very feast at which it was feared, because of the presence of his friends, to arrest him. It seems to me that the Viscount has the best of it. As I have said, I have not read the book for some years, and do not remember the Viscount's reasons for his assertions, and have therefore given such as occur to me. But I think them amply sufficient.[1]

So, also, it seems to me that Amberly is correct in the assertion to which the Bishop objects: that "Judas is pointed out to all the eleven as a man who is about to give up their master to punishment. . . . The announcement is taken as quietly as if it were an every-day occurrence that was referred to."

The Bishop says: "Nowhere does He mention the name of the traitor. He referred in such an obscure way to the person who would betray Him, that while the guilty conscience would make him understand, the others did not perceive to whom Christ had reference." My Bible (Protestant) says, Matt. xxvi., 21–25:

> "And as they did eat, he said verily I say unto you that one of you shall betray me. And they were exceeding sorrowful, and began every one of them to say unto him, Lord, is it I? And he answered and said, He that dippeth his hand with me in the dish, the same shall betray me. The Son of Man goeth as it is written of him: but woe unto that man by whom the Son of Man is betrayed: it had been good for that man if he had not been born. Then Judas, which betrayed him, answered and said, Master, is it I? He said unto him, Thou hast said."

And *this* account does not say that no man heard him.

If I understand this passage—and the Bishop only quotes a part of it,—it means:

    1st. That Jesus informed them *all* that one of them was about to betray him;

    2d. That they were "exceeding sorrowful."

---

[1] At this time, and for a long time afterwards, the book was lent to various friends, and I have never since examined it. My quotations in my first paper were from my notes.

3d. That he said, "He that dippeth his hand with me into the dish . . . shall betray me"; and, as if this were not plain enough,

4th. That when Judas said "Is it I?" Jesus replied "Thou hast said."

If Matthew tells the truth—and I doubt if the Church will attempt to impeach him,—every man at the table knew that Judas was the traitor. And how was the announcement taken? They were sorry, very sorry, exceedingly sorry. As if Jesus had told them he had a bad cold, or a severe headache, or was going away from them for a few days. When a teacher, a leader, not to say a God, announces to his chosen intimates and disciples that one of them is about to treacherously lead him to a cruel death, and points that one out to them; and they say nothing, and do nothing, but only feel sorry; it is putting it very mildly to say that they took it "as quietly as if it were an every-day occurrence"; and if they said or did any more than I have here set down this Gospel does not inform us of it.

So much for Matthew's account. Mark and Luke give substantially the same, but omit to say that Judas asked and was answered in the manner narrated by Matthew. Of course it will not be claimed that this omission disproves or contradicts Matthew's statement; these latter simply do not go so much into details. They seemed to have thought that Judas was sufficiently indicated by dipping his hand into the dish.

But there is another difference between them which is much more significant. Matthew says that when they heard what Jesus said they were "exceeding sorrowful"; Mark is not so emphatic; according to him "they began to be sorrowful." While Luke says nothing about their sorrow, but states that there was " a strife among them which of them should be accounted the greatest " (Luke, xxii., 24), each evidently having an eye to the succession as head of the Church,—which must have noticeably moderated their grief.

It will be noticed, therefore, that in each of the three synoptical Gospels (which are all the Viscount referred to) it is indicated with distinctness that one of those present is about to betray him, that in Matthew Judas is directly and distinctly pointed out as the man, and that in the other two he is sufficiently indicated to put any one who felt any interest in the matter on guard, and cause, at least, further inquiry; but nothing of the sort was done. As Amberly puts it, " no step was taken or even suggested by any of them to either impede the false disciple in his movements, or to save Jesus by flight or concealment." And while Jesus was praying in the garden they felt so little interest in the matter that they went to sleep while he had left them to watch. Was not the Viscount, as I said before, putting it with extreme mildness when he merely said they treated it like an every-day occurrence?

He adds that John tries to avoid this difficulty, but thinks that he fails—as he evidently does,—for even there the announcement is distinctly made to all that one of them is about to betray him, and the traitor is distinctly pointed out to John and Peter. And, by the way, although Amberly distinctly states that in the first three Gospels Judas is pointed out as the man, the Bishop is reduced to such straits that he tries to disprove that statement by quoting from the fourth. Again the Viscount has the best of it.

But it seems to me that, if the Christian theory be

true, there is a great deal of unnecessary sympathy displayed for Jesus and his passion. Considered from the Church's standpoint, the scheme was his own, even in its details; and the good to be done—the saving of all humanity present and to come—was so great that the sufferings of his temporary body sink into comparative insignificance. Not that we should not regret the necessity that called for such physical sacrifice and pain, but because so many others have suffered more for a less result, with a smaller motive, and sustained by hope instead of certainty. And especially does it seem inconsistent to ascribe such sorrow to Jesus. The result of his passion was to be the attaining of his wish to rob death of its sting, the grave of its victory; his sacrifice was his own wish, his own scheme, the crucifixion was the end of his self-imposed troubles, the successful consummation of his plans, and he was to resume his Godhood in a form unmixed with humanity, and forever free from physical and mental pain and suffering. It seems that such a result, even at the cost of a few hours' suffering, should have made the arrival of the preordained end a cause of gratulation, not of grief, more especially to Jesus himself. As the human soul within them has enabled so many martyrs to mount the scaffold, and to brave a far more cruel death at the stake, with a smile of triumph and a hymn of thanksgiving, because of the crown of glory for which they hoped, so, as it seems to me, the *God* within Jesus should have enabled him to meet his fate, less cruel than the stake, with other feelings than sorrow "even unto death." As God he must have known his future, while the martyr had but his hopes. Is a human soul sustained by hope stronger to suffer than God and certainty?

Thus the conclusions to be legitimately drawn from this story of the Betrayal seem also to point with unerring accuracy to the absurdity of the theory that Jesus was God, and to tend to establish, what is getting to be the belief of the most intelligent and least prejudiced minds of the present age, that he was an earnest reformer, honestly trying to free his countrymen from what he recognised as error—an infidel to the creed of the past, an apostle of the creed of the future; but whose doctrines and designs were misconstrued and misrepresented by ignorant or designing followers, seeking by their misrepresentations to advance their own or their Church's interests so soon as his lips were sealed in death—thrusting on him, as I have already said, divine honors, which, were he alive, he would most certainly have rejected, that they might profit from the reflected glory.

THE ARGUMENT.

PROPOSITION VI.

VI. The Bible is not a divinely inspired book; and being untrustworthy as to its facts, cannot be relied on as to its theories.

If the Bible be a divinely inspired book, as is claimed, I believe, by the Christian Churches as to both the Old and New Testaments, and by the Jews as to the Old, it all being spoken of indifferently as the "word of God," it is clear that it must be inspired in whole, or in part. If in whole, then everything in it must be true; if in part, we have no means, so far as I know, of ascertaining which are the inspired, and which the uninspired, portions; which would, of itself, greatly detract from its usefulness.

But it may, I think, be safely concluded that if it positively and unequivocally asserts any important thing to be an absolute fact, and it is demonstrated that such thing is not a fact, and is not, and never was, or could be, true, then the sacred character of the book is lost, and its power as an authority before which even reason must bow, is gone. If it misleads us, and is ignorant, unreliable, and absurd as to its *facts*, it certainly cannot be depended upon for the correctness of its theories. The statement of this proposition is its sufficient proof; it only remains to be seen if the Bible is correct in its statements of facts.

It had been my intention, in discussing this proposition, to have commenced with the cosmogony of the first chapter of Genesis, and to have shown how science has absolutely demonstrated its utter incorrectness in every detail; but the proportions already assumed by this argument, and the vast amount of material at hand with which to demonstrate the unreliability of the Old Testament, warn me that I must omit much that I would like to say.

I can only repeat that science has shown with entire certainty that the history of the first six days as given in Genesis is wrong, impossible, and absurd, because in direct contradiction to what is known of God's records and God's law. So true is this that I presume no one pretending to any knowledge of the present condition of geology will venture to deny it.

I know not what position the Roman Catholic Church holds on this point; but such educated Protestant theologians as I have spoken with about it hold that the six days of creation mean six periods, each of vast extent, and thus attempt to meet some of the facts of geology. But that does not explain how the account is so incorrect as to the order of creation of vegetable and animal life, nor as to the earth being made as we know it before the forming of the sun, nor as to the creation of light, and its separation from darkness (whatever that may mean) on the first day, while the sun and moon were not made until the fourth day. Nor do these apologists seem to reflect that there are *seven* days spoken of, one of which is devoted by God to rest, and that as there is no intimation of any one of the days being different in duration from the others, He must have rested as many millions of years as they assume a " day " to have contained.

The truth is that educated theologians, feeling their

ground giving away under them, grasp at any straw, no matter how slender, to save themselves. But I cannot dwell on this point.

Perhaps one of the most remarkable stories in the Old Testament is that of the deluge, and, as the demonstration of its absurdity is not so generally known as that of the cosmogony just referred to, I will consider it at some length.

The introduction to the story is in these words, Gen. vi., 5, *et seq.*:

" And God saw that the wickedness of man was great in the earth, and that every imagination of the thoughts of his heart was only evil continually. And it *repented the Lord* that he had made man on the earth, and it *grieved him* at his heart. And the Lord said I will destroy man whom I have created from the face of the earth, both man and beast, and the creeping thing, and the fowls of the air ; for it *repenteth me that I have made them*. But Noah found favor in the eyes of the Lord." (The italics are mine.)

Here we have it represented that the great and only God of the universe, maker and sustainer of all things animate and inanimate, omnipotent, omniscient, and prescient, *repented* what He had done!

This one word, if it means what it says, destroys the divinity of the Jewish God. To repent can only mean that events had turned out differently from what He had anticipated, or that He had changed His mind.

The first is evidently what is meant here, for the reason of the repentance, so far as man is concerned, is given : man had become corrupt. No reason is given why he repented having made the lower animals.

So (1) either God did not know that man would become corrupt, and therefore, when he found that he had, really repented,—became sorry—that he had made him, which deprives God of His attributes of prescience and omniscience; or (2) He made him with the full knowledge that he would become corrupt, and allowed him to so become —for if He is omnipotent He could have prevented it,— and thus destroyed him for being what He permitted him to become, He foreknowing from the beginning both the crime and the punishment—which takes away His attribute of justice—(in which case the account is incorrect when it says, and makes God say, He repented, for He would, in this view, have been merely carrying out what He had determined on from the beginning, and, without warning or notice of any kind, would have visited on His unprepared creatures a terrible and vindictive punishment under what was, to them, an *ex-post-facto* law); or (3) He knew man would become corrupt, and did not originally intend to punish him, but changed His mind (repented) and did inflict an unexpected (even to Himself) penalty.

Turn it as you will, this passage alone is sufficient to show that the *God* here portrayed is only an ideal of ignorant barbarians. How the Roman Church gets over this word "repent" here and elsewhere in the Bible I do not know; but learned Churchmen of other denominations have endeavored to explain it to me thus: the people to whom the word of God was originally addressed were incapable of grasping high metaphysical ideas, and could not comprehend the true reasons which actuated God, and therefore they were given one which was suited to their comprehension. They could not receive the *true* idea, therefore they were given the nearest approach to it they could comprehend. I suppose this is about as good an explanation as can be given; at any rate it is the best I have heard.

This explanation shifts but does not lessen the difficulty. It means that God, feeling that some explanation was necessary, or at least advisable, gave a *false* one, His reason being that the people could not comprehend the true one. Apart from the fact that it is difficult to understand *why* God should give to His creatures any reason for His acts, it is purely an assumption, and, I think, an unwarranted one, that He would depart from that truth which is a part of His essence, and lie to His people for fear they might not understand Him if he spoke the truth. It passes belief; the explanation needs at least as much explaining as did the original statement; the remedy is even worse than the disease.

The truth is the Old Testament merely records the ideas which the ancient Jews had formed of the Divinity which they supposed to be their especial God, and whom they represented as possessing the principal characteristics, good and bad, which they knew in earthly rulers; and this passage is but another proof of it. They felt the need of a God, and manufactured one just as every other people did. Or perhaps it would be more exact to say they felt there must be a God, and, as they knew nothing of Him, they invested Him with attributes which seemed very proper to them, but which to a more enlightened and cultivated people are simply blasphemous.

So much for the introduction. We now come to the event as narrated in the book. I will be as brief as the importance of the point will permit.

God having thus resolved to destroy everything in which was the breath of life, except Noah and his family, and a sufficiency of the animals, etc., with which to start the world afresh, determined to execute his plan of destruction by means of a flood, and that those whom he wished to spare should be saved by an ark, the size and structure of which was dictated to Noah by God Himself. It is to be observed that the entire account avoids referring anything to miracle; the whole affair was to be, and by the account was, accomplished by the use of purely natural means. We of the present age know that for this story to be true would have required a greater variety of miracles, and of a more stupendous character, than has ever been attributed to any God; but to the people who invented the story nothing could be more natural.

A large vessel was built, it was stored with provisions, Noah and his family, and specimens of every living thing on earth (except fish, which it appears escaped the general condemnation and were the only living things God was satisfied with—which may account for their being considered, to some extent, as sacred food to this day), went on board; a heavy rain came, lasting forty days and forty nights, and covered the entire earth, mountains included, with water, and drowned all that were not in the ark.

The account as given must be true or untrue; difficulties are not to be explained away by saying that with God all things are possible, or by invoking the aid of special miracles. No miracle is mentioned or hinted at. The whole thing happened as it is described—that is, in a purely natural way, or it did not happen at all. I do not undertake to disprove statements that are not made, nor to combat theories that are not warranted by the narrative. I intend to take the facts as they are recorded and to deal with them alone.

The size of the ark is given at 300 cubits long, 50 broad, and 30 high. It was to be divided into three stories. It was to have one door (size not given) in the side, and one window, a cubit large above. The size of a cubit is variously estimated at from 18 to 22 inches, and we will consider it as of 22 inches. This would give the following dimensions: length 550 feet; width 91 feet 8 inches, and height 55 feet. The floors must have been strong, so the stories were probably of 17 feet each. This would make the total cubical contents of the ark, supposing it to be square at the ends, about 102,000 cubic yards. Scott in his commentaries estimates only 69,120 cubic yards, but we want all the room we can get. Each floor contained 5,601 square yards, and the three floors together 16,803 square yards total standing room in the ark.

Into this space were to be put:

Birds, according to Lesson (cited by Hugh Miller), 6,266 species—and Noah being directed to take of fowls of the air by sevens, male and female 87,724
Unclean beasts, 1,825 species, by pairs, 3,650
Clean beasts, 177 species, by sevens . . 6,128 } 9,778
Land reptiles, 457 species, by pairs . . 914
Insects, large and small, 754,600 species, by pairs 1,509 200

Then the food for all these for one year and seventeen days. The hay for such animals as eat that food is estimated at 105,300 cubic yards, or more than the entire capacity of the ark. Then consider the grain, fruit, fresh meat for the carnivorous animals, fish for the fish-eating beasts and birds, insects (other than those to be preserved) for certain birds and beasts, and the other varieties of food necessary, and it at once appears how utterly absurd it is to suppose that Noah had all that in an ark that could not have held the tenth part of it if packed like sardines in a box.

And we cannot assume that the animals were without food, and were miraculously preserved, for God expressly ordered Noah to provide food for them all, and nothing is said about its being condensed or compressed: everything appears to have gone on naturally.

Consider also the difficulty of getting together specimens of the entire fauna of the world; how, and by whom, it was determined what particular pair, or seven pairs, were to be selected, and how they were to be conveyed from arctic, antarctic, temperate, and tropical regions, and how they were to withstand, and live under, the great climatic changes. And as all the species mentioned exist now, and the natural changes by evolution are so slow that the number of species could not have been much less at the time of this supposed flood than they are now (and if evolution is untrue all these varieties existed then, as we have no dogma of new creations so far as I am informed), it cannot be said that Noah did not take them all on board, unless we consider the flood as partial, not universal, and this point is considered further on. And whether they came or were brought, the difficulty is the same; and we have no right to claim a miracle where none is even hinted at.

And the same difficulty which attended their collection must also have attended their dispersion, with the additional most serious difficulty of how, and where, they were to live until nature had time to produce their proper food, vegetable and animal.

Again, as these beasts, birds, reptiles, and insects were in confinement, they required attention. Imagine the eight persons in the ark giving them food and water, and cleaning up their filth. In our days, in menageries, one man cares for four cages—cleaning and feeding the animals. In the ark, each person, women included, must have attended, each day, to 10,964 birds, 766 beasts, and 114 reptiles, besides the almost innumerable insects, and all in the dark, there being but one window, 22 inches square, in the roof, and one door in the side, and that shut. And the ventilation! the smell!—but I forbear.

The Bible says that "all the high hills that were under the whole heavens were covered; fifteen cubits upward did the water prevail; and the mountains were covered." And all this from a rain of forty days and forty nights! The heaviest rain recorded in modern times is 30 inches in 24 hours; such a rain as this, had it fallen over the entire globe (which is, of course, impossible, naturally) for forty days and forty nights would have been but 100 feet, which would not have covered the hills, much less the mountains. To cover the highest mountains it would have to rain, instead of 30 inches, 700 feet a day for forty days. But there is not water enough in the atmosphere, according to Sir John Leslie, to form, if all precipitated at once, a sheet more than five inches thick over the surface of the globe—that is to say, if all the water in our atmosphere were added to all on earth. Then where could the water have come from? That quantity of water does not exist in, on, under, or above the earth. And where could it have gone to when the flood was over? It had no place to run off to, and evaporation was the only way to get rid of it. Accordingly it is said that "God made a wind to pass over the earth." For this wind to have removed the water from the surface of the earth, it would have been necessary to have blown away an ocean 125 feet deep, over the whole earth, every day for eight months! But even this does not explain where the water went to. Certainly it did not stay within the sphere of attraction of this planet.

I might go on for many pages in the same way, showing the utter absurdity, viewed naturally, of the account, but hardly think it necessary. Those who desire to go still further into the details of this subject are referred to a lecture by Prof. Wm. Denton, the geologist, called *The Deluge in the Light of Modern Science* from which I have condensed my facts and figures in this connection. I quote from that discourse, pp. 29–31:

"Geology furnishes us with evidence that no such deluge has taken place. According to Hugh Miller, 'in various parts of the world, such as Auvergne in Central France, and along the flanks of Ætna, there are cones of long-extinct, or long-slumbering, volcanoes, which though of at least triple the antiquity of the Noachian deluge, and though composed of the ordinary incoherent materials, exhibit no marks of denudation. According to the calculations of Sir Charles Lyell, no devastating flood could have passed over the forest zone of Ætna during the last twelve thousand years.'

"Archæology enters her protest equally against it. We have abundance of Egyptian mummies, statues, inscriptions, paintings, and other representations of Egyptian life belonging to a much earlier period than the deluge. With only such modifications as time slowly introduced, we find the people, their language and their habits, continuing after that time as they had done for centuries before. Lepsius, writing from the pyramids of Memphis, in 1843, says: 'We are still busy with structures, sculptures, and inscriptions, which are to be classed, by means of the now more accurately determined groups of kings, in an epoch of highly flourishing civilization, as far back as the fourth millennium before Christ.' That is one thousand six hundred and fifty-six years before the time of the flood. Lyell says that 'Chevalier Bunsen, in his elaborate and philosophical work on Ancient Egypt, has satisfied not a few of the learned, by an appeal to monumental inscriptions still extant, that the successive dynasties of kings may be traced back, without a break, to Menes, and that the date of his reign would correspond with the year 3640 B.C.' That is nearly thirteen hundred years before the deluge! Strange that the whole world should have been drowned, and the Egyptians never knew it!

"From *The Types of Mankind*, we learn that the fact is 'asserted by Lepsius, and familiar to all Egyptologists, that negro and other races already existed in Northern Africa, on the upper Nile, 2300 years B.C.' But this is only 48 years after the deluge. . . If all the human occupants of the ark were Caucasians, how did they produce negro races in 48 years? The facts again compel us to announce the fabulous character of this Genesicle story of the deluge."

This is, of course, on the idea that the flood was universal. What the Roman Catholic Church teaches on the subject I do not know, and the Bishop has never replied to this argument. It was originally believed, I suppose, by all Christendom, that the flood was just as it is represented in the Book, *i. e.*, universal—over the whole earth. But when science demonstrated that that could not have been, many Churchmen, and Christian geologists, claimed that the flood was only partial, and that the difficulties of the narrative may be so explained and removed.

This is an old device, as J. T. Sunderland, *What is the Bible?* 1878, p. 27, says:

"Almost every scientific theory that comes into existence is found to conflict in some point or other with the theological notions which an unscientific past has handed down. But the theologians are ever on the alert; and war to the knife is at once declared against the scientific intruder. All friends of the Bible are summoned to the Holy War. The conflict rages fiercely and shows no signs of abatement until it is seen that the scientists are getting the day, when it begins to be discovered by the theologians that after all the new theory is harmless, indeed there is no discrepancy between it and the Scripture. The discrepancy that had been supposed to exist grew out of a wrong Scripture interpretation. In fact, instead of the two being in conflict, the scientific theory is really taught in the Bible."

And Letourneau, *Biology*, p. 303 (as quoted by Sunderland):

"The doctrine of evolution is already almost triumphant. There scarcely remains for the recalcitrants any other resources than to demonstate its perfect agreement with the (theological) dogmas they are not willing to abandon. The thing is in process of execution. The interpreters are skilful, the sacred texts obliging, the metaphysical theories ductile, malleable, flexible.

Courage! we must be very narrow-minded indeed not to recognize in the first chapter of Genesis a succinct exposition of the Darwinian theory."

But this accommodating power of changing and modifying interpretations of Scripture ought not to apply to any Church claiming to be infallible, unless, indeed, it also claims that, no matter what it taught, it always knew what was right, and, after the example of God (according to the word "repent" as explained by the apologists), only submitted to the people such truths as it thought they could comprehend or stomach. I suppose when no one knew any better, and everybody believed in a total deluge, all of the Churches so believed, and should yet unless, still after the example of God as indicated in the Book, they have changed their views.

But this is unimportant. If any Church believes, or believed, the deluge total, it is, or was, as we have seen, wrong; if it believes, or believed, the deluge partial, it equally is, or was, wrong, as we are about to see. I quote again from Denton's lecture on the deluge, p. 31 *et seq.*, as to a partial deluge:

"I read (Gen. vi., 7) 'I will destroy both man and beast and the creeping thing.' How could a partial deluge accomplish this? (vi., 13) 'The end of all flesh is come before me. I will destroy them with the earth.' How could all flesh be destroyed with the earth by any other than a total deluge? (vi., 17) 'I do bring a flood of water upon the earth, to destroy all flesh wherein is the breath of life, from under heaven, and every thing that is in the earth shall die.' Not only is man to be destroyed, but all flesh wherein is the breath of life, from under heaven, and everything in the earth is to die. Can this be tortured to mean a partial deluge? (vii., 19) 'And the waters prevailed exceedingly upon the earth; and all the high hills that were under the whole heavens were covered; (21) and all flesh died that moved upon the earth, both of fowl, and of cattle, and of beasts, and of every creeping thing that creepeth upon the earth, and every man. (22) All in whose nostrils was the breath of life, and all that was in the dry land, died. (23) And every living substance was destroyed which was upon the face of the ground, both man and cattle, and the creeping things, and the fowl of the heaven ; and they were destroyed from the earth, and Noah only remained alive, and they that were with him in the ark.'

"Had the man who wrote this story been a lawyer, and had he known how these would-be Bible believers, and, at the same time, geologists, would seek to pervert his meaning, he could not have more carefully worded his account. It is not possible for any man to express the idea of a total flood more definitely than this man has done. He does not merely say the hills were covered, but '*all*' the hills were covered ; and lest you should think he certainly did not mean the most elevated, he is careful to say 'all the *high* hills' were covered ; and lest some one should say he only meant the hills in that part of the country, he says expressly 'all the high hills that were *under the whole heavens were covered*,' lest some one in its absence might still think that the deluge was a partial one. To make its universality still more evident, he says 'all flesh died that moved upon the earth.' This would have been sufficiently definite for most persons, but not so for him ; he particularizes so that none may escape—' both of fowl, and of cattle, and every man.' To leave no possibility of mistake, he adds, ' all in whose nostrils was the breath of life, and all that was in the dry land, died.' Can anything more be needed ? The writer seems to see that some theological professor may even yet try to make this a partial deluge ; and he therefore says ' every living substance was destroyed which was upon the face of the ground, both man and cattle, and the creeping things, and the fowl of the heaven ; they were destroyed from the earth.' Is it possible to add to the strength of this ? He thinks it is ; and he therefore says, ' Noah only remained alive, and they that were with him in the ark.' Could any man write this and then mean that less than a hundreth part of the earth's surface was covered ? If not a total flood, why save the animals—above all, the birds ? All that Noah and his family need to have done would have been to move out of the region till the storm was over. If a partial flood, how could the ark have rested on the mountains of Ararat ? Ararat itself is 17,000 feet high, and it rises from a plateau that is 7,000 feet above the sea-level. A flood that enabled the ark to float on to that mountain could not have been far from universal, and when such a flood is accounted for on scientific principles, it will be just as easy to account for a total flood.

"' *The flood was only intended to destroy man, and therefore only covered those parts of the earth that were occupied by him.*'"

(The Professor here supposes an objection.)

"The Bible states, however, that it was intended to destroy everything wherein was the breath of life, and your account and the Bible do not agree. But if man was intended to be destroyed, the flood must have been widespread.' We know that Africa was occupied before that time, and had been for thousands of years, by various races. We learn from the recent discoveries in the Swiss Lakes that man was in Switzerland before that time; in France as Boucher's and Rigollet's discoveries prove; in Great Britain as the caves in Devonshire show; in North America as the fossil human skull beneath Table Mountain demonstrates. Hence, for the flood to destroy man alone at so recent a period, it must have been as widespread as the earth.

"Even according to the Bible account, the Garden of Eden where man was first placed, was somewheres near the Euphrates; and in 1600 years the race must have rambled over a large part of the earth's surface. The highest mountains in the world, the Himalayas, are within 2000 miles of the Euphrates. That splendid country, India, would have been occupied long before the time of the deluge; and on the flanks of the Himalayas man could have laughed at any flood that natural causes could possibly produce.

"'*How do you account, then, for these traditions of a deluge that we find all over the globe?*'"

(Another objection.)

"Nothing more easy. In all times floods have occurred; some by heavy and long-continued rains, others by the bursting of lake barriers, or the irruptions of the sea; and wherever traditions of these have been met with, men, with the Bible story in their minds, have at once attributed their origin to the Noachian deluge."

I have quoted at length because to have condensed was to have spoiled. In fact the first portion of my remarks on the facts of this remarkable myth, condensed from this admirable lecture, has very little of the force with which Prof. Denton urges his criticism. Still I think that the matter is even here stated with sufficient clearness and strength to demonstrate that the account, as given in the Bible, is simply the rather clumsy invention of a primitive people totally unacquainted with many now well-known facts clearly set forth in what is undoubtedly God's revelation to man, the Book of Nature, a book which speaks everywhere and to all men the same language, and tells the same sublime story, free from all vain imaginings and false teachings; a book which, though hard to read and oftentimes misconstrued as to its higher teachings, is simple and plain as to its more necessary lessons, and which would have been now far better understood, because more universally studied, had not the Church discouraged all investigation which pointed to conclusions differing from those begotten of superstition and taught of ignorance.

But an important corollary may be drawn from the exposure of the fallacy of this account as indicated above. It is not given to us—as in truth it is—as one of the barbaric theories of the past, or even as a purely human history. It is held up as divine; God Himself is supposed to be the author of the story; and as this narrative rests on the same authority as does the entire Old Testament, an assumed communication between God and man; and as the Old Testament is the foundation on which is built the New, the demolition of this story is the demolition of all—that is, the demolition of the divine origin of all. And as Jesus is represented as endorsing this most absurd and impossible legend by saying: "But as the days of Noe were, so shall also the coming of the Son of Man be. For, as in the days that were before the flood they were eating and drinking, marrying and giving in marriage, until the day Noe entered into the ark, and knew not until the flood came and took them all away: So shall also the coming of the Son of Man be" (Matt. xxiv., 37-39); we can but conclude that, as a man, living at the time he did, and knowing no more of nature than those around him, he, as was natural, believed with reference to supposed ancient history, what was believed by his contemporaries; but this one fact that he believed in the reality of the occurrence and truth of the Mosaic account of the Noachian deluge, should, to every thoughtful, well-informed, impartial, and unbenumbed mind, at once deprive him of that Godhood which since his death the Church has thrust upon him.

If it were an easy task to point out an almost unlimited number of absurd stories and barbaric conceptions of God contained in the Old Testament; the material is abundant and readily accessible through the labors of others, and my only task would be to transcribe. But if the foregoing argument is as conclusive as I think it is, further evidence is unnecessary; still I cannot forbear, in conclusion, referring to Exodus xxxii. and Numbers xiv., where Moses represents himself as having an argument with God, and getting the best of it by appealing to His vanity, telling Him what the Egyptians would say of Him, as specimens, not of what God is, but of the Jewish conception of Him —a conception outgrown by all the civilized world except the adherents of dogmatic Christianity.

THE ARGUMENT.

PROPOSITION VII.

VII. *Arguments directed especially against the Roman Catholic form of orthodoxy:*

Saying masses for the dead—for a pecuniary consideration—is either obtaining money under false pretences, or is selling the grace of God;

If repentance and confession are necessary to and will secure salvation, charity, and other good works cannot affect our future condition—unless the forgiveness of God can be bought;

And the Church practising the one and teaching the other is in error and not infallible.

The Roman Catholic Church claims infallibility; if any of her teachings or practices can be shown to be wrong or inconsistent with other of her teachings or practices she must give up this pretension; and, having built herself up on this theory, must fall with it.

I have seen circulars and other advertisements distributed in and posted on the walls of Roman Catholic cathedrals and churches, claiming on their face to be by the authority of the bishop of the diocese, in which it is stated that by the payment of a specified sum of money any deceased person whose name is given by a subscriber may participate in the benefits to be derived from certain Masses which were to be said at certain times and places.

The practice is a common one, I believe, and extends to wherever there are priests to say the Mass.

These official announcements can mean but one thing: if I pay the required sum it is my privilege to name any deceased person, and the benefits of the Mass are extended to him; if I fail to pay such sum the deceased person does not get the benefit of the Mass. In other words, no one gets the benefit of these particular Masses except those for whom the benefit is bought.

I believe that requiem Masses also are charged for, and that they will not be said unless the price demanded is paid; such at least is the custom in such Roman Catholic communities as I am familiar with. If this be true generally, the remarks I am about to make will apply to them also; if not true generally, they will apply so far as the custom exists.

A Mass for a dead person either does good or it does not do good; is either valuable or worthless.

The Church, if infallible, must know whether it does good or not, because if the Church thinks it does good and it does not, the Church is in error, and therefore not infallible; and I will not ask the Church to admit that it sells Masses either knowing or believing them to be worthless; for if the Mass is worthless, and the Church so thinks, or knows, my money is obtained by her under false pretences, and I am defrauded in the name of God.

If the Mass does good, is valuable, that necessarily means that because of the Mass God does something which without it He would not have done, or omits to do something which without it He would have done; for if the Mass in no way influences Him, it does neither good nor harm.

Now, whether the Mass is or is not said for the deceased person, or, in other words, whether or not the deceased person obtains whatever benefit may arise from the saying of the Mass, depends on whether or not a certain sum of money is paid; that is, if the money is paid on his account he receives the benefit; if it is not so paid he does not; for it is distinctly stated that he will receive the benefit IF the money is paid; and if he would receive the benefit without the money being paid—if he would be as well off without paying as with,—the person who has been induced to pay the money is defrauded, not having been put in possession of all the facts, but having been led to believe that the benefit depended on the payment of the money.

And if the benefit does depend on the payment of the money, then the grace of God is for sale.

There is no escape, so far as I can see, from this dilemma, if the Church be infallible—for if she be infallible she certainly must know the value of her own rites and ceremonies; and either the Church obtains money under false pretences, by offering for it a service which she knows to be worthless; or, if she knows it to be valuable, she sells the grace, the forgiveness, of God, by limiting the benefits of the Mass to those who have paid for it.

Again, if I have correctly understood the doctrinal sermons I have heard, and even the argument of the Bishop in this discussion, it is taught by the Roman Catholic Church that repentance and confession are essential to, and sufficient for, salvation. That is to say, as I understand it, a full absolution, after all sins have been repented and confessed, insures salvation; but a sin, to be forgiven, must be repented, and, where a priest can be had, must also be confessed, and absolution be obtained; otherwise, if repentance alone be sufficient, confession, not being necessary, is valueless, except to give the clergy the immense advantage of an exact and intimate knowledge of the personal characteristics, traits, and affairs of their people.[1]

Therefore, if there remains one sin unrepented and unconfessed (the sinner having had opportunity to seek absolution), that sin must remain unforgiven, and the sinner be damned, or else an unrepented and unforgiven sin will not prevent the salvation of the wicked.

Then I have heard the faithful urged to give money to the Church, to build another edifice, to repair or improve the old one, to further complete a new one, to support the clergy, and for various other purposes; and I have understood it to be held out, sometimes directly, sometimes indirectly, as an inducement to give and to give liberally, that it would be a good act which would be remembered by God to the advantage of the giver hereafter, with a strong intimation that the future advantage was to be proportionate to the amount given—not the actual amount, perhaps, but proportionate to the relation of the amount given to the ability to give.

All of which suggests this: suppose one (we will suppose a member of the Roman Catholic Church) has committed a sin which is unrepented and unconfessed (with opportunity of confession) and so dies, how will the money which he may have given to the Church help him? Will God say, or think, that as he had given money to help build Him a temple or to help support His clergy, or for any other Church purpose, his unrepented and voluntarily unconfessed sin will be forgiven unasked? If yes, then repentance and confession may be rendered unnecessary

---

[1] I am informed that there is a repentance—that flowing alone from the love of God—which is so efficacious that it needs neither confession nor absolution. Of course my argument applies equally to repentance alone, where confession is unnecessary, as to the two when they are required to be combined.

by good works, and the forgiveness of God has been bought with money (if money-giving be the particular good work), even if He looks only to the intention with which the money has been given ; if no, then his liberality to the Church will have availed him nothing, and he will be punished just as his sin deserves, without reference to his gifts.

Or, if his sins be all repented and confessed, and absolution obtained therefor, he is sure of salvation—or else full absolution for all sins is meaningless—and the money so given avails him nothing ; he is safe without reference to his charity.

So the ground upon which the money is sought to be obtained, and the rewards held out as an inducement to give, seem to me to be entirely unsubstantial, illusory, and deceptive, if the teachings of the Church be true, even if they be held out in good faith by the clergy.

And it will not do to say that such charity will not procure the forgiveness of an unrepented, unconfessed sin, but will go to the credit of the sinner, and lessen his punishment ; it is still forgiveness *pro tanto*, and to that extent has been bought.

From my standpoint I can, and do, believe that every good action, done with a proper motive (without which it could hardly be called really good), will bring its reward here and hereafter; for while I believe that " faith without works is death," I also believe that works without faith may be life, though every sin must be punished, proportionately, not eternally. But from the standpoint of orthodoxy I find it difficult to see how good works will benefit a man unless he also repents and is forgiven for all his sins, in which case I cannot see that he needs the help of his good works.

CONCLUDING REMARKS.

THE foregoing seven propositions cover the entire discussion with the Bishop. My last letter has remained unanswered, and although I have frequently met him since he received it, he has never even alluded to the subject.

Of course he does not feel that he is unable to answer: he could undoubtedly write thousands of pages in response. I suppose he has merely concluded that further correspondence would be a waste of time without advantage to either side. If such be his conclusion, he is right to a certain extent. Judging from the past, every argument which he can adduce is, when properly considered, but additional evidence of the weakness of his cause. The argument on both sides is of long pendency. Every year brings new light and power to the opponents of orthodoxy, but the argument on the side of the Church remains unchanged, and by the very theory of the religion must ever so remain.

That theory is, as I understand it, that some 1893 years ago God became incarnate in the person of Jesus of Nazareth for the purpose of redeeming mankind, and, during that incarnation, established his Church on earth to be, in future, the only medium through which he should communicate with man.

The facts upon which the theory is based are of such a character as to appeal to faith, rather than to reason, and no new facts having been developed, or, indeed, being possible, the argument is necessarily of great sameness. It may be brilliant or dull, interesting or tiresome, learned or foolish, eloquent or flat, according to who is the speaker or writer; but in its last analysis it is always the same, the same old argument in a circle, before alluded to: Jesus was God, and having established a Church and promised to be with it always, and that the gates of hell should not prevail against it, the Church is not subject to error; and we know that Jesus was really God because the Church, thus shown to be infallible, tells us so. Such, at least, has been my experience of the argument. Whenever I have heard that any one has successfully undertaken the defence of orthodoxy, I have, when practicable, examined his arguments, and, so far, every one of them assumes as his premise some of the very points in dispute. If there be any other argument I have not been fortunate enough to have met with it. I have not studied or written for the purpose of self-deception, nor with the desire to mislead others. My attention was drawn to the subject by the conviction of its vast importance, and I wanted nothing but truth. Believing, as I most firmly do, in a future life which is, to a great degree influenced, certainly at its commencement, by our life here; and our life here being in great measure controlled by our religious belief, I felt that I could not afford to follow false Gods, to hold false doctrines. I have therefore given to this all-important subject the deepest thought and most earnest study of which I am capable, and if my conclusions are wrong I am more interested in finding my error than any one else possibly can be; and, if I know myself, I am perfectly sincere when I say that any argument which will lead me to TRUTH will be most heartily welcome, no matter what that truth may be. And one of the reasons why I have consented that the foregoing discussion should reach the publicity of print, is the hope that it may draw forth the fullest and freest criticism of the argument (as an argument, not as a literary production), that its weak points may be discovered, and strengthened or abandoned. And here, perhaps, I might with propriety leave the matter with the public. I opened the argument, the Bishop followed, I answered, he replied, and I concluded. I had taken the affirmative, the burden of proof was on me, and I had the right to the opening and conclusion. So this is as it should be. But I yield to the temptation to summarize a portion of the argument already given in order to apply it in a somewhat different manner.

Most of us who are born in this or any other so-called Christian country are, while yet children, imbued with the prevailing ideas and beliefs, and, growing up with them, very naturally consider them as most certainly true. We surround them with all the sacred affection of our earlier associations, our helpless infancy sustained by a mother's and a father's love and devotion; and they are strengthened and supported by the very superstitions they have evolved. Hence the first time any of these cherished ideas is attacked, we feel a shock, more or less violent according to the interest felt in the subject, and a very slight argument against what we consider a blasphemy, and in favor of what we already believe an unassailable truth, completely satisfies the mind. And it is only after repeated and long-continued assaults that we ever, if we do at all, begin to feel the force of the attacking power. This is the case with the thoughtful, and those who feel an interest in the matter. The majority of those who conform to the prevailing faith do so simply because it is the prevailing faith, and say, and think, that the religion which was good enough for their parents and other ancestors is good enough for them, and dismiss the subject from their minds as one promising more trouble than benefit,—more evil than good. Such, of course, will never read this discussion; they can be reached only in conversation by their more thoughtful friends, those who, like myself, realize the importance of having a true religion—and it is to such that I now address myself.

But instead of attacking the Church, entrenched as she is behind so many loving memories, protected by so much affectionate reverence, supported by such strong superstitious instincts, and upheld by an almost irresistible force of habit; let us change places, and make her the attacking party, giving her all the weapons she is in the habit of using except reverence, superstition, and force of habit, which she could not use in an attack, and let us see what her real strength is.

Let us, then, suppose a full-grown person, fairly educated in science and scientific methods, having an average intellect, and tolerably well acquainted with nature as known and understood at this time, of a religious or spiritual turn of mind, but with no knowledge of any so-called revealed religion. Then let us suppose some learned Churchman endeavoring to convert such person to the dogmatic Christianity of the present day.

Clearly, the most important point to be established by the Churchman, the one on which all the other dogmas are based, or to which they point, is the divinity of Jesus, or, in other words, what the Bishop has called the fundamental doctrine of all Christianity, the Incarnation. If this doctrine be true, the others *may* follow; if it be false, they *must* fall.

The supposed fairly educated person has learned from his studies that the earth, on which he lives, is one of a series of planets revolving around the sun. That as to size, location, composition, it is neither the most nor the least favored. That Mars, which we have the best chance of observing, closely resembles Earth, is divided into continents and seas, is cold at both poles, and has an atmosphere. There is no reason that he can conceive of why Mars, at least, should not be inhabited by beings similar to those in this world. The same is true of Venus. Hence he concludes that the probabilities are that the other planets of our system are, have been, or are getting to be, in a similar condition, as the process of formation of all the planets in our system is evidently the same—from a nebulous, to a liquid, to a solid, to a cool state, indicating birth, infancy, youth, and maturity, to be followed, probably, by old age and decrepitude, as is supposed to be the case with our moon.

So he reasons that during the period of maturity all the planets must be fit for human life as we know it. There is unity of design in all organic life on this planet, there is unity of design in all the planets; why should not the unity of design in all that is seen be assumed to extend to that which is not seen? Or perhaps it would be better to say why should we assume that the unity which runs through all we see ceases with our range of vision? Why should we assume that all these planets, fitted for the highest known forms of life, should be left as waste places in the universe, useless for every purpose of which we can conceive? No reason can be given; on the contrary analogy would seem to indicate that in our system, at least, there is every reason to believe that many, if not all, of the planets, are, have been, or will be, inhabited by intelligent beings similar, in at least many respects, to those of earth.

Then, going beyond our solar system, he finds innumerable quantities of what are called fixed stars, so called because their vast distance from us renders their motion almost imperceptible. These stars are known to be vast globes of matter shining by their own light. Hence, by analogy, they are assumed to be suns similar to our own; and it is also supposed that they are, each of them, centres of solar systems like ours, and, almost necessarily, like ours teeming with intelligent life. How many of these systems there are we cannot possibly conceive, since we can neither conceive of space without limit, nor of space with limit. We cannot comprehend either eternity or infinity, though we are driven to the conclusion that both exist from our inability to conceive of the cessation of time, or of what could have preceded or can follow its existence, or of the cessation of space or of what could lie beyond its limits. So, then, as it seems to our student, he must conclude that the universe includes an infinity of worlds which are, which have been, or which will be, like ours, and equally inhabited by intelligent beings.

It is true that this conclusion is largely speculative, but it seems to be entirely justified by the facts. What is absolutely *known* is only what we learn from the telescope and the spectroscope. They tell us that space is filled with bodies composed of the same materials as our sun, and in the same condition, and of even greater magnitude. Reasoning from the known to the unknown, we conclude that they are suns, and planetary centres, and can conceive of no reason why in all this illimitable universe an average planet, of an average solar system, should be the only one possessing intelligent life. The logical mind revolts from the idea. There is, as we have seen, nothing remarkable about the earth in its composition, situation, or condition to exalt it above its fellows. There is absolutely nothing unusual about it: why then should we assume, while it is, to say the most for it, only an average world so far as we know other worlds, that it is so immeasurably superior in all those points upon which we know nothing about all other worlds? Such an assumption is utterly without any reason to sustain it.

Hence we have a reasonable degree of certainty that the entire universe teems with intelligent life; and we know that the whole observable universe is governed by fixed law.

All this points to a God; not because we can comprehend what God is, or why, or how, He should exist; but just as we are forced to admit eternity because we cannot conceive of anything before or after time; to admit infinity because we cannot conceive of anything beyond space; nor even think of the non-existence of either; so we must, as it seems to him, admit God, because we cannot conceive of universal law, order, and intelligence, without also conceiving of a universal source, or centre, from which they flow, of which they are a part, or an emanation; for law, order, and intelligence imply design, and design cannot, by its very nature, be self-originating.

That we cannot tell the origin of this source, or centre, does not affect the argument, because we cannot tell the origin of either time or matter, though both assuredly exist. We can only go back within finite limits; and when we have gone back to the earliest source of which we can conceive, that is, for us, the first Great Cause, that must be our God; and if there be any other cause or source beyond that again, It is what we mean when we think of God; for this source, or centre, or primal cause, is what we call God, the Supreme Intelligence, and must, from its nature, pervade all time and space, past, present, and to come, must, in a word, be eternal and infinite; believed in because felt to be a necessity indicated by all Nature, but incomprehensible, because above, beyond, superior to, and out of the realm of our reason.

This God, revealed to man through His own works in nature, is, and from the nature of the case must be, as we are taught by nature, omnipresent, omnipotent, omniscient; and, consequently, as we have already seen, He cannot be angry, because anger necessarily implies discontent, and discontent means disappointment—that matters have not gone to suit Him. We also know, from the same teacher, that He never interferes with His works because they were and are perfect, and in accordance with His perfect plans; that He sustains, not alters; and hence is unchangeable. That He is Love and Truth, and neither hates nor deceives. That He acts through Law, and evolves, rather than manufactures; and necessarily governs and maintains all things in accordance with His original, eternal design, unchanged and unchangeable because now and always perfect even in its minutest details.

Such would be, in brief, the views of Divinity entertained by such a person as I have supposed, being what a religiously disposed, highly spiritualized, but healthy and sane mind, would naturally deduce from its study of nature.

The truth of his belief may not be outwardly demonstrable; but I know of no argument that can disprove it. It is, to a great extent, a matter of faith, but of that higher faith of which I have already spoken, which only assumes to control in regions where reason admits her inability to penetrate; that truer, purer faith which believes nothing which reason rejects, and relies on that only which reason may accept.

What, then, is this man asked to believe? That the God whom he adores made man so bunglingly that His expectations of him were not realized. That He gave His creature, man, free-will, power to oppose Him, to thwart Him, and that man used this perilous gift in such a manner as to cause God to repent that He had ever created him, and to determine to destroy him. That He did destroy him, all save eight, and started a new race, a new experiment. That the new experiment succeeded no better than the first, and the first remedy, destruction, having proved of no avail, He determined to try another plan, atonement. That one of the necessary details (and the chiefest of them all) of this plan was what is now called the Incarnation. That He accordingly caused a maiden, who was espoused to Joseph, but who had never known man, to become *enceinte* by the Holy Ghost, through an unexplained process, to bear her child for the usual time, to be purified after its birth (though purification for giving birth to God would seem to have been somewhat unnecessary), and to raise him up to the carpenter's trade until he was thirty years of age. That this child so begotten, born, and reared, was God Himself veiled as a man. That Jesus was very man and very God. That there is God, the Father—God, the Holy Ghost—and God, the Son—yet not three Gods, but one God. That although in the world of which science takes notice 3 times 1 are 3, in the world of which theology assumes control, 3 times 1 is one. That this new and remarkable experiment has not succeeded in 1893 years, but is still progressing, and there are strong hopes that it will succeed yet,—in fact it must succeed—as it is God's own plan—but when is not yet known.

Our supposed student would very naturally suggest that this is a very remarkable story; that it shows a very childish (perhaps I should say primitive) conception of God; that it is at variance with all experience, and all that is known of nature; that it represents Him as uncertain, changeable, and not very wise; and respectfully begs to know what is the evidence to support so strange a tale.

In reply he is referred to the Holy Scriptures, comprising both the Old and New Testaments, with the assurance that they are the word of God, and are the source of all our information on the subject, except such as we derive from the traditions of the Church; but as such traditions are in confirmation of the Scriptures, and their authenticity and validity are dependent upon the infallibility of the Church, which infallibility is founded on the Bible, the Bible is really the all-sufficient basis of the whole system.

As our unregenerate friend is supposed to be entirely ignorant of any revealed religion, he, of course, cannot make any analytical comparison between other religions than that which he is invited to adopt; and we will also assume that he knows nothing of the history of the Bible —not Bible-history—but the history of how and when the books of the Bible were written. He is therefore compelled to rely upon the book itself, without outside aid. Hence he will carefully study it, not as it is studied by those who accept it before they know anything whatever about it, and take it all as a matter not to be questioned; but fairly, candidly, and earnestly, and equally without prejudice for or against it. But he studies it critically, and for this reason: he knows that the book he has been trying to read, Nature, is God's word, and that the only element of error which he has hitherto had to contend with was false interpretation of what he saw; while in the book now offered to him as God's written word the elements of error must be legion. The inherent inability of human language to always accurately convey human thought, let alone Divine wisdom; the possible carelessness, incompetency, or even design, of the original writer, or of some of the numerous subsequent scribes; the mistakes or interpolations of translators; the suppressions or additions of interested editors; the facility with which marginal glosses, conveying the ideas of the copyist, or editor, may be by some subsequent copyist or editor incorporated into the text; and many, many more fruitful sources of error, intentional and unintentional, will suggest themselves to him, and any one of them may materially change the original meaning. He therefore naturally requires pretty clear evidence to convince him, when the Bible is in conflict with Nature, that the Bible is right and Nature wrong.

Commencing then, at the beginning, he discovers that the account of creation, as contained in the first chapter of the first book, is not only inaccurate, but actually absurd; that the story of the creation of man is utterly at variance with well-known facts of ethnology; that the dates and order of the various events recorded are totally inconsistent with the demonstrated facts of Geology and Archæology. That the story of the Deluge, a little farther on, whether it be viewed as universal, as it is distinctly and clearly stated to have been, or partial, as some apologists now claim, is simply an imaginative account of a physical and natural impossibility which could have originated only among a people entirely ignorant of the plainest facts of nature, and which can be believed only by those who are equally ignorant, or else who refuse to apply their knowledge to the story but "swallow it whole," as the whale, still farther on, is said to have swallowed Jonah. And he finds that the farther he goes into the book, the more of such impossible stories does he discover.

Further examination satisfies him that it is unlikely that Moses wrote the account of his own death and burial, announcing where he was buried, his age at the time of his death, and the lamentations over his loss, with the additional fact that no man knew the exact locality of his grave; and that as such details are a part of the recognized text of Deuteronomy, and written in the same style as the other portions of it, the probabilities are that some one else than Moses wrote the whole book. An examination and comparison of dates makes this still more clear, not only with reference to this, but with reference to all of the five so-called books of Moses, and to those of other reputed Bible authors, leaving such books to stand without the sanction of even a mythical name. Further, he observes that if Moses be the author of the Pentateuch, he represents himself as advising God, arguing with Him, and inducing Him, God, to change His, God's, intentions on account of the new light thrown on the subject by him, Moses; and concludes that either Moses is a very unreliable reporter, or the God he writes about a rather inferior sort of a deity.

Again, he finds that this Moses, who is considered the great lawgiver and chief teacher of the Jews, God's chosen people, this "man of God," either did not know anything of the immortality of the soul, or else thought the information not worth giving to his people, for nothing in his books teaches that doctrine.

Then he observes that God, in the Old Testament, is represented as countenancing almost every conceivable wickedness, provided it is done by His chosen people, though unforgiving and vindictive as to anything which seemed to interfere with, or reflect upon, His own personal pre-eminence; and, finally, that the record nowhere claims for itself that it is either inspired or infallible—its inspired infallibility being a discovery of much more recent date.[1]

Certainly, so far, he has found nothing to make him wish to substitute the Jewish conception of God for that which he has derived from Nature, and very naturally concludes that a book so untrustworthy as to its facts cannot be infallible as to its theories.

He now takes up the New Testament to investigate the Incarnation, feeling that the all-wise, all-powerful, all good God whom he adores, if He had taken that extraordinary step—if He had so honored this infinitesimally small and apparently unremarkable part of His universe,—would certainly have so arranged it that there could be no question about the fact; especially as the success of

---

[1] Paul says, 2 Timothy iii., 16, Protestant version: "All Scripture is given by inspiration of God." The Catholic version is not so strongly put, but is: "All Scripture divinely inspired is profitable to teach," etc. But in either version it was merely Paul's opinion or assertion, as to the holy writings as then known and recognized, and those holy writings do not seem to have claimed inspiration for themselves; such expressions as "the Lord saith," "thus spake the Lord," etc., etc., when used by the writer, being no more a claim of inspiration for themselves or their writings than when the same or similar language is used by a writer of to-day; it is merely the recording of a belief or tradition, that the Lord had at some time and in some place spoken such things, and that the writer was narrating the circumstance as he understood it. And these remarks apply equally to 1 Peter i., 20, 21, often cited as claiming inspiration for the Bible; and, besides, Peter expressly limits inspiration to prophecy.

the plan depended more on its being known and believed than on its being performed. For he has been assured that the object of the Incarnation was to save mankind, but that no one can or, rather, will be saved who does not believe in it; hence, as just indicated, the most important part of the whole scheme was that it should not merely be consummated, but believed; and as God could, being all-powerful, have so arranged the event, or, at least, the evidence of it, as to have produced that belief, our friend turns to the New Testament with a feeling of relief —that he will now surely find something to satisfy his mind, something to bring conviction. This is what he reasonably expects—let us see what he finds.

He finds four Gospels asserted to have been written by four of the followers of the Incarnate God, Matthew, Mark, Luke, and John. He finds that two of them, Mark and John, give no account of the Incarnation. Either they did not know of it, or did not think it of sufficient importance to mention or refer to; since this omission could scarcely be because it is mentioned by Matthew and Luke, for Mark and John tell of a number of things of comparative insignificance which the other two also recount, while this event was the most important of all that could have occurred, the supernatural character of Jesus' birth being the sanction of his authority to teach. Besides, the two stories of the Incarnation related by Matthew and Luke differ, showing that either one or the other was wrong, or that neither knew the whole history of the affair, but related only a part of it. So that so far from the narratives of Matthew and Luke being a reason why the matter should not have been referred to by the others, the differences in the accounts afforded an excellent opportunity to Mark and John to explain and reconcile if they knew of the story and its relation by the others; if they did not know of the story, it would be conclusive evidence against its truth, and their failure to allude to events that never occurred can be understood; but if they knew of the story, and did not know of its relation by the others, it is in order for our teachers to explain their silence.

All this is rather discouraging, and our friend's expectations are not as great as they were. Still, he turns to Matthew and Luke for light.

So far as he can see, according to Matthew the only reason for believing in the supernatural conception is a dream of Joseph, after Mary's condition is known to him; according to Luke, a vision of Mary, before the conception, and the interview with Elizabeth. Each evangelist apparently tells all he knows about it, and neither alludes to the story told by the other, and as each is supposed to have been inspired of God (for the value of their writings is from their supposed inspiration), and hence to have known all about it from high authority, besides what he may have learned from Mary and Joseph, the two accounts are really irreconcilable. But assuming that the two writers were not so fully informed, but only wrote what each knew, or what he thought he knew (which would effectually dispose of the inspiration theory), the whole story, combining both accounts, amounts to this: Mary, at the time of her espousal to Joseph, found herself in a condition which imperatively demanded explanation. She explained it by telling of her vision; Joseph, a just man, and, from the little we know of him, probably a weak one, and very much in love with Mary, slept over his troubles, and dreamed that her explanation was true. This must, as it seems to him, have been the case if there was any truth at all in the story. But it is to be observed that it is merely *announced* that Mary and Joseph had such vision and dream; it is not claimed that even they so asserted; the authority for the story is not given. And the story of the interview with Elizabeth adds absolutely nothing to the evidence of the truth of the incident. So much for the conception; now for his life.

After his birth Jesus lived just as other children, so far as we are informed, and he learned and followed his father's trade as a carpenter until he was about thirty years of age. Is it likely that his mother and Joseph, had they known of his miraculous conception, and that he was very God, would have so treated him? Would their poverty have caused them to allow their God-guest to work for his food and clothes? It seems hardly probable; his Godship must have been veiled even from them. And that it was so veiled, even from Mary his mother and Joseph, is made still more apparent (Luke ii., 46-50) by the fact that, when Mary and Joseph found him in the temple disputing with the doctors, his mother reproached him for leaving them, and on his replying that he must be about his Father's business, she and Joseph understood not what he meant.

But further than this, if God had incarnated Himself in this extraordinary manner, and made the belief in such incarnation the most important matter of salvation, is it conceivable that he should never once allude to the wonderful circumstances of his birth? Or that, having alluded to it, such allusion should not have been recorded and preserved? Yet it does not appear that he even knew of such a report.

And those living in the house with him (his "brethren") did not believe in him; and they and his mother interfered with him and tried to interrupt his preaching, which would hardly have been done had they known, or believed, him to be God-incarnate.

And to the very last some of his disciples doubted, even if any ever believed in, his divinity, and there is no proof that any of them ever did so believe, and if there were, it would not be evidence of his divinity, but only evidence that some thought him divine then as many do now.

Again, he finds upon examination that the so-called prophecies, said to have foretold Jesus' coming, have no more reference to him than to us. That the "inspired" genealogies of Jesus fatally and absurdly vary, and that the attempt to explain the variance by supposing one genealogy to be that of Joseph and the other to be that of Mary, is without authority or reason, because nothing of the sort is said or intimated in the account, and the Jews never traced descents through the female; that, however, even if this explanation were true (which, of course, is not the case), it would still leave the absurdity of tracing Jesus' descent from David *through* Joseph while claiming that he was not descended in any manner *from* Joseph. Further, that if the Messiah was to be of the line of David, Jesus could not have been the Messiah, because He was not of David's, or any other human line, but was direct from God, nay, was God.

That Jesus, if ever claiming to be more than man, did so in such ambiguous terms as to allow of different constructions, or in so contradictory a manner as to throw doubt upon the claim, and to throw doubt upon a matter the belief of which was essential to salvation would have been a crime, and totally foreign to Jesus' character.

That the miracles ascribed to Him, and even His resurrection and ascension, though not doctrines, but described as facts, and the most wonderful and important facts in the history of the world, and said to have happened within historic times, in the midst of numerous contemporary writers who, recounting many very much less important and interesting events, would hardly have failed to notice these stupendous ones, and which should therefore be sustained by overwhelming contemporaneous evidence, are, on the contrary, without further proof than the bare assertions of those who were forming a sect, and therefore interested in having such things believed, but who do not even pretend to have themselves witnessed these occurrences.

Is the evidence sufficient to the end? Could any reasonable man, with his mind free from bias, be satisfied with such testimony? Would any one believe the Church's dogma who had not been taught to believe it before he could think and reason, while yet a child, or in the mental condition of a child? Is there any reason why all nature should be false, and the Hebrew-Gentile Bible true?

Verily, we cannot blame our friend if he thinks the Incarnation lacks confirmation, and declines to change his views and lower his conception of his God; refuses to believe that God would make man's salvation through all time and eternity depend upon his believing an asserted phenomenon which is contrary to all experience, and which is supported by evidence so flimsy that it failed to convince those living at the very time and place where it is claimed to have occurred. The New Testament seems to him no better than the Old, and both to conflict with what little we do know of nature and of God.

And if his would-be teacher can show him wherein he is wrong, he is wiser than the teachers I have met.

I have thus epitomized some of the points made in the

foregoing argument for the purpose of illustrating how weak the cause of the Church really is when deprived of the mere sentiment and force of habit that sustain it. I have nowhere gone into the question of the authenticity, correctness, or age of the books of either Testament, I have merely referred to it, for my purpose, as I have said, has been to present a plain, common-sense view of dogmatic Christianity as it exists at the present time, and to discuss and point out what I conceive to be its errors in a way that may be understood without previous theological study, and without too close application. But to those who desire to know more on the subject, as well as to have a much more complete argument against ecclesiasticism, I suggest the reading of the books already referred to, and quoted from by me.

As to the position so frequently taken by those who fail in the argument in behalf of orthodoxy—that the fact that so many great, wise, and good men and women have believed, and do believe, in the Church's dogmas and doctrines, should be considered as an argument in the Church's favor, and that some religion is necessary to man, and that the Christian religion is the best form known, and should not be interfered with, even if it be full of errors, I have already so fully discussed, and, as I hope, disposed of, these points in considering the influence of the Church on man, that I do not care to add to, or even summarize, what I have there said; but I will give some additional illustrations of the harm that is yet being done by a dogmatic Church, whether it teach the best-known form of religion or not, though in doing so I necessarily repeat and enlarge upon what has been said before.

In this, and most other civilized countries, the Protestant division of Christianity is allowed quite a large latitude in matters of doctrine, and many who deem themselves very orthodox reject much that is held to be essential by the Roman Catholics, and even by some sects of Protestants. But there are certain doctrines taught from all orthodox pulpits, so far as I am informed, which seem to me not only erroneous, but to work great harm; and I now briefly notice one or two of the more prominent of these.

The doctrine that Jesus is God gives, as I think, not only a false but pernicious conception of Deity. It may increase our idea of our own importance and dignity, but it does it at the cost of lowering our conception of the Almighty; for to suppose Him anxious to save mankind from His own vengeance, to make them friends with Him, to reform their evil ways—all of which, by an all-powerful God could have been done by the mere exercise of His volition,—by incarnating Himself in a fœtus for nine months, and in a child, youth, and man for thirty years, before He should begin to act, and then acting in an inefficient way for three years, and dying prematurely on the cross, and after some 1893 years of waiting to be no nearer the attainment of His wishes than at first, certainly seems to me to be a low conception of God; and it is no answer to say that we have no right to question His acts, or His wisdom, and that because all this is mysterious and incomprehensible, it is none the less true. I admit that we have no right to question either the acts or the wisdom of God; but as I have said before in this connection (Prop. I. *b*.) it certainly is our right to be assured that the act IS the act of God before we yield to it the respect to which it would be thereby entitled. We may admit the possibility of even the Incarnation, on the ground that all is possible with God; but this does not preclude our examining to ascertain if this possible, but improbable, thing was really done. The mere fact that the story is mysterious and incomprehensible does not prove it true, and the narrated event to be the act of God, though some would seem to think so. On the contrary, it would seem that if a purely human and finite mind can see how an object could have been actually attained by simple and natural means, the probability is that Infinite Wisdom would have seen as much ; and when we are asked to believe that Infinite Wisdom rejected the natural, obvious, and effective plan and adopted one mysterious, incomprehensible, and entirely inefficient, we should require indubitable proof before throttling our intelligence and surrendering our reason.

Without further discussing the reasons for believing in the divinity of Jesus, or the contrary, leaving the truth of the belief to be determined from what has already been said, let us see wherein it is pernicious.

We are told that Jesus was the only perfect man, and that he was perfect only because he was God. That we must try to be perfect even as he was perfect, but that we cannot succeed, not being, as was he, divine. This discourages many from attempting to follow the impossible-of-attainment example of his life; whereas if they were taught that Jesus was but man, and that it is possible for any other man to live as pure, holy, good, innocent, and useful a life as he did, many would be encouraged to try it. In this way the example of his life would be utilized, and not wasted as it is under the Incarnation theory. *Then* it could be held out as a point of perfection to be reached ; *now* it is set up as an example impossible of imitation ; and the really sublime lessons of his life and actual teachings are lost sight of in the assumed benefits of his death.

Again, while told that we must follow his example, though without the possibility (he being God) of doing so successfully, we are further told that, no matter how good we may be, no matter how near we may come in acts to imitating his, no amount of honesty, honor, charity, morality, and virtue will avail in the slightest degree to save us, unless we also believe that Jesus was God, that he died to save us, and that we can be saved in no other way. As I have fully argued, and, I trust, established, *belief* is beyond our control. Hence many who feel the impulse to lead virtuous lives, but who are utterly unable to believe those dogmas, but do believe what they have been taught about the effect of such unbelief, determine that if they are to be finally damned in any event, they will have a " good time " while they are here, and so fall into various kinds of immorality, the religion they have been taught making them believe that virtue of itself alone is worthless in the sight of God.

Besides, taught that God has made a man's salvation dependent on something beyond the man's control—belief ; knowing that the belief which a man holds when grown depends in most instances on that of his parents, and, hence, on the circumstances in which God has caused him to be born ; that if he examines into the question for himself his belief must be determined by evidence and argument and not by volition ; that God could have given satisfactory evidence of what was true, or could have so arranged that the truth should be known to and believed by all men, and would not ;—his mind refuses to believe in so monstrous a conception of Deity, and knowing none other, he flies to materialism pure and simple, and dies uncheered by any hope of a higher life ; and, unless he is naturally good and philosophic, he will not live a life of as much purity and usefulness to his fellow-men as he would were he otherwise, and truly, instructed.

Again, the doctrine deduced from the Incarnation and its sub-theories, that, on account of Jesus having, by his death, taken away the sins of the world, a man may live a life utterly at variance with all morality and virtue, and yet, by a tardy repentance and belief, be relieved from the penalties and consequences of his vicious acts, and be forever blessed, causes many to persist in living more in accordance with the promptings of the flesh than the aspirations of the spirit, trusting to wash out all the past with the atoning blood of Jesus.

Thus this one dogma, with the doctrines necessarily flowing from it, has within it not only error, but the potentiality of great harm; and that potentiality has acted, and is acting now, to the great injury of humanity and human progress by driving many of the most earnest and thoughtful of our race out of the paths of rectitude and beyond the pale of all religion.

Then the doctrine of future punishment, as punishment, generally supposed to be endless,—the great dogma of hell,—has the effect of hardening the heart and deadening the sensibilities, lessening the appreciation of justice, confounding degrees of crime, and tending to develop the most heartless selfishness, by teaching that it is divine justice, wisdom, and mercy to punish forever and cruelly the sin of a moment; that cruelty may be justice, and may be deserved; that crimes of action are as nothing compared to the crime of unbelief; that one unrepented sin is as bad as another, and the moral man who doubts the Church worse than the murderer who finally believes it; and that we may enjoy not only contentment, but supreme bliss and happiness, in heaven, with the dearest and most beloved wife, child, or parent in hell; and by making us suppose that God *triumphs* (rejoices over success—see Webster) over His enemies—His own creation, His own children, and ever absolutely helplessly in His power.

And the idea inculcated by the Church that the true believers are especially marked out by God as the recipients of His favors and blessings, while those less favored receive His frowns and curses, must arouse a personal vanity and overbearing pride that cannot but interfere with our consideration and treatment of those whom we look upon as our less fortunate fellow-men.

But I pause. If I have shown, as I believe I have, that dogmatic Christianity tends to debase our conception of God, and to give us false ideas of our relations to our surroundings, then I have done all I wish—I will have shown it to be a bane, not a blessing, to man.

I have said that I do not oppose religion but only ecclesiasticism. I may say that I do not oppose true Christianity. I make my meaning plainer.

I believe that Jesus of Nazareth did actually exist, and did teach many great, though not new, truths. I believe, further, that many, if not all, of those truths, though not new to the world, were new to him, and that they were evolved out of his own consciousness and thought, under and through the laws of God, and were to him, and those to whom he spoke, true inspirations: for I believe that God is truth; and any truth—whether it first reach the world from the lips of Jesus or Pythagoras, from Christian, Pagan, or Infidel—is an emanation from Him—is Divine Inspiration.

Hence his ethical teachings, with but few exceptions, I believe to be right, and they, in my opinion, constitute true Christianity. The dogmas and doctrines devised by the Church to reconcile obvious discrepancies, and to forward its own interests, I would reject, as also such portions of the Bible, whether in the Old or the New Testament, as are plainly repugnant to reason.

For a creed, I would offer:

"I believe in God the Father Almighty, maker of heaven and earth; and in a life everlasting."

For a rule of conduct:

"Thou shalt love the Lord thy God with all thy heart and with all thy soul and with all thy mind; and thy neighbor like thyself."

And to those who require any outside sanction to cause them to observe the law, the teaching of nature that every infraction of her laws, whether physical, mental, or moral, carries with it fixed natural consequences, in the nature of punishment, because disagreeable, certain, and proportionate, but not eternal; and that man must work out his own salvation, and not depend on the mediation of others; and that instead of praying to be saved on account of Jesus' death, we had better strive to win our own redemption by following the example of his life.

In other words, let men live good moral lives, attending to their plain duties here on earth, as indicated by the precepts and example of Jesus and dictated by a sound philosophy and enlightened conscience, and trust the rest to God. This seems to be the extent of the knowable. As to that which lies beyond this world and this life, let men believe what they please, it is but theory after all, and while we may, as I do, try to convince our fellow-men of the truth or falsity of various beliefs, no one should be persecuted, even to the extent of being shunned or reprobated, because his theory may differ from that generally accepted; certainly we should not try to force him to adopt our belief in matters of mere faith, under the threat that if he does not conform to our views we will not only not aid him to get to heaven, but will do all we can to send him to hell, by cutting him off from our Church fellowship and our social influence.

Such is my creed; and though much of it depends on faith, it is that nobler, truer faith of which I have so often spoken, and none of it seems to me to be repugnant to reason; still I do not think it an essential to salvation that even my creed should be believed, for much of it is deduction only, and though I think mine are more logical and reasonable than the deductions drawn by the Church, they are deductions still; and no belief in any doctrine or dogma, which is a *deduction*, no matter how clear, should or can be an essential to salvation, because what is perfectly clear to one is by no means clear to another, and the condemnation for disbelief would be for having either too much, or too little, brains to believe it; and in either case the sentence would be equally unjust, being an endless spiritual doom for a temporary physical defeat.

I believe the ideas advanced by me, and, as I think, unsuccessfully controverted by my opponent, lead to a peace of mind, a fulness of faith, and a consciousness of truth, unknown to the orthodox; we do not have to try to become as little children—to pray for imbecility—lest we may not be able to avoid seeing the errors of our creed; and when we say, "Lord, we believe," we are not obliged to add, "help Thou mine unbelief," for our belief comes from the head as well as the heart, and is mental conviction, not mere acceptance. And they certainly tend to elevate our ideas of our duty to ourselves and others, and to raise our conception of God from that of a changeable, uncertain, rather bungling, personal interferer in our affairs, to that of an all-pervading, living, unchanging, perfect God, ruling by fixed and immutable laws, and those laws Evolution, Progress, Compensation, Love.

Surely the changed conception cannot be regretted even if to bring it about we have to differ in our theological views from the pioneer thinkers of an infant world. God's children, the sons of Earth, have progressed in knowledge, in accordance with His laws, in everything pertaining to their physical nature; shall we believe that physical progress alone is possible? That the Spiritual, which if it exists at all, being eternal, must be the Real, alone is cut off from God's great law of growth? Rather would I believe, as I do, that the more important the faculty, the greater the capacity for progress, and that in the spiritual as well as in the physical world the mistakes of the past are the stepping-stones to the truths of the future; and that spiritual truths will always be provided for the yearning human soul which shall thereby continue to grow and progress higher and higher, purer and purer, wiser and wiser, happier and happier, here and hereafter, through all time and eternity.

THE END.

www.ingramcontent.com/pod-product-compliance
Lightning Source LLC
Chambersburg PA
CBHW021623250426
43672CB00037B/1973